Ralph Bates

A Biography

by Christopher Gullo

Midnight Marquee Press, Inc.
Baltimore, Maryland, USA

Copyright © 2018
Interior layout: Gary J. Svehla
Cover design: Susan Svehla
Copy editor: Janet Atkinson

Without limiting the rights under copyright reserved above, no part of this publication may be reproduced, stored in or introduced into a retrieval system, or transmitted, in any form, or by any means (electronic, mechanical, photocopying, recording or otherwise), without the prior written permission of the copyright owner or the publishers of the book.

ISBN 13: 978-1-936168-77-4
Library of Congress Catalog Card Number 2018952703
Manufactured in the United States of America

First Printing by Midnight Marquee Press, Inc., August 2018

Ralph Bates

A Biography

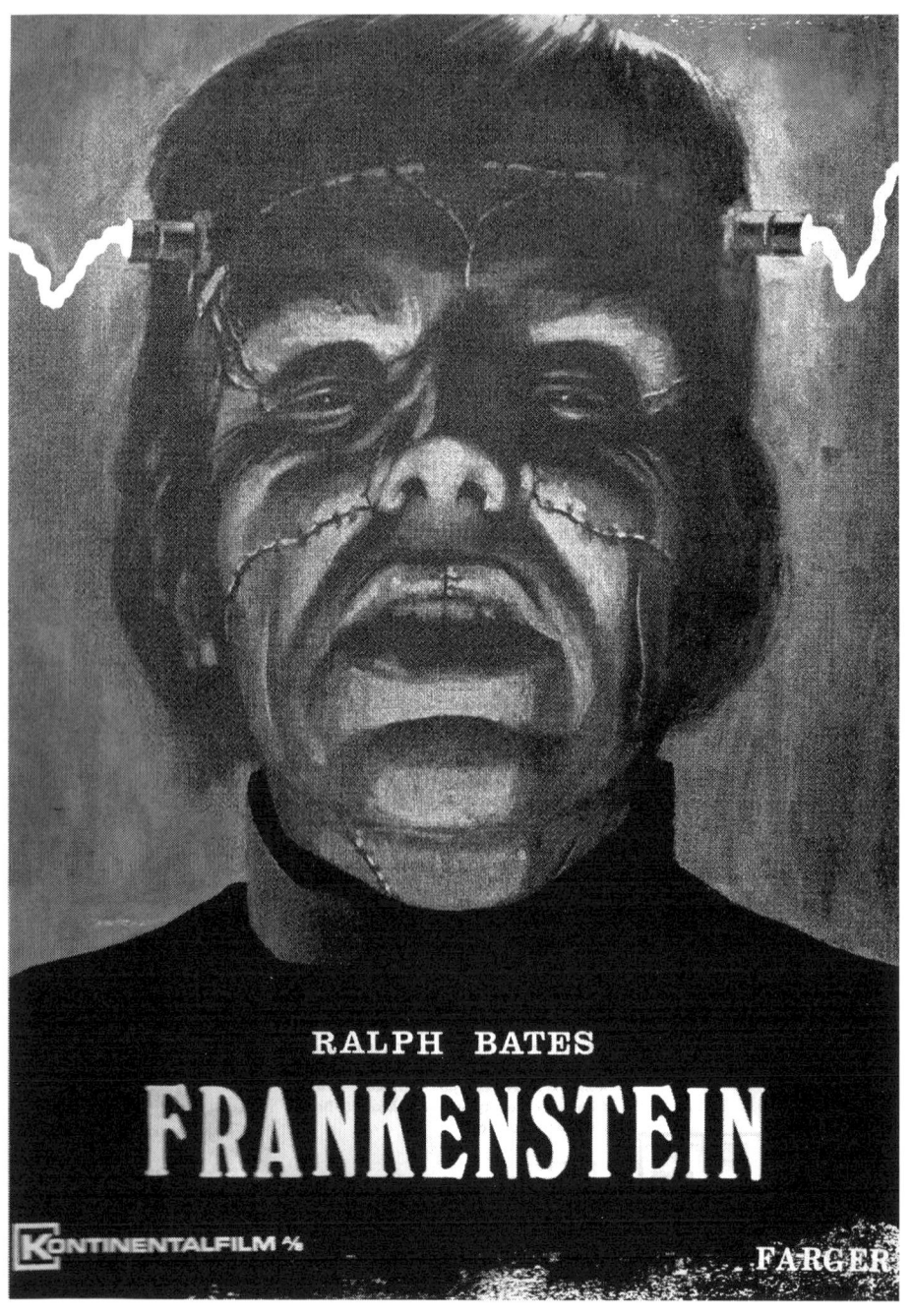

A Norwegian brochure created for *The Horror of Frankenstein*, with artwork created by Tom Chantrell, illustrating a caricature of Ralph Bates as the Frankenstein Monster, while ironically he in fact played Dr. Victor Frankenstein in the Hammer Film Production.

Dedication

To my son Anthony Gullo,
who continues to make me proud at every moment of his life,
and to Ralph Bates, for providing so many enjoyable performances.

This film is filled with...
SHOCK
...VICTIM AFTER VICTIM DIES HORRIBLY IN THROAT-CUTTING ORGY!
AFTER SHOCK
...UNNATURAL LABORATORY EXPERIMENTS PERFORMED BEHIND BARRED DOORS!
AFTER SHOCK
...ONCE AGAIN HE WILL CHANGE SEXES AND KILL, KILL, KILL!
WARNING!
THE SEXUAL TRANSFORMATION OF A MAN INTO A WOMAN WILL ACTUALLY TAKE PLACE BEFORE YOUR VERY EYES!
PARENTS: Be sure your children are sufficiently mature to witness the intimate details of this frank and revealing film.
DR. JEKYLL AND SISTER HYDE
An American International Release
STARRING
RALPH BATES Co-Starring MARTINE BESWICK · Also Starring GERALD SIM · LEWIS FIANDER
PG PARENTAL GUIDANCE
In COLOR
Screenplay by BRIAN CLEMENS · Produced by ALBERT FENNELL & BRIAN CLEMENS · Directed by ROY WARD BAKER · EMI Film Productions Limited presents A Hammer Production
72/106

Table of Contents

8	**Foreword**
10	**Ralph Bates Appreciated**
11	**Acknowledgments**
12	**Preface**
14	**Chapter 1: "How about you let me go to university then?"**
36	**Chapter 2: "Any means is worth the end result"**
53	**Chapter 3: "The supreme prince of darkness …"**
113	**Chapter 4: "Excuse me my dear, I have some work to do"**
136	**Chapter 5: "Well, don't you think that's funny?"**
149	**Chapter 6: "It will all pass too quickly"**
166	**"Death of an Actor" by Ian Blake**
170	**Afterword by Dr. John Glees**
171	**Notes/Bibliography**
177	**Photo and Art Acknowledgments**
181	**Index**
186	**About the Author**

Foreword
by Virginia Bates

In spite of stabbing me in the back on the first day we met (*Dr. Jekyll and Sister Hyde*), Ralph and I instantly became great friends. He lived close to my shop and he would bomb down Portland Road on his Harley-Davidson, improving my street cred to no end. He was unbelievably cool and quite beautiful with his long, straight raven-black hair and unique style. He'd wear skinny velvet or leather trousers or faded blue jeans, and sweatshirts with sleeves cut off to the elbow and ripped-out collars.

Saturdays after closing the shop a gang of us would pile into his 1950s Dodge or Volkswagen Camper and hang out in hamburger bars, which were then the new scene. He had a habit of filling my bag with peppermills, which I'd only discover when I got home and would then have to return the following day. Without a doubt the funniest man I've ever met, Ralph was a great listener, a cultured and informed *Guardian* reader, a cook and raconteur. His passions included cricket and boxing, and later sailing. He was always curious about people and his interests widened, as he got older.

The biography that Christopher Gullo has written almost 25 years after Ralph's death is painstakingly researched and documents Ralph's work, his life and his times. Without the various contributors to this book, the past could not have come together in such a compelling

Virginia Wetherell Bates (middle) in *Dr. Jekyll and Sister Hyde*

reminiscence, and I am so thankful to them, and to Christopher.

Ralph invited me to a screening of *Dr. Jekyll and Sister Hyde* when it was playing all night at the Jacey Cinema in Piccadilly Circus, and for the one pound ticket you were also given a snack box with a sandwich, an apple, juice and a piece of cheese. In those days cinemas ran movies in continuous performances and it seemed that every tramp had taken refuge in that warm cinema. The noise of snoring and the stench were unbearable! I refused to sit on a seat and crouched at the back on the floor with the star.

We married in 1973 and had two children, Daisy and Wills. Our life was never dull, often hilarious, and always frantic in the days leading up to a show. Those times could be intense, trying to keep the house quiet, while continually running lines. But then I'd come home from the shop to find Tommy Cooper pulling our pet rabbit out of a champagne bucket, or the cast of *Dear John* playing cricket in the garden. I remember once finding Ralph with Jimmy Sangster trying to knock down the wall between the sitting and dining rooms, until I stopped them. Sundays were open house and lunch could go on for days, even weeks.

Virginia Wetherell Bates as she appears today

While starring in the West End in *Run For Your Wife!*, Ralph was diagnosed with pancreatic cancer and given six weeks to live when he was only 50 years old. He'd never been ill and it was impossible to believe that he wouldn't recover. But pancreatic cancer is unforgiving and it did get the better of him. I was determined to fight back and started a charity for pancreatic cancer in his name.

Ralph is buried in Chiswick Cemetery, in West London. A photo of his burial plot was chosen to be included for the *Page 3 Sun* calendar, a copy of which hangs in the gravedigger's hut, which appropriately faces the actual burial site. As Ralph was half French, I brought a large ironwork cross back from France and a blacksmith installed it on his gravesite gate, which includes a butterfly, roses, and a sunflower (the Research Fund's symbol).

A mist of lavender rises over the grave every summer. These days a menacing tramp has taken up residency opposite the grave. He washes his socks under the communal tap then hangs them out to dry on Ralph's ironwork. That's so very Bates.

—Virginia Bates, 2016

Ralph Bates Appreciated
by Richard Klemensen

"Dick, you Bastard!" That was Ralph Bates on the telephone to me in April 1980. Of course, it isn't how it sounds. My first wife, Karla, and I had gone to England to attend the initial Hammer Con in London, at the Kenilworth Hotel. Among the many Hammer guests were Ralph and his wife, actress Virginia Wetherell (who brought along their two young children, Daisy and Will). Ralph, in particular, had fun handling the props from Hammer's 1969 *Taste the Blood of Dracula*, which was his first film he made for the company. He had fun drinking out of the goblet and trying on the long Dracula cape (brought along by Mike Tilley, a SPFX assistant to Les Bowie on the film). Ralph's co-star from Hammer's 1970 *The Horror of Frankenstein*, David Prowse, was also there. The producer/director of the film, Jimmy Sangster, who became a great friend of Ralph's, said it was the most fun he ever had making a movie. You could see it was true by the kidding that Ralph and David engaged in that spring day.

During our time with Ralph and Virginia, I had given Ralph a copy of the 1978 issue #4 of my magazine, *Little Shoppe of Horrors*, which was an in-depth study of Hammer films. As Ralph elaborated after cursing gleefully at me, "I spent the whole night reading your damned magazine." Then he laughed and we chatted. Before Karla and I left England, I was calling all the people we met and spent time with. In the case of Hammer make-up artist Roy Ashton, Karla and I traveled around Southern England with he and his wife Elizabeth, seeing all the sights. Roy left us for several days with fellow Hammer make-up expert Phil Leakey, and his wonderful wife, Gladys. This was the first time I ever had clotted cream at a meal. For that matter, the first time I ever had lamb. So you can imagine that the conversation with Ralph was especially fun as we talked about how we were so glad to have met.

Ralph would end up doing five films for Hammer—*Fear in the Night*, *Dr. Jekyll and Sister Hyde* and *Lust for a Vampire* being the other three. There was the thought in the Hammer camp that he, along with Shane Briant, could be the heir apparent to Peter Cushing and Christopher Lee. Sadly, the declining state of Hammer and the British film industry prevented that, and Hammer would be in bankruptcy by 1979. But for Ralph, he continued to do excellent television work (*Poldark* and his much beloved series, *Dear John*, being among the best) and theatrical films, such as playing Suzan Farmer's husband in the first Tyburn film, *Persecution*.

And during the period, he remained close to his fans. They loved him and he loved them back. We were lucky to run two interviews with Ralph in our magazines, and he talked with affection about his fantasy films and the people he worked with, such as Lee and Cushing. Then at the young age of 51 he succumbed to pancreatic cancer. The world not only lost a wonderful actor, but it also lost one of its nicest people. All of us who knew Ralph and Virginia miss him to this day.

—Richard Klemensen, 2016
Editor/publisher of *Little Shoppe of Horrors*

Acknowledgments

I would like to thank the following individuals and institutions for their invaluable assistance in the research and writing of *Ralph Bates: A Biography*: Virginia Bates (for kindly approving of my proposed tribute to her husband and for all her generous help), Elisabeth Eidinow (sister of Ralph Bates who kindly provided much of the early family history), Will Bates, Daisy Bates, Joanna Van Gyseghem, Terence Brady, Tim Goode (for editing my manuscript and who also had the enviable task of sorting through Ralph Bates' personal boxes), Richard Klemensen (for his wonderful poignant tribute), Ian Blake (for his lovely and touching poem, dedicated to Ralph Bates), Sam Irvin, Carlos Aguilar, Ton Paans and Ian Woodward (for kindly allowing their interviews with Ralph Bates to be used in this book), Jonathan and Glennis Johnson, Steve Hackett, Michael Bogdin, Peter Cocks, Brian Clemens, Peter Sasdy, Wanda Ventham, Mia Farrow, Sir Peter Blake, Leslie Lawton, Braham Murray, Peter and Ros Duffell, Shane Briant, Ray Cooney, Alan Strachan, Veronica Carlson, Brian Cox, Jill Townsend, Martine Beswick, Wendy Allnutt, Robert Wilkinson (for kindly researching *The Beaumont Review* for Bates' early plays as well as contacting many of Bates' fellow Beaumont alumni), John Wolff, Barrington Tristram (for supplying an early Beaumont photo of Bates and assisting in editing), Henry Stevens, Michael Parker, Robin Mulcahy, Felicity Kendal, Patrick Malahide, Linda Hayden, Robin Ellis, Rachel Bell, Jon Jory, Renée Glynne, Phil Campbell, Brian Reynolds, Dave Prowse, Michael Briant, Gerald Harper, Edita Brychta, Ian Cullen, Terrence Hardiman, Carol Hawkins, Martin Thurley, Neil Dickson, Gareth Jones, Joanna Monro, Christopher Olgiati, Jeremy Burnham, Viviane Ventura, John Miller, Richard Wilson OBE., Eric Carte, Dick Sharples, Judy Matheson, Hugh Dickson, Peter Blake, Garrick Hagon, Stefan and Jean Gates, Julian Glover, Paul Spurrier, David Delve, Angela Pleasence, Cathy Munroe, Shelagh Bourke, Peter Bowles, Anne Rutter, Michael Shilling, Jacqueline Clarke, Bruce Hallenbeck, Serena Cairns, Bruce Arnold, Donald Douglas, Ellen Sheean, C. Courtney Joyner, Wayne Kinsey, Andy Roffey, Pip Evans, Denis Meikle, Sherry Gregory-Hansley, The Yale University Library, Neil Robinson (Marylebone Cricket Club library), Stephanie Rolt (The Theatres Trust), Clive Limpkin, Judith Noble, Anthony Battock, Salvador Fortuny Miró (for his translation of a Spanish Ralph Bates interview), Dima Ballin, Daniel Bouteiller, Mark Myler, Steve Thompson, Matt Gemmell Robertson, Timothy Scrafton, Tony Crawley, Andy Roffey, Moyb Ullah and of course, my wife, Beth Anne Gullo, and my son Anthony, for their support.

Preface

Where does the time go? As I double and triple check my works cited section, I see that the research I did for this book started back in 2013. Five years later and here we are, with you the reader about to digest an in-depth look at the life of Ralph Bates. The lengthy time from start to finish had mostly to do with my personal schedule—a delicate balance of research, contacts, interviews, family, teaching and a newly started side career with the fire department and as an EMT. As it turned out, slow and steady won the race—one lead often would turn up additional leads, and the added time allowed for many interviews, which might have been skipped had I rushed through the writing of this biography. Some of the most important bits of the book actually came toward the end of the writing process, an example being the interviews with Bates' fellow Beaumont College alumni, who shared stories of the very beginnings of what would become his career in acting.

The first time I ever saw Ralph Bates was on a rather unseasonal-like sunny Halloween when I was about eight years old. I was manually turning the channel dial on the television set in my grandparents' living room and immediately stopped when I saw a baron hiding a huge monster in a giant vat. The baron, sporting long jet black hair, then argued with the constable, who had barged into the laboratory, and in the chaos an inquisitive little girl accidentally hit a lever that wound up giving an acid bath to the poor monster inside the vat. The film, of course, was Hammer's *The Horror of Frankenstein*, which left an indelible mark on my youthful psyche that seemed to be tuned to classic horror. I would eventually see Bates again in *Taste the Blood*

Author Christopher Gullo (right) with Virginia Wetherell Bates and son Will Bates

of Dracula and then his other three Hammer films, followed years later by his performances as George Warleggan in the series *Poldark*, which aired on PBS in America.

While I was always a big fan of Hammer horror stalwarts Peter Cushing and Christopher Lee, I also enjoyed watching Ralph Bates perform and did not understand at the time why he was not in more films. Of course, what I did not realize was that Bates came into the Hammer stable late in the game and, when the company petered out in the mid-1970s, he moved on to various television episodes and series, most of which did not air in America. It has been a true delight for me when writing this biography to watch Bates in many performances that I got to see for the very first time. I felt like a kid again sprawled out on the carpet of the living room floor in my grandparents' house watching Bates in *The Horror of Frankenstein*.

I think what makes Ralph Bates stand out to me was his genuine approach to the many characters he played throughout his career. It did not matter if he were Baron Frankenstein, Dr. Jekyll, Caligula, George Warleggan, or John Lacey; I believed him in each role, which to me is the benchmark of a good actor. Ralph Bates was also blessed with cinematic good looks, with his thick mop of jet-black hair, his handsome face and deep soulful eyes. He was someone I wanted to know more about but there was always very little information about him other than the occasional article or interview in a magazine. Besides being a history teacher, I segued my love of research into a side career writing biographies of actors that I admired. My first book was on Peter Cushing, which I followed up with my second book devoted to Donald Pleasence. When it came time to write my third book, Ralph Bates was right at the top of the list of people I wanted to research. I reached out to Bates' wife Virginia and was delighted when she agreed to give her permission to authorize a biography of her late husband. As Bates sadly died young from pancreatic cancer, I also wanted to help the charity created in his name that Virginia initiated and so I am donating all my personal profits from the sale of this book to the Ralph Bates Pancreatic Cancer Research Fund. I encourage everyone reading this book to visit the Fund's website at http://www.ralphbatespcr.org.uk/ to learn more about the charity and the disease. If you are reading this book you are most likely a fan of Hammer horror and I hope that you too enjoy learning about Ralph Bates' other work outside of the studio that brought him worldwide fame. I know that I have enjoyed the journey in writing this book and I hope it honors the memory of Ralph Bates.

—Christopher Gullo

P.S. The quotes that begin each chapter come from dialogue that Ralph Bates said during his career. Try to figure out which character and production belong to each.

Chapter 1
"How about you let me go to university then?"

In the cramped laboratory at the Rue D'Ulm, a figure cloaked in a long white lab coat eagerly sets to work in the meticulously clean surroundings. Upon closer inspection, the figure is a tall, handsome man with dark hair and rock steady hands that reach out for the beaker to conclude his experiment with anticipation. A bead of sweat runs down his forehead as he concentrates on pouring the exact amount needed for the test. As he waits for the concoction to properly mix, the man dutifully takes notes of every step he has taken for the experiment. Working with the goal of furthering science, the man hopes that this time the results will yield success for the vaccine. In what could have been a scene featuring actor Ralph Bates portraying Dr. Jekyll in *Dr. Jekyll and Sister Hyde*, it is instead an experiment of Bates' maternal grandfather—Dr. Adrien Charles Loir, assistant and nephew to the famed biologist Louis Pasteur and a notable scientist in his own right.

The story of how Dr. Adrien Charles Loir came to work for Pasteur begins with his father, Professor Adrien Joseph Loir. Twenty-seven-year-old Louis Pasteur, who was quickly making a name for himself in France and had recently worked as a professor of physics at Dijon Lycée, came to the University of Strasbourg located in Alsace, in 1849, where he was assigned as a professor of chemistry. While there, Pasteur met Marie Laurent, daughter of the University Rector, and became smitten with her. After a brief courtship Pasteur married Marie on May 29 of the same year. Marie's brother-in-law happened to be Adrien Joseph Loir, who was also working in the scientific field. Loir wound up researching his thesis overseen by Pasteur, a sure benefit to his own career. This eventually paid off when the newly married Pasteurs began to start their family in 1850, and Loir became his successor at the Faculty of Pharmacy. Like Pasteur, Loir also married one of the Rector's daughters, Amelie Laurent, whom he courted upon arriving at the University. After the University, Loir continued his career in the field of science and did eventually become dean of Faculty Sciences at Lyon.[1]

After having a son Maurice in 1852 and a daughter Elisabeth in 1856, Adrien Joseph Loir's wife, Amelie, gave birth to their second son on December 15, 1862, whom they named Adrien Charles. The young Adrien Charles Loir grew up in the company of Louis Pasteur, who referred to him as "mon neveu," my nephew. The admiration was mutual and Adrian Loir was soon following in the footsteps of Pasteur to eventually become a bacteriologist. By the time Adrian Loir was 19 in 1881, he had begun working as a picker in the laboratory at the chemistry faculty at Lyon that his father chaired. By the following year Adrian Loir had transferred to Rue D'Ulm and was working in the laboratory of Pasteur, who had taken him under his wing while he continued his medical studies.

Pasteur had suffered a series of strokes during his lifetime, starting in 1868, and was finding it increasingly more difficult to carry out his experiments as a result of a weakened arm, and so he began taking in assistants when needed. It was only a matter of time before Adrian Loir became Pasteur's most trusted assistant and he started major research into the effects of swine fever. As part of his duties, Adrian Loir began to travel and in 1886 he headed the first anti-rabies clinic in Saint Petersburg, Russia. Two years later Loir journeyed to Australia where he studied the effects of anthrax and pleuropneumonia.

While in Australia, Loir worked to reduce the massive rabbit infestation that was brought on in 1787 when the Great Fleet of Britain introduced the species. With no known predators, the rabbit population exploded and became a serious problem to agriculture. The New South Wales government, in response, offered a large reward with the purpose of cutting down the rabbit population. Loir introduced chicken cholera bacillus to the rabbit population, which, while not a runaway success, did introduce biological attempts that would eventually prove fruitful.

In 1888, a year before Loir made his first journey to Australia, the very first Pasteur Institute was created. It was a non-profit foundation that promoted the study of biology and vaccines against diseases. Loir founded a Pasteur Institute in Tunisia, North Africa in 1893 and served as a professor at a colonial school there as well. The success of the institute in Tunisia led Loir to open many additional institutes throughout the world, including Rhodesia. He also served as Director of the Health Bureau of Le Havre, France in 1909 and soon after became the curator of the Natural History Museum of the city. Loir was forever grateful to his mentor Louis Pasteur and in 1937 published a series of essays about Pasteur, which were published in the French journal *Le Mouvement Sanitaire*. [2]

Louis Pasteur, mentor to Dr. Adrien Charles Loir

In Loir's personal life he married twice, first to Marguerite Morache and later to Hélène de Montès. Loir's marriage to Hélène resulted in three children raised in their Roman Catholic family. The middle daughter, Lilian Adrienne, was born in Paris in 1903. Following in the medical career of her father, Lilian would grow up to become qualified as a medical doctor in Paris and worked at the Pitié-Salpêtrière Hospital specializing in venereal diseases. While at a medical conference in Paris in 1933 she met the love of her life, Ralph Marshall Bates. He was born in Shanghai, China in 1902, the second child with an older sister. Bates' father worked on the Shanghai Stock Exchange. The family returned to England at the turn of the century and settled in Saltash, in Cornwall. After his education in the medical field at Plymouth College, Bates

A Biography

Ralph Bates' paternal grandparents, Ralph and Jose

entered the London Hospital where he qualified as a surgeon specializing in brain surgery earning his FRCS (Fellowship of the Royal College of Surgeons). Bates later on developed an interest in psychiatry, and at the time of the medical conference where he met Lilian, he was already established as a psychiatrist in his post at Stoke Park Colony in Stapleton near Bristol. The Colony featured the Stoke Park Hospital, which was founded in 1909 by Reverend Harold Nelson Burden and his wife Katherine and would become the very first institution set up to care for mentally handicapped patients.[3]

Bates courted Lilian and they married in 1934, before moving to England. The family had settled in Bristol at Stoke Park Colony, so Bates would be close to his job. Lilian had given birth to the couple's first child, Lilian, in 1934, and a second girl Elisabeth, in 1936. By the time the Bates' only son Ralph was born in 1940, his father had become Medical Superintendent at Stoke Park Colony. Bates was highly regarded at the hospital and had papers published, one example being "Three Cases of Phenylpyruvic Oligophrenia" (1938).[4]

In 1947 the family moved to Colchester, Essex, where Bates took the job of Medical Superintendent of the Royal Eastern Counties Hospital for the mentally handicapped, and he remained there until his retirement. The Queen eventually decorated him with the Order of the British Empire (OBE) for his work in the medical field. Lilian also continued her career while in England, qualifying in psychiatric medicine and specializing in child development.

Colchester is noted for being Britain's oldest town on record and a stopover for the Romans during the time of their Empire. Emperor Claudius, uncle to the previous emperor Caligula (who Ralph would eventually portray to great success in the television series *The Caesars*), had claimed the town then known as Camulodunum and made it the first Roman capital of Britannia, which had become a province of the Empire.[5] The town was then repopulated with retired Roman soldiers, a coincidence considering during World War II the same town was occupied with British troops who used it as a base.

While the Bates family permanently resided in England, Lilian felt the importance of instilling a love of her home country in her children and throughout their childhoods she maintained a very French household. When they were young, they all had to speak to her only in French; English was forbidden. Holidays were spent with the family in France and inevitably young Ralph grew up bilingual. Ralph's childhood was spent in the countryside, spending his time fishing, catching butterflies with long nets, playing on hayricks or skating on frozen flooded fields, which were his natural pastimes. As his sister Elisabeth recalls, Ralph was very good at roller-skating backwards. He also learned to ride on his sister's pony named Snowball. During these formative years his father would treat him to the movies, where Ralph enjoyed seeing the films of Buster Keaton, the Keystone Cops, Max Miller, Spike Milligan and Kenny Everett. Seeing these classic comedians sowed the seeds of a possible future in entertainment for young Ralph.

Ralph's first school experience started at the age of seven in 1947 at St. Mary's in Colchester. It was and still is predominantly a girls' day school and Ralph attended with his two older sisters. Among the many girls there, ranging in age from five to 17 years old, were approximately 10 young boys ranging in age from five to eight years old. The boys and girls were taught together in the same class. One of the fellow boys in Ralph's class was Jonathan Johnson, who would become a close friend. "I had been at St Mary's a term or two when Ralph first arrived," remembered Jonathan. "We were exactly the same age. My first recollections of Ralph were that he was rather lonely and shy and seemed a little bit of a lost soul. We got along very well, as did our sisters who attended with us. We attended St. Mary's together from 1947 until 1948 and Ralph actually stayed on until the following year, before we met up again at Orwell Park Prep School. During this time, the Second World War was coming to an end, and Colchester, being a military town, saw many patrolling soldiers all the time. St. Mary's is located on Lexden Road and I recall the British troops would come marching down the road in front of the school with their motorized Bren Gun carriers.

"The headmistress at St. Mary's was quite strict and we received what I call proper teaching of reading, writing and what seemed like an endless reciting of our times tables. What I think wound up working to Ralph's benefit was that he was bilingual, speaking fluent French, which his whole family very often spoke at home. At the end of the school day we would all trundle off home in the late afternoon. Ralph and his sisters lived about three miles away from St. Mary's, so their parents collected them, while my sister and I lived closer and walked.

Top: Bates' father, Ralph, Sr.; Bottom: Ralph as a young boy

A Biography

Ralph as a young boy riding in his model toy car.

"I was a guest at the Bates house quite often and sometimes would stay overnight. My sister would stay as well, as she was a friend to Elisabeth (called Babette at the time, the French shortened version of Elisabeth). The house the Bates lived in, Braiswick Lodge, was a fine house with a drive through driveway built around 1800. It was a large house with gardens and stables where they kept a pony who was cared for by a stable hand named Mourie. On the property was a large Wellingtonia tree with a soft bark, which is also known as the California giant redwood. Inside the house in the drawing room were fine furniture and old French tapestries hanging on the walls and there was also a grand piano as well as a harp, which Ralph's mother played. Being children, we were all not allowed in the drawing room unless we were invited in. By the early 1950s I remember they had gotten a television, which they set up in a separate room. It was a well-appointed house. The property is now a residential home for the elderly.

"My family saw a lot of Ralph's mother Lilian. She was a very neat and petite French lady. So French was spoken at Braiswick Lodge a lot. They even had a French cook who came every day to the house to prepare meals. Sometimes my entire family would be invited over for supper at the Bates' house, which was a great treat, especially for the cider given to us children, which was very much looked forward to! Lilian was also a doctor and worked in Chelmsford, a town about 20 miles away from Colchester where she would drive in her little Daimler car. She was a very kind lady and also a very good harp player.

"Ralph, Sr. was a rather distinguished looking gentleman, with his silver hair always very neatly combed. He was a very handsome man and also a doctor of psychiatry. He was the chief of the psychiatric hospital in Colchester, which was a large institution for the mentally ill. He usually wore a bowtie and was well dressed. I remember that he was particularly interested in antiquities, especially Oriental porcelain. He had quite an interesting collection including Ming dynasty plates, which intrigued me. This connection with Chinese antiquities was due

An Orwell Park Prep School photo, 1949, shows Ralph sitting in a chair, far right.

to his family ties to the country. Another hobby he had was collecting coins from the Roman Empire period, especially those featuring the emperors. I recall that once he dug up in his very beautiful rose garden, at Braiswick Lodge, a silver Elizabethan (Queen Elizabeth I) three pence bit (from the mid-1500s). He was an extremely keen gardener and often spent time working on his rose garden. He also smoked a pipe or cigars from time to time. He drove an Armstrong Siddeley to work, which was a rather fine looking large automobile. He was what I call a gentleman, quite softly spoken. He was good-natured and never seemed to get angry or raise his voice, and I have no doubt he certainly had opportunities with Ralph and me for some of our antics! Another hobby he had was collecting cameras, and he had what in those days was quite rare, a movie camera. I remember that he took quite a number of moving films in Technicolor. One of the films he presented to Orwell Park School was a film of the summer of 1949 sports day at the school. This was the term where Ralph first went to Orwell Park. This film was noted in the Orwell Park magazine of that year and the students had a special assembly that autumn to view it.

"Orwell Park Prep School was (and still is) a well-known traditional boys day school, all boarding where you would live for the whole three months of the term, with three terms in a year. This was a preparatory school for the English public schools, which are private schools. Orwell Park School seemed like living in a stately home to me. It was set on a large 90-acre park filled with Cedar trees leading down to the river. There was also a ha-ha recessed barrier to keep the deer away. Also on the property was an observatory with a well-known Tomline Refractor telescope. The school also had a clock tower, a walled swimming pool and a pond where we sailed model boats. There were 95 boys at the school. It was a disciplined school where you had to work. There were a lot of societies the students could join, like a photographic society or a bird watching one. On Sundays we would all attend and sing in Nacton Church, located on the school grounds. The school hosted a film show every other Saturday. Unfortunately the old projector had a bad habit of breaking down, but when it worked we enjoyed watching lots of films featuring Laurel and Hardy, as well as Charlie Chaplin. For fun, Ralph and I and the other boys built small tunnels in the nearby woods with sheets of corrugated iron used for the roof—it was exciting times for us.

"It was at Orwell Park that Ralph first got involved in playing the sport of cricket. We both played in the under-12 division and later on the Orwell Park Second XI. Ralph's cricket skills had been noticed quite early at Orwell Park and in the school magazine for the 1949 summer term it noted, 'Outside the Second XI and the Under-12s, both Johnson and Bates showed exceptional promise for their age'. During the break in between lessons during the summer, you would be sort of an apprentice to one of the older students who played in the Orwell Park XI and he would throw cricket balls at you while you went forward and back. This sort of peer coaching helped us hone our skills. There were also cricket coaches to train us before the season began and Ralph, myself, and some of the other Essex cricketers were under the excellent tutelage of quite famous English cricketer Trevor Bailey. Known by the nickname Barnacle Bailey for his forward defensive stroke, our 'coach' became England's leading all-rounder after the Second World War. Bailey would coach us at the Castle Park ground in Colchester during the school Easter holiday.

"Ralph, like his father, always seemed good natured and never really had a bad temper. I do recall the first record Ralph bought when we were teenagers in 1955 was Bill Haley and his Comets *Rock Around the Clock*. We were about 15 years old and, although the rock and roll movement had been in America for sometime, it was only just arriving in England. Ralph played the record all the time at Braiswick Lodge. *Veni Vedi Vici* by Ronnie Hilton was another record Ralph was very fond of. Going along with the rock and roll movement was the desire to smoke cigarettes, which everyone was doing back then. Ralph and I started experimenting with cigarettes at age 14, although Ralph's father was not very keen about that and went out and bought both of us smoking pipes and tobacco from Fribourg and Treyer, famous pipe makers from the West End of London. But we didn't get on very well with the pipes and secretly went on smoking cigarettes. Among Ralph's other interests were radio and he was always listening to either *The Goon Show* or a mystery series called *The Third Man*. On the television Ralph was keen on a program by comedian Tony Hancock called *Hancock's Half Hour*. Both Ralph and his father loved that show, and when it came on, they would head down to the little television room to watch it.

"While we were on holiday, Ralph and I enjoyed going to movie theaters in Colchester. Among the ones we visited sometimes twice a week were The Regal, The Playhouse, The Cameo, The Hippodrome and The Empire. There was also a repertory theater in the town. We would go to just about any film we wanted to, as we had a lot of choices with the five cinemas. Mainly we would seek out Westerns that were playing, as we found them quite exciting. It was cheap entertainment for us only costing about a shilling or two.

"I kept in touch with Ralph after school, but we didn't see a lot of each other because he went on from Beaumont College to Trinity College in Dublin, and I went to London and joined a company called Brooke Bond, who were big in the tea trade and I eventually was posted to Java in the Far East. I met him again when I returned to England when he was married to Joanna Van Gyseghem. Ralph's parents by then had sold Braiswick Lodge and moved to a house called The Cannons on Layer Road in Colchester. It was a similar sort of house, with lovely gardens and of course two cannons outside the front door. The last time I saw Ralph was when he was doing the theater production of *Run For Your Wife!*, which was staged in Norwich where my family and I lived. My wife, my daughter and I met him after the production and we had coffee and a chat, which was the last time I saw him sadly. I attended Ralph's funeral with Elisabeth and I just cried and said he was my best friend. He was such a lovely man."[6]

Cricket coaching at Colchester Castle Park under the tutelage of famous cricketer Trevor Bailey. Ralph is wearing the black jacket with a white piping.

At age 13 during the autumn of 1953 Ralph entered Beaumont College in Berkshire, a school run by Jesuits. The Jesuit priests were very strict and infused their ideology, which had a big impact on Ralph's faith. It was also at Beaumont that Ralph realized he would not be following in the family profession. "Unfortunately, at college I was the sort of fellow who added up two and two and got five. I just couldn't pass the math exams to become a medical student."[7] And so Ralph's attention gravitated toward the arts and dramatics and he soon caught the acting bug. By 1955, as part of the Lower Line (the junior half of the school), Ralph made his acting debut on stage as Mrs. Tickle in the production of the farce *Baa Baa Black Sheep* by Ian Hay and P G Wodehouse. *The Beaumont Review*, the school's magazine that came out each term, made mention of this gender-bending role: "Some experienced hand produced most credible examples of young and attractive womanhood and it is always a revelation to see how the boys can assume such alien identities."[8] In November of 1956, Ralph had gravitated to the Higher Line production of *The Magistrate*, a farce by Sir Arthur Pinero, in which he played the lead role of Mr. Posket. This role earned Ralph his first name mention in *The Beaumont Review*: "Bates rendered a very able Posket: querulous and weak good nature: the head of a Victorian family who is the reverse of assured of his domestic status as an autocrat: the magistrate who pays his victims' fines: the virtuous man who finds himself, without knowing how, almost before his own Bench."[9] Also in the cast, along with Ralph, was fellow student and friend Matthew

A Biography

The Beaumont College production of *The Housemaster* (1955); Ralph Bates is seated at the desk on the far right; Matthew Guinness is center wearing a bald wig.

Guinness, son of actor Alec Guinness, who played the role of Cis Farringdon and was noted for his complete confidence and accomplishment. In December of the same year Ralph had a cameo as the Demon Nasser in the school Pantomime of *Robinson Crusoe*. Already showing a penchant for comedy, Ralph continued to showcase his abilities in the December 1957 Pantomime of *The Sleeping Beauty*, which he not only wrote but also appeared in a cameo role as Komik. Once again, Ralph was highlighted in *The Beaumont Review*: "Highest praise must undoubtedly go to Bates whose 'Komik' acts were just that, quite admirably carried out with the able assistance of Barrington Tristram as his 'stooge.' Their contortions with a ladder were, in particular, in the best tradition of slapstick." [10] By the end of his time at Beaumont, Ralph was convinced that acting was for him. It would not be an easy journey, but for Ralph, his dream of entertaining others would be a richly rewarding career that he would continue for the rest of his life.

Besides his budding interest in acting, Ralph also continued learning the game of cricket at Beaumont College, which never left his heart. Ralph practiced to become a spin bowler, which involves putting such a spin on the ball that when it bounces it leaves its straight course making it difficult for a batsman to make contact. Later in life he even got to wear the famous red and yellow necktie, the symbol of the world-known Marylebone Cricket Club at Lords. When Ralph captained Beaumont College against the Oratory School at Lord's Cricket ground in London (The Mecca of Cricket), he felt he had made it. [11] He continued to play the sport throughout his life and became a prolific and accomplished cricket player, playing in many charity matches and even teaching the game at his son Will's primary school.

One of Ralph's friends at Beaumont, Henry Stevens, recalled their time at school together. "Ralph was a great pal of mine. We lived in the same town of Colchester and grew up together. We both were part of a small group of friends who always hung around together. I used to catch a ride with him back to school as, at the time, we only went home once a term. Ralph was like a magnet—he always seemed to attract people. This was due to his charismatic personality and a great sense of humor; he could always make you laugh. Ralph was an avid fan of *The Goon Show*. He could imitate Peter Sellers' voice perfectly. I think Ralph was always destined to be an actor. His pranks and sense of humor were always way ahead of his contemporaries at school. He wasn't a great cricketer but captained the first XI as a very good natural leader. People always wanted to do their best for him. We were lucky as Beaumont was one of the very few schools in all of England that got to play at Lords, which of course was incredibly popular being the home of the sport of cricket. I remember one time he made a stunning catch at Lords without touching the ball. It shot straight into his midriff and got stuck in his crotch! We all laughed—it was just so Ralph—it summed him all up." [12]

Bates (right) poses with his school mates.

Robin Mulcahy remembered Ralph being a member of a unique bunch of friends at Beaumont. "I did have a brief but close relationship with Ralph at Beaumont as Chief Gherkin of the Ole Society, along with the other members John Wolff and Matthew Guinness. This was an epicurean gathering feasting largely off the purloined goodies of our unbeknownst parents. All so innocent. I remember one particular occasion when the school matron roasted a chicken for us!" [13]

"It was always clear to me that despite the presence of some good actors (Beaumont had a strong tradition in the theater), Ralph stood out and took the lead in most productions," recollects Michael Parker. "It seemed very likely that he would follow this route to a professional career. Ralph was also a talented sportsman playing both cricket and squash for the school. He captained the first XI in 1958 and this proved to be a happy and successful side due in large measure to his charismatic influence. He was always great fun and a good friend to many; myself included, and is still much missed."[14] "I met Ralph on our first day at public school at Beaumont College in October of 1953," recalls John Wolff, one of Ralph's close friends. "We were both 13 years old and had been told to look out for each other by our older sisters, who knew each other at a convent called New Hall near Chelmsford. My sister was friendly with Ralph's second sister, Elisabeth. Ralph became a close friend of mine from then on. He was lucky in a way because he knew what he wanted to do in life even then—act—when most boys had no clear idea what they would do for a living. The Jesuits who ran Beaumont encouraged acting as part of the curriculum. Ralph was in a junior class play, which was considered one of the best ever at the school, an extract from *Journey's End* by R.C. Sherriff about being in the trenches in the First World War. As he progressed he took leading roles in senior school productions. During the holidays he used to go watch wrestling back home in Colchester.

A Biography

He enjoyed the theatrics of it. To raise money for charity he coached a number of us and under false names we put on a performance at Beaumont in the school boxing ring, causing a lot of laughs!

"Ralph was also on the school squash team. In addition he captained the first XI cricket team. This was an inspired but risky decision by the coach because Ralph was not one of the stronger members of the team. But he proved to be a good captain and tactician and the team was nearly unbeaten. As Ralph was not one of the better bowlers or batsman, he trained himself to become a very good fielder and specialized in fielding directly in line with mid on and very close to the batsman, a brave position called the Silly mid on. Ralph had a kind of mind over matter facility if he really wanted to do something, which was evident in his fielding that position and in learning long parts for theater productions at short notice.

Bates makes an impressive diving play at school.

"Years later I went to see him and Terence Brady and others in a review in London at that time. He was truly honing his craft as an actor. I was studying in Germany then, around 1960, and he visited me for a weekend from Dublin. I remember that he was wearing a jumper with 'Guinness' written across the front, which caused comments. Although common now, company logos on clothes were rarely seen in those days. I also saw him later in the productions *Run for Your Wife!* and *Hedda Gabler* on stage in London.

"I only found out Ralph was terminally ill in February of 1991. From his initial diagnosis of pancreatic cancer, Ralph only had about 12 weeks to live. I managed to see him in the hospital. He told me he had been through the whole range of emotions from fear to consolation but I think the main one was still shock at the severity of his illness and the short time he had to live. He kindly sent me a card thanking me for coming, which I still hold on to. I was very fond of him and it was tough losing a close friend at such a young age." [15]

"I came to Beaumont effectively a year early, so spent two years in the first year group, but was a few months younger than Ralph," recalls Barrington Tristram. "I think Ralph may have spent his first year in the A stream, but from year two, aged 15, we went up the school together. However at age 16, because my parents had moved to Windsor (and were short of money), I became a dayboy, one of a small group of about 10 boys, a number of who were sons of lay masters, and which included the future Nobel Laureate Prof. Anthony Leggett. I commuted from home, initially on a motor-assisted pedal bike and later on a 98cc James motorbike. It was in our 15-year-old class that we acted in an adaptation of *Journeys End*, which was directed by our class teacher Reverend Malcolm Clark SJ, who was a very intelligent but not very charismatic Jesuit, at the time a 'scholastic,' that is not yet ordained as a priest, and who subsequently became a noted theologian and I believe later left the priesthood. The occasion of the play was an annual one-act play competition for the seven classes of the junior school, and indeed the production was of a high standard for our age group. Ralph played the disillusioned company commander Stanhope, I played the keen newly-joined subaltern (Raleigh), Matthew Guinness was the other officer and Michael Patterson had a successful cameo as the batman. I can't recall other actors, in which case it would seem we were some way from the 'all-inclusive' approach to a class play that would be de rigueur today. Ralph played the lead in Pinero's *The Magistrate* and Ian Hay's *The Housemaster*, which were annual plays presented by both the junior and senior schools and attended by parents etc., and which were always in my opinion very competently directed by members of the staff. These two were both, I believe, directed by Reverend Fr R.C. Ezechiel SJ.

"At the end of the winter term of our last year, it was traditional to organize a pantomime, replete with in-jokes and impressions of staff idiosyncrasies. Ralph and I did a lot of work on this in 1957, although we had a script from a boy called Kevin McGrath. In our working scripts we had referred to ourselves as Komics, intending to adopt some such persona as 'the brokers' men,' but in fact we were still billed as Komics when the program was printed (by The Scout Press at school, who undertook all such work). All I can remember of our act is a very unhealthy safety episode with Ralph hanging on top of a ladder as I staggered round the stage carrying it.

Bates reads and relaxes at school.

"Once in the sixth form, boys at Beaumont moved from dormitories to rooms, some single and some, as I remember, shared. As a dayboy I needed somewhere to do my homework and study in free periods and thus I moved in with Ralph. I think we spent 18 shillings on a toaster, and 'improved' the decorative effect by pasting newspapers on the walls in lieu of wallpaper. As I had my small motorbike I had more freedom than most, and at some stage in our careers I used to ride, with Ralph on the pillion, to a pub in Old Windsor, virtually the last building before one of the entrances to the Great Park, called The Union Inn (because it was adjacent to the old workhouse). This was a beerhouse (no license to sell spirits), so we didn't get into too much alcohol trouble. We used to drink beer and play dominoes with the locals. Our school friends also used the pub, as it was virtually certain that no member of staff would ever go there, but of course it was more of a slog to get there by bike (if you had one), but I think that it was Ralph and I of our generation who discovered it. Opening hours were elastic. The village PC used to drop in for a couple of drinks when he came off duty at 11pm, although closing time was 10.30.

"A major shared interest from the age of about 15 was *The Goon Show*, which of course fed into Ralph's general theatrical interests. There was a radio in the common room and Ralph and I would huddle over it every week to listen to the latest episode, and of course, like half the country at the time, revert to the catch phrases and silly voices at the drop of a hat. Neither of us could have done much work in the sixth form, Ralph was of course heavily involved in cricket.

"Another 6th form memory is of the Debating Society. I recall that at the beginning of the first term I wrote a speech for Ralph that he memorized and delivered brilliantly, in order to be elected a member. Although I was also elected, my own speeches were often inadequately

A Biography

Beaumont vs. Oratory, the 1958 match card

prepared and less effective. I don't recall being his speechwriter again, so maybe Ralph made his mark and then turned to other activities. I have a copy of the scorecard for the annual match with the Oratory School at Lords, which Beaumont won in the year of Ralph's captaincy. He was not only a spin bowler rather than a speed merchant, but he was also a leg spinner. On a suitable pitch as you may well know a leg break bowler can be deadly, but on a flat surface he can be expensive. As our home ground was usually a pretty good batting wicket, I have no idea what his bowling average looked like at the end of the season, but as John Wolff said, he was at 18 years old a mature individual, with a sense of humor, who was an admirable captain of a team with a number of either younger or more volatile characters. While I never had any contact with Ralph during the holidays, I did see his father once when he supervised a visit a number of us made to London to see the original production of *Waiting for Godot*.

"After I left school I never saw him again; however, when I was serving in the regular army in Belize in 1970 I wrote to him care of Hammer Films. I received a warm and friendly letter in return. After that the necessity to earn a living after leaving the army, and getting married and having two children in the first three years put a reunion on the back burner, and sadly Ralph's early death intervened before I tried to make any arrangements to meet up."[16]

"At 17 Ralph bought a small ex-Navy motorbike," recalled his sister Elisabeth. "The wheels were so small that he appeared to be sitting on the ground as he flew down the country lanes, his ex-Navy duffle coat billowing behind him. As he got older, he enjoyed visits to the local repertory theater. This was not met with a lot of enthusiasm by his parents who had hoped their son might follow in their footsteps and go into the medical field. The acting profession was extremely difficult and even more so to make a living. Still, Ralph hoped to pursue his dream and began doing a stint in 'rep' while trying to seek an agent to represent him. He built up his experience at Colchester Repertory Theatre, and it was, necessarily, mighty hard work. Playing one part, rehearsing another and learning a third, week after week, was what being in repertory theater meant." [17]

Although Ralph was born in England, as were his two sisters; he was not officially considered "English" until he actually turned 21. As Bates explained in an interview with Ian Woodward, "I was raised part of the time in France, and I spent a lot of time in the South during school holidays, with the family there. I know the French can sometimes be pig-headed, but if the chips were down and they said, "Okay, you have a choice of living in Britain or France," there would be no question that, despite all the pitfalls and all the uncertainties of earning a living, I'd go to France. My mother had given me a French passport but, at 21, you have to opt for either French or British nationality and I chose to be British." [18]

Bates in a rowboat circa 1956

After Beaumont Ralph went to North East Essex Technical College before going on, in 1959, to Trinity College in Dublin, where he first studied Law for a term before switching to General Studies, which allowed him to study French and left time for his true passion, acting. It was only a matter of time before Ralph joined the Players acting amateur troupe, Trinity's famous undergraduate theater company. Many of their major productions were staged at the nearby Olympia Theatre on Dame Street. Bates' first stage appearance after joining the Players was in fellow alumni Bruce Arnold's December 1959 production of *The Life and Death of Sir Walter Raleigh*, in which he played the role of Lord Cecil. Featured in a courtroom scene taking place at Winchester, Bates' first lines in a Players production were: 'My Lords, I would hold your attention for one moment. I like not these dealings we have with Raleigh. I disliked equally our dealings with Cobham. But we are none of us our own masters. We have done the King's service and not our own, and that only partially. Let us swiftly away with the rest of it.' [19]

It would not be long before Ralph's talent earned him a nod in the University newspaper, *The Trinity News*, which revealed: "The acting redeemed the evening and the Players can be sure of a better future with better plays if they can retain the services of the Freshmen in *As We Were*. Ralph Bates will find it hard to throw off the name of 'Trinity's Louis Jourdan,' but he would do well to copy that actor's more forceful delivery and not be too pianissimo." [20]

In an interview many years later with Suraya Al-Attas, Bates reflected on his time at Trinity. "It was a struggle but I managed to pull through with an MA. I was already interested in acting while in college, but my parents wouldn't hear of it until I completed my studies. My parents were both psychiatrists but they weren't against my choice of a career at all. In fact, they were very supportive. They just wanted me to finish school first, and looking back, I know they've put the right kind of barriers." [21]

It was in the Players Dramatic Society that Ralph would meet another student who was interested in acting and would become very important in his life, Joanna Van Gyseghem. They were often cast in opposite roles with her as an old woman and Ralph as an old man. Joanna explained their time at Trinity: "We were all in our twenties and were very young and just left school not long before. We were very lucky as a group of people, some of whom went on to become actors, working for the BBC or becoming producers. It was an extraordinary group of people with Terence Brady, Michael Bogdin (future theater director), Ralph and me, along with some others. One of his good friends at Trinity was Roger Ordish, who shared flats with us. He went on to become a big producer for the BBC. He was a great mate while we were finishing up at Trinity. He and Ralph were like terrible twins behaving very silly and always doing comedy stuff to each other.

"Ralph was absolutely the sweetest person. He was very funny, gorgeous, handsome and French. He was quite cool even doing the simplest things. An example being just putting on a pair of jeans, and he was immediately cool, whereas other people might not be so cool. Remember, this was the 1960s! We did a lot of stuff in the Players Theatre together at Trinity." [22]

Besides Joanna, some of Ralph's other fellow alumni were Shane Briant, who would also go on to become one of the "next generation" of Hammer horror stars, and another person who became one of Ralph's best friends, future actor/playwright Terence Brady. Sharing his memories of Ralph, Brady explained: "I did quite a lot of plays and revues with Ralph. I was two years ahead of him at Trinity, and when he arrived, I was already Chairman of the Players Dramatic Society. I was writing scripts and plays for the society by then, and when Michael Bogdin arrived, who, after he left Trinity, changed his last name for professional reasons to Michael Bogdanov, I began collaborating with Mike for the many revues the Players staged and toured. Ralph joined the Players that year, as did Joanna Van Gyseghem. They were strangers to each other before going to Trinity, and their romantic association didn't begin until they were leaving. Ralph came to Trinity with a girlfriend already in his life (someone he called Fluff), which was quite a long association. Joanna soon became involved in a relationship with another student called Bart O'Brien.

"I think the first performances Ralph and I did together were most probably in the summer revues. He was certainly the second leading man in the revue *Way Out*, written by Bogdin and myself, with myself as lead. Ralph and I worked together in *The Hole* by N. F. Simpson, *The Long and the Short and the Tall* by Willis Hall and probably most notably in the two handed *The Dock Brief* by John Mortimer, for which we won the Best One Act play at the Universities Drama Association Festival in Galway, where I also won Best Actor for performances in

Bates poses at the side entrance to Braiswick Lodge (1957).

The Dock Brief and *The Long and the Short and the Tall*. The Players Company were then invited to appear at Joan Littlewood's famous Theatre Royal in Stratford East, London, where we performed *The Dumb Waiter* and a revue called *Would Anyone Who Saw The Accident*, again written by Bogdin and myself. The show got very well reviewed in London and led to a lot of interest in the cast, including Ralph—probably where he first got noticed. By then I had already graduated and remained in London, where

Bates and his school chums pose by an airplane.

I was invited to take over from Peter Cook in *Beyond the Fringe*, in which I appeared for two years at the Fortune Theatre, London.

"In terms of Ralph's acting I felt that his good looks were a great help, as was his own personal style, but I always thought he was far better in comedy than in straight drama. That's a compliment, by the way. I think comedy is far harder than straight acting and, because Ralph could do deadpan so well, I loved to act with him in comedy. Our very different styles worked very well together, and one sketch we performed called *Time* (written by Bogdin and Brady) showed Ralph at his very best. It also drew complimentary notices from none other than Samuel Beckett, who whenever he was in Dublin would attend performances at Players, although I don't think Ralph was ever aware of Beckett's admiration. Beckett was a very private man.

"For a long time Ralph was my best friend. We struck it off from the moment we met and I counted him as one of my closest friends while I was at Trinity and for a short while afterwards. He was very generous—absurdly so sometimes, funny, obviously, and good company (when he left his French side behind)—stylish, ridiculously so for a student in those times, and attractive to both sexes. I don't mean sexually; I mean he was equally at ease with his men friends as he was with his girl friends. He was demanding and sometimes petulant, but he was half French and inclined to quite a lot of introspection. He also greatly enjoyed indulging in what he called *subterfuge*, which normally entailed playing off one friend against another. He attracted great loyalty in his own coterie, a power that he did not always use for the common good. Yet when you were on the inside it was a very good place to be. He was also capable of becoming quite jealous, sometimes extremely so—which is where he needed the counsel of his friends—and which he did not always get, since most of them were entirely enthralled by his charisma. I'm not sure which Ralph I loved best, the friend or the actor, for when you are such close friends, these sort of identities are inclined to merge together. Perhaps finally I would have preferred him as *schoolmate* than as *acteur*.

"I can say Ralph and I always laughed and laughed and laughed whenever we worked or played together. Once when we were doing *The Dock Brief*, because I was playing an older man and because Ralph and I were obsessed with make-up (as actors were then), I was wearing nose putty and it was such a hot day and the theater so small, my nose melted and Ralph had

Bates and Babette in a rowboat (1959)

to play opposite me during a 10-minute meltdown until I ended up looking like an old turkey. And there was the time during *The Long and the Short and the Tall* when the actor shooting the Japanese prisoner while aiming his blank-loaded pistol managed to hit the electrician in the leg with the wad, and the electrician fell out of his box onto the stage. And then there was the time—no. Too many were the good times. And those are what I remember.

"Ralph was enormously helped in his career by the fact women fancied him, and having spent two years sharing a flat with him in Dublin, sharing the typical adventures of wayfaring undergraduates, I saw this close up. As you probably know, the secret to attracting women is both to like women and to listen to them. Ralph checked off these two boxes. After he broke up with Fluff he then had a serious relationship with an American student, Jodie Saugsted, which I seem to remember he was still involved with when I left Trinity. He was not going out with Joanna then. I was delighted when later I heard he had become a Hammer films star, although I was also surprised because, of all the actors I knew, I would never have cast Ralph in such roles. To me he was still a young Buster Keaton, with a very poetic style and a sweetly mournful expression. I think he liked acting with me as much as I did with him. I know we loved doing *The Dock Brief,* which we played not only in Dublin and Galway but also back in England. After our last performance, Ralph gave me a memento in the shape of the notes I took nightly as Morgenhall, the solicitor (Ralph played Fowle, the convicted murderer), framed and mounted and inscribed by Ralph with the message, '*Brady at his best.*' It still hangs in my study. He then went on to achieve national television fame in both drama and comedy and was certainly a very popular and attractive actor." [23]

Bates (left) and Babette (right) relaxing outside

Michael Bogdin, who also became good friends with Bates, shared his memories of Trinity. "The first time I met Ralph was by accident as I had picked up my mail from the post box at Trinity College and, along with mine, was one letter for an R. Bates. I hadn't realized it until I got to the Players Society and inquired if anyone knew whom he was; I was directed over to Ralph and that is how we first met each other. Rather quickly, Ralph, myself, Terence and Joanna became close as a quartet at Trinity.

"I had become quite good friends with Ralph and I was Best Man at his wedding to Joanna. Ralph would sometimes visit me at my place in Ruislip, which is a suburb of London, and I would also visit him at his place. We used to travel together to Trinity. Ralph had a Bubble car, which was a funny looking little car, with three wheels, and literally looked like its name implied. So we used to travel across to Dublin in this bubble car. We usually stayed the night somewhere around Birmingham before getting to the ferry and going over to Trinity. We could sometimes cram about four people into that bubble car with arms hanging out. It was a wonderful little car. We also used to take the trip together to Clare Island, which was a nice place to visit.

"On one of our trips to Birmingham we wound up in this extraordinary pub and actually created our own dance. It was the time that Roy Orbison had his hit song *Only the Lonely*, which was all the rage. Ralph and I devised this dance we called the Brummy to Orbison's song. We gave it that name, as we created it in Birmingham, and that is what someone from there is called. It was a strange dance with our feet kicking out and our hands almost swinging like a breaststroke. We kept that dance up for several years and we even taught it to other people." [24]

While at Trinity, Bates' acting talents blossomed and he was judged Best Actor in the University's Drama Association Festival at Belfast, in 1962, for his portrayal of Stavrogin in *The Possessed*. The production, by director John Jay, was also awarded Best Three-Act play and the Sunday Review Cup for Best Production. The Players received many accolades in the *Trinity News*, following their five U.D.A. awards won at the 1962 Festival held in Belfast. The paper noted the difficulties the Players faced for the Festival:

Players are particularly to be congratulated as they had very little time to rehearse and accustom themselves to the rather unusual stages; the three-act plays were performed on a stage wider than that of the Olympia and no higher than the Players stage, and the one-act plays were presented on a stage so small (nine feet square) that three people fell off it during the run-through of the *Bald Prima Donna*! [25]

In Michael Bogdin's "revuesical" entitled *Bricks*, Bates also received praise:

It is the first half that has the entertainment and the zip of the Revue. Ralph Bates and Roger Ordish lead the cast and captivate the audience, never faltering in the smoothness of their performances. [26]

Another Trinity alumni with fond memories of Bates is Scottish poet and author Ian Blake. "Ralph took the lead in my play *The Meeting* which won the Best Original Play award at the 1963 Irish Universities Drama Festival," recalled Blake. "We both acted in Players—the drama group at Trinity College of Dublin. We were both in a production of *The Hole* by N. F. Simpson in my first term festival, and also in *The Long and the Short and the Tall* by Willis Hall, which was a great success with audiences at the 1961 Irish University Drama Festival in Galway.

"After Trinity and time spent as a Research Scholar for the British School of Archaeology, I eventually began teaching English at Charterhouse and, meeting Ralph by chance, I asked him to talk to some pupils interested in acting to share his experience. This went over very well and as a result I remember his daughter Daisy came to the school as a Sixth Form student. She was an intelligent and interested student who became a fine young actor in her own right.

"I last saw Ralph not long before he died at his home in Chiswick. He gave me a photograph of three of us (Michael Bogdin was the third) as farcical Roman Soldiers in a 1960 revue at Camberley, Surrey, which I keep framed above my desk. On the photo Ralph had written, "I only work with the greatest!" It is a tragedy that such a talented actor should die so young. After attending Ralph's funeral, I was inspired to write a poem as a tribute to him entitled "Death of an Actor." [27]

Bates continued to thrive in the Players and by 1963 became the Chairman of the group. He was even profiled in *Trinity News*, along with his friend Roger Ordish, for a tongue-in-cheek student biography. As reported on Bates, "He has more often been criticized for his impressions of senile men in wire glasses. He is currently appearing in *Cuchulain* where, typecast once more, he is playing the fool. Although he started in Law School, Ralph soon found his level in General Studies in French (he is half-French), Mental and Moral (he is half mental and half moral) and History (no comment). Moore is his favorite philosopher and fellow Player Joanna van Gyseghem is his fiancée. He persuaded her to accept by offering her a surname which she would be able to spell." [28] In a *Trinity News* review of *Cuchulain*, Bates was singled out for his performance, "Ralph Bates, the Fool and W.B. Yeats proved that he is the only truly versatile actor in Players." [29] For his performance in *Cuchulain*, Bates once again received the Best Actor Award in the University's Drama Association Festival in 1964. [30] During his time at Trinity, Ralph and a number of his fellow students decided to take a trip to America, where as he described it, "We just wanted to see the place, and we travelled all over the country on buses, just seeing the sights. It was great!" [31]

Michael Bogdin, who came along for the trip to America, shared his memories of it. "I did go to America with Ralph and some other friends. About 20 students from Trinity had all decided to make the trip, but only Ralph, myself and Peter Bell decided to travel the country. We planned the whole trip together and Peter had chartered an airplane that cost us virtually nothing. We started out in Rhode Island and stayed at the home of a lady called Eliza Collins, whose mother was a painter. She had a house on Payton Avenue, right near the beach. Ralph, Peter, and I stayed up there to start and then we went down south. Ralph and Peter went down ahead of me to New Orleans on a Greyhound bus and I decided to hitch there. In fact I still have a letter that Ralph left for me in New Orleans to say where he was, so we could meet up again. Then Peter and I hitched on down to Mexico and Ralph took the bus over to Los Angeles, to Jodie Saugsted's place. Her father was a photographer for Warner Bros. We all later met up at Jodie's and then I hitched on back. After meeting up again on the East Coast we all went home together." [32]

Scottish poet and author Ian Blake

With his interest piqued, Ralph had a desire to eventually return and even did American studies as a subsidiary bit of study at Trinity, but before pursuing his overseas goal, he decided on a more personal goal to marry Joanna Van Gyseghem. The two hopeful thespians had been dating for a while at Trinity and decided to marry. Ralph then applied to the prestigious Yale University in America on an acting scholarship and was accepted. Joanna Van Gyseghem described their wedding and time spent in America: "We had a big wedding in London, which made the papers as my mother was very well known as an actress (Jean Forbes-Robertson) and the press picked up on that. It was all rather glamorous and good fun. Ralph's family was absolutely great. We really had a great time in those days when we were all young and foolish. We were still in Dublin when we got married.

"Ralph always wanted to be an actor, as far as I remember. While we were in Dublin, we had some very good friends who managed one of the theaters there called The Gas Company. It got its name from literally being located directly above a gas company. Ralph and I thought we would like to put on a production or two, so we pooled our money and formed our own little company. We hired actors with whom we were friends and eventually put on the play *Private Lives*, by Noel Coward. Although I was involved with Ralph in the theater, I did not plan on going into acting at this point and spent time studying for exams. Ralph did not act in this production, as I remember, but it was still good fun. He did get a bit part in a documentary film entitled *Street and Sand*, while we were in Dublin in 1961, and that was quite exciting." [33]

Michael Bogdin explained his role in the production company: "We later on started our own theater production company at the Gas Company Theatre on St. George's Street in Dun Laoghaire, which is 10 miles outside Dublin. Ralph and Joanna put up the money and I directed the shows. We did three shows there altogether: *Private Lives*, *Wolf's Clothing* and a revue called *Patterns*, which was a compilation of the work of R.B.D. French. Ralph and Joanna didn't perform in them and in fact Ralph and Joanna went back to Britain. Ralph came out to see a couple of the shows." [34]

Ralph Bates' first wife, Joanna Van Gyseghem (Getty Images)

Now married and contemplating his next steps towards an acting career, Bates decided to return to America. He hoped to get accepted to one of the universities there to continue his education and get to travel the country again as he did previously with his friends from Trinity. As Joanna Van Gyseghem explains, "Ralph also had a desire to go to the States. A lot of us who were born around the War had a very wonderful romantic feeling about America and Americans. He did feel he ought to have some training to become an actor. He didn't want to go and spend three years at some proper drama school so he cleverly applied to Yale for a scholarship. And it was only one semester. We went October and by the summer we were already driving all over the States. We sailed over America, as Ralph hated flying. We were in no rush and we went on the original Queen Mary. We had married in June and went to America in October. Being the fall season, the ship was not really full and it was a beautiful ship with its 1930 décor. We went to our cabin, which was the cheapest one we could get; it faced the inside which we thought was not the greatest, so Ralph went to the steward, and being a bit bold, said: "I don't suppose there is any room we can get upgraded to?" and the steward said to Ralph, "follow me sir." Ralph went off with this steward into the depths of the ship. Ralph said to me later he did not know what to expect but it turns out the steward just wanted a little extra something in the hand, so Ralph gave him a pound and we were moved to a room overlooking the sea, with a beautiful view. We then traveled to New Haven, Connecticut. It was strange for us but great there and we got a real cheap flat. The Americans were so nice to us there. The Dean and his wife were especially kind to us when we arrived. They took us over to their house and fed us. Ralph did some very good stuff there including the George Bernard Shaw play *Arms and the Man*, and he played the lead, which was absolutely lovely. Jon Jory played opposite Ralph and became good friends with us. Jory went on to become a theater director and founded the Actors Theatre of Louisville.

"During this time I got the odd job helping a bit with our finances by selling lingerie in a Macy's department store. They kept saying, "Oh I love your accent!" Then we took some time off at the end of the semester and we bought a car to travel around. Ralph always loved flashy American cars. He loved big cars that in those days were very cheap. He bought this beautiful red Chevrolet Impala. And we drove off down to Houston, Texas with a friend who lived there and we stayed to visit. Afterwards, we drove across to California to see some other friends and it was 1964, Beatles time. Everyone kept asking us, "Oh do you know the Beatles?" We ended up playing along and said, "Yeah, we met," and they all believed us. It was all very hippy, lovely and West Coast. On our first wedding anniversary we were driving up the coast not knowing were we were going to stay. We did not see any hotels but eventually we saw lights, which turned out to be the Big Sur hot springs. The people there were really kind and brought us flowers and breakfast in the morning for our anniversary. You could sit in these hot springs overlooking the ocean and the view was gorgeous. The Big Sur hot springs was quite a famous place and very trendy, but we didn't know anything about it until much later of course." [35]

Besides playing lead in *Arms and the Man* while at the Yale School of Drama, Ralph also performed in a feature role in the 1965 production of *Masquerade*, a collection of three plays by Bill Kelb. In the play *Honeymoon in Haiti*, Bates played the lead character of the Prince. [36]

Bates' friend and fellow alumni Jon Jory recalled their time acting together at Yale: "I only worked with Ralph once. He played Bluntschli and I played Sergius at Yale. It was a bit dismaying. I was young, he was young, how was it that he seemed … well … so much better? Because, you see, he was a prodigy. He was an actor in his early 20s who simply had 40-year-old skills when he woke up in the morning. He didn't gloat. Actually he seemed unaware. He just went out nightly and wiped me off the stage. To top it all off he was generous, kind and definitely kept the lid on his ego. Ralph was utterly at home on stage and probably had been for a long time. It would have been nice to think that there was endless work to achieve his ease, but I viewed him narrowly and had to conclude the ease was innate. I wish I could have seen him at work later in his maturity, but I never did. With all the buffeting that life so kindly provides, he must have deepened and broadened and sharpened but, honestly, he was amazing enough at 20." [37]

While Yale was a good experience for Bates, he did feel that the timing could have been a bit better for his stay at the University, "I then went to Yale in the United States and studied acting there for a year. Unfortunately, the year after I left, they revamped the whole film department and became very modernized; I was taught by the same old people who had taught people like Van Heflin years and years ago; acting has changed since then." [38] However, the University was not without its benefits, "I used to sit behind a glass partition and read all Paul Newman's letters." [39]

Like many actors, dreams of starring in Hollywood productions no doubt crossed Ralph's mind upon finishing at Yale, but this was not to be. The American actors' union was quite protective and Ralph was unable to get a work permit there, which would have allowed him to act professionally. [40] Ralph and Joanna returned to England and decided to take fate into their own hands.

Chapter 2
"Any means is worth the end result!"

The swinging 1960s brought big changes to British theater. In 1961, Peter Hall, the director of the Shakespeare Memorial Theatre, announced the formation of a permanent company known as the Royal Shakespeare Theatre. This transformed an annual festival of plays into year round productions in England. Competition came in 1963 with the formation of the National Theatre, under the leadership of Laurence Olivier. The National Theatre, which also previously put on various productions, established itself that October with an opening performance by Peter O'Toole in the lead role of the production of *Hamlet* at the Old Vic Theatre. With the establishment of these two major theater companies, the acting profession received a major boost and shine in the public eye. In addition, a number of big name actors were getting much praise in the public spotlight during the prime of their career, including some of Bates' favorites: Laurence Olivier, Albert Finney, Tom Courtney and Richard Harris. By the time Bates and Joanna returned to England, there were loads of opportunities for young actors looking to make a start to their career.

It was not long before Bates would make his professional debut in 1964 with the Edwards-MacLiammóir Company in their production of George Bernard Shaw's *You Never Can Tell*, which was performed at the Gate Theatre in Dublin. Bates was on hallowed ground at the Gate Theatre, for a number of legendary actors had gotten their start on this stage including Orson Welles and James Mason. The building that houses the Gate Theatre was built in the late 18th century and originally served as the Great Supper Room of the Rotunda Maternity Hospital.

In 1928 Hilton Edwards and Micheál MacLiammóir converted it into a theater featuring sphinx reliefs above the stage to bring European and American theater productions to Dublin. The Gate Theatre is still very much active and is located on Parnell Square in Dublin, Ireland. Following his debut, Bates went on to join the Colchester Repertory Theatre for two years and also appeared with local production companies including Richmond, Plymouth, and the Glasgow Citizens Theatre.

As Joanna Van Gyseghem explained, "When we went back to London we had our little house, one of the few people of our age group to be able to do so. Everyone used to come around to our place and we played games of *Risk* and would chat for hours. It was a very good time really. Ralph got jobs

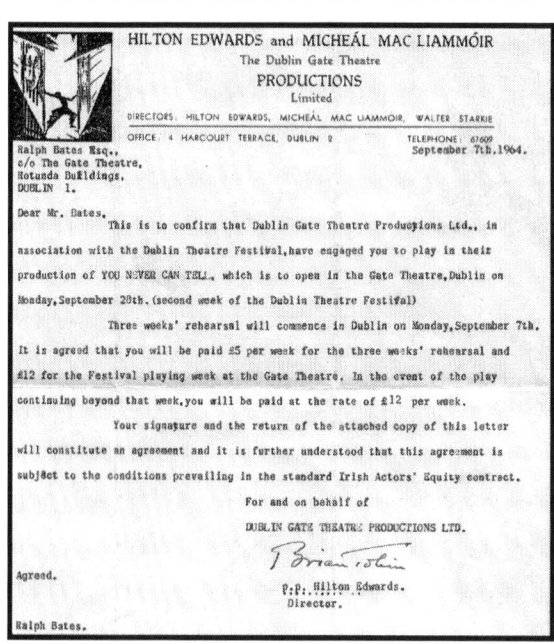

Bates' theater contract for *You Never Can Tell*, his professional debut in 1964

here and there and then we went into repertory together and spent two seasons doing all sorts of plays.

"We were in a play called *You Never Can Tell*. It was a Shaw play and Ralph and I were cast as twins. I had a dress that was made with a zipper up the entire back, which it shouldn't have had. I was behaving silly because we were playing these twins and I suddenly felt the zipper go and the entire length of the dress from my neck down to my underwear was exposed in the back. I knew what had happened but nobody else on the stage could see it. I also knew that I couldn't turn around, but Ralph and I were supposed to make this big exit together. Then we were to turn around, walk back upstage and off. But I couldn't do that, as I knew my dress was completely open. I remember Ralph tried to wrench my arm around and whispered come on now while I'm going—no no! So eventually I staggered off backwards. And then somebody had to find a lot of safety pins!

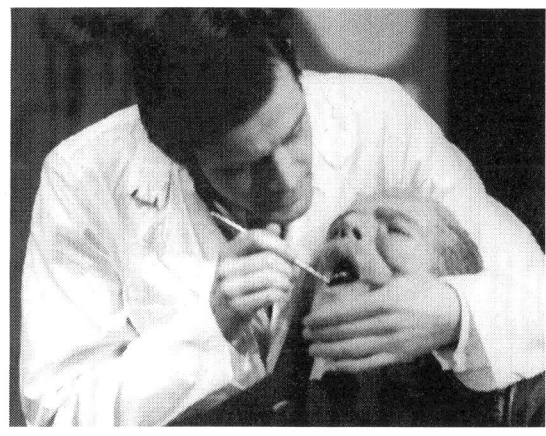

Bates examines Geoffrey Hutchings in *You Never Can Tell* (1964).

"I remember that Ralph was very nervous in the theater. In fact, at the time he was nervous about acting in general, often standing in the wings shaking with nerves. Which is sort of unusual for someone in the prime of his or her acting career. It usually happens much later, funnily enough. However, that being said, I think that Ralph preferred working in theater as opposed to film or television. In theater you always had another chance the next night with a different audience. Ralph may have been nervous before going on stage, but he was always fine once he went on." [41]

You Never Can Tell was reviewed by *Theatre World* magazine and the young Bates couple was noted for their performance. "The revolutionary Shaw has settled into the Festival's "classic corner" and *You Never Can Tell* was presented at the Gate during the second week, under Chloe Gibson's direction, and it delighted full houses. The amusing and incisive dialogue was well delivered by the whole company, and the three sets by Alpho O'Reilly were of a high order. Joanna Bates was Dickensian in appearance and deportment. The twins (played by Joanna and her husband Ralph) scored by taking full advantage of the freedom the author had given them." [42] While Bates may have been nervous about performing, he continued to improve in his craft and by the mid-1960s he was appearing on television. One of the first television exposures for Bates came in the 1965 series, *Broad and Narrow*, written by his good friends Terence Brady and Michael Bogdin. The six-episode series was a late night revue show for ATV that satirized the current events of the time. Also in the cast were Joanna, Brady, Roger Ordish, Bill Wallis and Chris Serle. The idea of a cast of young actors satirizing everything around them was a novel and fresh idea at the time; four years later another group of British actors would take this idea to new heights and fame with *Monty Python's Flying Circus*. Sadly, the series, like some other early Bates' television work, is missing and has not been seen since it was originally broadcast.

Joanna Van Gyseghem shared her memories of the show: "I have lots of fond memories from the series *Broad and Narrow*. Terence and Michael wrote for the series, which was basically

Bates in Night Must Fall *(1965)*

a sketch show that we did on television. There was Ralph, myself, Terence and Michael, along with another couple of friends in it. ATV produced and they were very brave to give us that job because we were completely unknown, just students beginning to become professionals. It was a very offbeat comedy, pre-*Monty Python*. This was before all that type of comedy began to become mainstream on television. It was very bold to give us the chance because we weren't very experienced and the guy that directed it didn't seem to understand the jokes at all. But it was all a very good experience for us. Thinking back you would never get away with what we did now. A company would never let a group of students get up on stage and do a television series. They would have to preview it and god knows what else." [43]

Terence Brady offered his take on *Broad and Narrow*: "Michael Bogdin and I wrote a television series together called *Broad and Narrow*, which has been described as the precursor to *Monty Python* in television revue form. We drew the cast mainly from our repertory of players from Dublin, including Ralph and Joanna. The show was a *success d'estime*, in spite of the host television company moving it to an impossibly late hour because they thought it so alternative! Again Ralph was well noticed in the reviews and the show possibly kick-started his career in the U.K. That was the last time we acted together, although in later years when I was writing successfully for television and the stage, my wife and writing partner Charlotte Bingham and I often tried to get Ralph cast in our work, but he was either already booked or didn't make the cut with the producers.

"Although we were out of touch for a while after Trinity, once we re-met on *Broad and Narrow* we became good friends again. Ralph and Joanna had moved into a mews house in Holland Park near where we lived in our first house in Hillgate Village, Notting Hill Gate. So we became both friends and neighbors. Ralph's house was always full of ex-Trinity people, while Charlotte and I did our best to keep the still-bachelors at bay. But during *Broad and Narrow*, cast and hangers-on invaded our houses, as indeed they were during that year's World Cup.

Sadly, *Broad and Narrow* vanished with the demise of ATV, even though it had been filmed. Since those were the days before VHS recorders, I doubt if anyone still has a copy, although perhaps something still exists through the companies that bought ATV. It is still talked about, believe it or not. A couple of years back I was in conversation with Sir Richard Stilgoe and he said one of the greatest influences on his young life as a performer and writer was *Broad and Narrow*. He loved the writing and particularly the performances of Ralph and

Joanna (and myself!). I think Ralph got a lot of notice from his work in that odd series ... thinking it was too esoteric." [44]

Michael Bogdin also shared his thoughts on *Broad and Narrow*: "In 1965, Terence and I were writing the local college revue after taking over from R.B.D. French, who was Percy French's grandson (a famous Irish song writer). R.B.D. French was also my tutor and he wrote all the revues up until the point where Terence and I arrived at the college. We had quite a successful partnership together writing sketches and songs. Terence was an absolutely brilliant performer, and Ralph was part of that revue team with Joanna, and also Roger Ordish. When we finished college we got permission to write a six-part series for ATV called *Broad and Narrow*. It was a very surreal and offbeat comedy series. It pre-dated *Monty Python*. One of the Stratford East shows I directed Ralph in, *Would Anyone Who Saw the Accident*, provided a lot of the source material for *Broad and Narrow*. Interestingly enough, it was one of the first shows they experimented with, not having a live studio audience. All comedy shows up until then had a live audience. We were used to the reaction of the audience for our sketches. We kind of got really low ratings, which didn't surprise us at all due to not having a live audience. There was not even canned laughter like modern comedy series use today—there was silence, there was nothing coming back at all for the performers. The guy who directed it was an old time variety director who had no clue how to direct our surreal sketches. *Broad and Narrow* was not a terribly successful experiment, though I still bump into people from time to time who remember the series." [45]

Bates as Aguecheek in *Twelfth Night* (1965)

Before his next few television appearances of 1967, Bates did a tour with the Citizens Theatre Company, based in Glasgow. Bates played Tranio opposite his then wife Joanna as Bianca in an October 1966 production of *The Taming of the Shrew*. In the story Lucentio (Edward Arthur) falls in love with Bianca but needs a distraction to get around her strict father, so he has his servant Tranio pretend to be him while he passes himself off as a Latin tutor to woo his true love. Michael Ashton was the director and would become the artistic director at Cheltenham's Everyman Theatre two years later. [46] Following this production, Bates took part in another Citizens Theatre Company adaptation, this time the classic Molière comedic play *The School for Wives*. The story involves a wealthy older bachelor named Arnolphe, who plans on wedding a young woman named Agnès, who he locked away in a convent to keep her naive. Trouble arises when a son of Arnolphe's friend also desires to marry Agnès, and the two

A Biography

men compete for her affections. The original French play *L'école des femmes* was adapted for the company's production by actor and writer Miles Malleson, who had appeared in *Dracula* (1958), *Hound of the Baskervilles* (1959) and *Brides of Dracula* (1960)—early hits for the film company Bates would later become associated with, Hammer Film Productions. Besides working with fellow actors Richard Wilson OBE, Susan Tebbs and Peter Kelly, Bates also starred in the production with his then wife Joanna Van Gyseghem. The Scottish tour ran from March 20 through April 16 1967 at several theaters, including the Cottage Theatre of Cumbernauld, the Palace Theatre of Kilmarnock and the Close Theatre Club of Glasgow. [47]

Bates (left) as Maurice in *The Creeper*

Richard Wilson OBE, a Scottish actor later known for his role as Victor Meldrew in the BBC comedy *One Foot in the Grave* and who also went on to become a theater director and broadcaster, shared his memories of the early plays with the Citizens Theatre Company: "Ralph Bates was charming, suave and a very funny man and he was great company and full of life. He was an excellent actor; very often good-looking actors tend to be a bit lacking in the acting stakes, but Ralph was an exception to that rule. Joanna, his then wife, was equally talented and they were a very happy couple. My abiding memory of our tour was that it was a very happy one. I had never really been in the Scottish Borders and the countryside was beautiful and the company was exhilarating. Besides Ralph and Joanna, I remember Jimmy Kennedy being a very good company member." [48]

By mid-1967, Bates came under the sole representation of agent Julia MacDermot. She started out as an actress working in repertory at Watford and Wolverhampton before becoming a casting director and, later on, a well-respected agent in the early 1960s. In the Spotlight casting directory Bates was listed under juvenile-character men with his given height of 5 feet 10 inches. Bates' first role that year was in the ATV series *Mrs. Thursday*. The comedy/drama starred Kathleen Harrison as Alice Thursday, a charwoman with a cockney accent who inherits £10 million and control of an estate and company from her employer when he passes away. Hugh Manning played

Bates in *A Christmas Carol*

Richard Hunter, who is Mrs. Thursday's butler, confidante and business liaison. Series creator Ted Willis (known for his long running *Dixon of Dock Green* police television drama) wrote the show in 1966, specifically for Harrison who, at the time, had turned to television after a long career in film. Originally planned to be a one-season show for Harrison, the series proved so popular (even topping *Coronation Street* in the ratings) that it ran another two years and revived Harrison's career.

Another photo of Bates in *A Christmas Carol*

In the episode *Charity Begins at a Ball*, Mrs. Thursday finds herself elected chairman of the Belgravia ladies' club, which is putting together a charity ball for underprivileged children. Also brought in to help with the event is organizer Nicholas Trevelyan, who sets up his headquarters in Mrs. Thursday's library, much to Richard Hunter's consternation. After a bit of sleuthing and role-playing, Hunter discovers that Trevelyan is in fact a crook who plans on swindling money from the charity and he sets out to expose the fraud before it is too late.

Bates had a small role in the episode as a dresser attending to Hunter in a fitting room. He does make the most of the role, portraying the dresser as a sarcastic and cheeky attendant. First seen trying to wrestle off Hunter's boot, Bates delivers a quite sarcastic, "Thank you sir," as Hunter sits still, non-helping. But the dresser gets his revenge as he squeezes Hunter into a waist band with a grin on his face and a retort of, "It does wonders for your waistline sir," following Hunter's query on whether the painful band is really necessary. A scandalous conversation heard from the next room brings the two men together though and the dresser has a cheeky smile on his face as he eavesdrops.

In Bates' second television role he would get the chance to take part in a Shakespearean play adapted for school children. The ATV produced drama series *Conflict* was presented in 25-minute specials for school presentations and was hosted by British acting legend Sir John Gielgud, who had a long and well-known connection performing Shakespearean plays in the theater. The programs would provide an analysis of each play and enacted scenes. In the 1967 episode production of Shakespeare's

Bates as Tim Bobbin in *Maria Marten*

Bates plays Oscar (bottom left) in *Naked Island*

Othello, Bates played Michael Cassio, lieutenant to General Othello, whom Edward Woodward played.

Following *Othello* he had parts in two productions in the ITV *Play of the Week*. The long running series adapted stories from various playwrights, such as Dennis Potter and Alan Sharp, and gave many actors a vehicle to showcase their talents. Granada Television's *Summer Playhouse*, episode eight, featured a production of *One Fat Englishman*. This production, based on the 1963 novel by Kingsley Amis, involves an overweight English literary agent, Roger Micheldene, who comes to America for a two-week trip in part for a publishing firm he works for. While in the States, the antagonistic Micheldene goes on booze-induced adventures and constantly tries to bed attractive women. Bates played Irving Macher, a young author, whose manuscript *Blinkie Heaven* Micheldene is considering publishing. His character pops up every now and then to counter Micheldene and provide some comic relief. Bates would also appear in the adaptation of D.H. Lawrence's *The Blue Moccasins*.

A string of television roles continued for Bates from 1967 into 1968. He appeared in the romance series *Boy Meets Girl* in 1967. The series, which sadly no longer exists due to the BBC purge of its tapes, adapted modern fiction for television. Mohammed Mrabet based the episode in which Bates appeared, *Love With a Few Hairs*, on the debut novel. Bates played the supporting character of Mustafa, in a story of teenage love set in Tangier. Also in the cast was actress Felicity Kendal, who played Mina in the production. She shared her memories of working with Bates: "*Boy Meets Girl* was one of my very first jobs on television ... I think it was probably quite appalling! I remember Ralph was very, very sweet to me. I was green and afraid and it was a love story and I found it all quite difficult, as the script was very lame but he got me through it and we bonded as pals. So when we were later cast in *The Woodlanders*, it was a joy to work with him again." [49]

Bates' first role of 1968 was as a café worker in the Granada Television-produced comedy drama teleplay *Sarah*. The plot involved a young woman from the north experiencing all the sights and thrills of swinging London in the 1960s. This ITV play of the week starred Wendy Allnutt in the title role; she would reunite with Bates again many years later playing his ex-wife in the popular John Sullivan series *Dear John*. Allnutt shared her memories of the production: "I remember that Ralph played the handsome Latin lover in the production and I have a particular memory of him wearing a floral shirt in character. This girl Sarah went through different kinds of men at different kinds of parties and Ralph was among them. There were various types of romantic interests, like a blond boyfriend, and then there was Ralph playing the dark-haired good-looking foreign interest. We filmed *Sarah* on location in London and it was fun to do." [50]

A quartet of roles followed later in 1968 starting with an appearance in the ATV series *Crime Buster*. Bates played the character Decre in the episode *The Third Thief*. The series starred Mark Eden as crime fighter Ray Saxon. The 13-episode series did not prove very popular and only lasted one year. Most of the episodes are missing; *The Third Thief* only exists with picture and no sound. Bates' next role was in the BBC produced *The Wednesday Play*, entitled *Hello, Good Evening and Welcome*. In the episode he had a supporting role as Alistair Gorringe. Ruth Trouncer, who played Betty Carter in the teleplay, also worked with Bates later on in the series *Poldark*, in which she played Mrs. Chynoweth. Robert Hardy, who starred in the production, had a long career as a character actor and gained recent fame playing Cornelius Fudge, the Minister of Magic, in the *Harry Potter* film series. Like some of Bates' other early television roles, the episode (and most of the series) is missing from the archives. Bates would appear as the character Chopankaway in another ITV Playhouse production entitled *Rogues' Gallery: The Misfortunes of Lucy Hodges*. The plot involves a young and naive country girl named Lucy Hodges, who is accused of murder and threatened with extradition to the United States for trial.

Bates poses in a publicity photo as Caligula for *The Caesars* (1968).

Every actor hopes to find that special role to bring them into the national spotlight, and for Bates that moment came in 1968 when he was cast as Caligula in the lavish historical series, *The Caesars*. Produced and written by Philip Mackie of Granada Television for ITV network, the series followed six of Rome's early rulers, beginning with Augustus and ending with Claudius. The series, made in black and white, would become somewhat overshadowed by the later 1976 BBC adaptation *I, Claudius*, which strayed more from the historical events. Still, *The Caesars* was a gripping drama and well cast with many veteran character actors appearing, such as André Morell as Tiberius and Freddie Jones as Claudius. After a string of small supporting roles, Bates' key role in *The Caesars* was a major step for his career as the series was met with rave reviews and thus helped bring him into the public eye.

According to the late director John Bartlett, it was Bates' starring role in his 16mm drama documentary entitled *Mayday* that helped obtain his role in *The Caesars*. Producers at Granada television had requested a print of the film to view before deciding to cast Bates in their own production.[51] Bartlett, who worked for Westward Television in Plymouth as a producer and director, had entered his film for the Irish Folk Film Festival. The judges were somewhat surprised

Caligula (Bates) with the guards in *The Caesars*

though as they were expecting a documentary on Cornish folk music but instead viewed a tale about a sailor (Bates) from Napoleonic times who survives a shipwreck and manages to wash up on an island, where it is no longer 1790 but instead 1970. Confusion, adventure and love await the intrepid sailor. The film even won the fourth prize at the Golden Harp Folk Film Festival.[52]

Bates was cast in *The Caesars* as Roman Emperor Gaius Julius Caesar Augustus Germanicus, better known by his nickname Caligula. This name, meaning "little boot," was given to him by his father's soldiers who noticed the young future leader dressed in a miniature soldier's uniform when he accompanied his father Germanicus. First appearing briefly as the future emperor in the October 13, 1968 episode four entitled *Sejanus*, Bates creates a character based in reality that was still prone to behavior and actions that would surprise and shock. As a guest of Tiberius on the island of Capri, one of Bates' first lines quoting Caligula's great grandfather Augustus acts as a foreshadowing of the young Roman's development: "Men are not gods." His character is quickly established as a man looking to get ahead in the Roman government.

Bates' next appearance as Caligula would be in the fifth episode aired on October 20, which traced his rise to power as the new Roman emperor. This episode marks the first time Bates would be the main featured actor in a television production and it certainly showcased his abilities in it. Starting out with a close-up of Bates still on the island of Capri, Caligula is quickly seen forcing himself upon Ennia (Wanda Ventham) just as her husband Macro walks in. Caligula, excited by this encounter, simply demands Macro divorce his wife when he becomes the new emperor and in return will make him the new chief minister. It is this brazenly bold and duplicitous nature of Caligula that makes him so fascinating to watch. In his game of human chess, Caligula refuses to visit his dying mother stating he never cared for blood relationships, only to later on conduct a special ceremony to bury her bones to win the love of the people when he is emperor.

It is when Caligula finally obtains the title of emperor that Bates ratchets up his performance a notch as the greed and power of the new ruler grows out of control the longer he is on the throne. Out of all the characters Bates played during his career, it is Caligula that is seemingly the most debased and evil, probably due to the character being based on the real Caligula and closely following the historic events surrounding his rule. After recovering from a serious illness, Caligula has a revelation that he is indeed a god and that everyone must worship him and bow to his demands and desires. Here an irrational and sadistic Caligula shows how dangerous he can be with the Praetorian guards behind him, forcing anyone who speaks back to him or refuses his demands to commit suicide before him, mockingly inflicting psychological torture on his uncle Claudius, and making the Senate bow down to his autocratic rule.

Bates' turn as Caligula ends in the last episode of *The Caesars* entitled *Claudius*. The insane emperor finally goes too far with his art of creating uncertainty and the very group that kept Claudius in power, the Praetorian guards, turn on their emperor to save their own necks. Compared to other actors who have played the infamous Caligula, John Hurt in *I, Claudius* and Malcolm McDowell in the 1979 film version *Caligula*,

Caligula shows his anger in *The Caesars*.

Bates' interpretation can be held as the most realistic and chilling as depicted on screen. Unlike Hurt's overly dramatic turn or McDowell's childlike deviant, Bates' portrayal is more cerebral. His Caligula is continually plotting, planning, feigning friendships and using his sarcastic nature to keep others in line. But it is his unpredictability that makes him such a scary figure, and the audience sympathizes with his uncle Claudius, who never knows when his nephew will finally demand his death.

Wanda Ventham, who played Ennia in *The Caesars*, shared her memories of the production and of working with Bates: "Working with Ralph on *The Caesars* was fantastic, that is where we first met, as I did not know him before. This was in 1968. I played Caligula's mistress in the production and of course Ralph played Caligula. We are all very young at the time. That part was the performance of a lifetime for Ralph. He did always seem to have a certain amount of nerves during the filming. He also always had an apologetic look on his face. He was extraordinary and a very bright young man. I'm not too sure that acting was enough for him. There was this terrific scene where he had to go absolutely mad. In this scene he had to jump on a very long table full of items. I can remember standing behind a pillar, waiting for the shot to begin. I remember Ralph saying, "I'm so scared." There was one young man just literally holding a spear and he had very few lines. I overheard him say, "Oh, for God's sake, it's the chance of a lifetime, give it to me!" The young actors in the production were quite envious of Ralph because Caligula was such a wonderful part. There was also a very distinguished cast of older actors as well and I don't think Ralph had a huge amount of confidence in himself in that situation. But I thought Ralph was fantastic in the role and he pulled it off, and his own slight neurosis suited the character of Caligula perfectly. A lot of people have played the part of Caligula since. *The Caesars* was done literally two years before television programs all went over to color. So our production was filmed in black and white. We did all get excited at one point as the producers were holding and storing the sets from *The Caesars* and told us that if we were all free they might do another version of *The Caesars*, but this time in color. Unfortunately, it never happened, which was a shame. I think that was a great pity for Ralph because it would have made all the difference had the series been done in color, as we had the most stunning sets. For a television studio, Granada, the sets were all very impressive. It seemed like we took up most of the inside studio space just to film the one dining scene, when Ralph had to fly across the table. Ralph never seemed to be quite free. I'm not sure how much he enjoyed being an actor. He didn't take praise well; he always thought people were comforting him rather than praising him. But *The Caesars* was a wonderful opportunity for Ralph and his performance brought him to the attention of other people and he did very well after that. Ralph was married to Joanna Van Gyseghem at the time and we all got on terribly well together, because Ralph said to me, "You know, you're the closest person that I've met who is like my wife." Indeed Joanna and I have similar personalities and we are still in touch to this day and still talk about Ralph. He also had a lot of friends and loved mixing us up, introducing people he liked to other people he liked. That was the peculiar thing about Ralph, he was always slightly apologetic about acting, and yet he was great socially. He loved getting all his friends together and he had a terrific sense of humor as well and so he was very popular. Ralph and I worked for similar people so we were always in a similar group of friends. I thought Ralph was terrific in the series *Dear John*, which John Sullivan wrote especially for Ralph. Although *The Caesars* was the only time I worked with Ralph, we remained friends until he died." [53]

Bates poses in a PR shot close-up for *The Caesars*

Joanna Van Gyseghem also chimed in on what impact *The Caesars* had on Ralph's career: "There was a television series he did in England called *The Caesars*. A lot of people think about *I, Claudius*, which came much later on. *The Caesars* was an absolutely brilliant television series written by Philip Mackey. Ralph played Caligula, which was a pretty major part, and it was a wonderful character. So that was a big step for Ralph to have gotten that role. It did terribly well, a very popular series, very well written. It helped that it featured top television actors of the day. That was quite a landmark for Ralph and his career." [54]

Bates' fellow *Caesars* cast member Wanda Ventham would also make a connection for him, which would prove quite advantageous when she introduced him to her agent John Miller, who would go on to have a long relationship managing Bates' career. As John Miller explains: "I first met Ralph just after he finished filming *The Caesars* for Granada. One of my clients, Wanda Ventham, told me about Ralph at the time and that he was not happy with his agent, Julia MacDermot. So a meeting was arranged and Ralph agreed to join me as I had formed my own agency. Previously I had worked with John Redway (who managed Peter Cushing) and also NEMS Enterprises Ltd., which handled The Beatles.

"In the early days when Ralph was with me, I remember that he was always short of money. When I would get a check in, Ralph would quickly come down to the office and we would go down to the local bank so he could draw out cash. At one point I went to Rome with Ralph for a screen test in some film. I paid for Ralph to travel to Rome by plane. We went out together and then he did the screen test, but when he got to the airport on the way back the Italians had failed to pay for his air trip home! So that was the last time we got involved in the Italian film business. (Author's Note: Although the name of this Italian film has been forgotten over time, Bates also alluded to it in an interview years later with writer Carlos Aguilar, "You know, producers have a mentality that is sometimes bizarre and strange. To give an example, one time an Italian producer said to me that I was clearly the ideal actor for a specific role and that there were no doubt about me getting the part. Then he asked my age and when I responded 29 he said that is a pity, as the character is 25 years old and then he took me out of the role!") [55]

Bates in a Colchester Repertory production

"Things started looking up when the producers at Hammer approached me to get Ralph for their film *Taste the Blood of Dracula*. That went very well and then I did the deals for his following Hammer films as well. When the film offers eventually stopped coming in, Ralph was happy to be working in television again, as that is what gave him his start and of course *Poldark* was such a great production for him, and he was fantastic in it.

"Besides his film and television work, Ralph always had a great interest in theater and I used to travel around to see Ralph in the stage plays that he did. I was his agent when he did the well publicized and well received play *Mary Rose*, starring opposite Mia Farrow. I went there for the opening night and was sitting near her mother, the actress Maureen O'Sullivan and Mia's husband, the pianist André Previn.

Ralph was just a lovely man, and was a very good and sensitive actor." [56]

In regards to flying to Rome as mentioned by Miller, Bates was not often eager to take to the skies. Joanna Van Gyseghem shared a situation in which Bates' feelings on flying affected

A Biography

their travel plans: "We used to go to his aunt's house in France. We would to fly to Nice from London. Ralph absolutely hated it and sometimes we did go down by train but mostly we had to fly and he sometimes had to take a valium in order to relax on the plane, while he gripped me by the hand. One time we were waiting on the plane in Nice getting ready to fly back to England. It was during a day in the week and there were a lot of businessmen on the flight reading their papers. Well the engines started and got up to a pitch and the plane started moving down the runway very fast and then suddenly the brakes went on. The sound of the brakes being applied was terrifying. It was a roaring screeching sound. You could see in Ralph's face his discomfort and in a very English manner he said, "I didn't like that."

Judy Geeson and Bates in *Happy Ever After* (1969)

A girl came on the intercom and apologized and said that we are just going to go around and will take off again, but she didn't say what was wrong. So we taxied around the runway again and Ralph was still saying he didn't like what happened, but I tried to assure him it would be fine. We went through it again and wouldn't you know it the same thing happened. At that point Ralph became adamant that he wanted to get off the plane, and kept saying he wanted to get off now. I tried to say we should stay on until he said something that always stuck with me … what you're saying is that you'd rather die than make a fool of yourself? And I thought about this and thought you know that Ralph was right, so we called the stewardess over. She explained that the plane did not have quite enough acceleration. Ralph then said, well, what if we get up in the air and we don't have enough acceleration? So we got off right in the middle of the runway—the stewardess came over and she said it would be fine and tried to keep us really quiet, saying the luggage would not come off and Ralph said he didn't care about the luggage. So the great big steps for the plane had to be wheeled out to us so we could get off. We got out and left and as we walked across the tarmac we watched the plane take off perfectly normally. And then we had a very pleasant, quiet and gentle ride back on the train from France." [57]

Back in England, proof of the impact of Bates' role in *The Caesars* and also John Miller's connections came quickly as he was given top billing in the 1969 episode *The Fifty-First State*, which was part of the ATV drama anthology *Happy Ever After*. Bates played the character Ross in a plot that explored whether the state would actually assassinate a young woman who may have accidentally seen one of their guarded secrets. Playing the young woman in peril (Susan Brown) was actress Judy Geeson; she would also play Bates' tormented wife in the 1972

Hammer psychological thriller *Fear in the Night*. While a number of the episodes from *Happy Ever After* are missing, *The Fifty-First State* episode, which marked the very first time Bates would have been seen by audiences in color, still does exist, though ironically only as a copied 16mm black and white print.

Bates' first project of 1970 was performing in an episode of the BBC mini-series *The Six Wives of Henry VIII*. The six-episode series focused on each of Henry VIII's wives and Bates would appear in the episode *Catherine Howard*, who was wife number five. The series also followed the actual historical events rather closely in detail. Actor Keith Michell played the title Henry VIII and was very well received by the critics, earning both a BAFTA in England and Emmy Award in the U.S. for his performance. Michell would reprise his role for the film adaptation of the series entitled *Henry VIII and His Six Wives*. The episode with Bates told the tale of Catherine Howard (Angela Pleasence), a teenager that her uncle, The Duke of Norfolk, uses to try and further his political ambitions. Norfolk introduces Catherine to Henry, who becomes smitten with her and they shortly after wed. Catherine is shocked upon her wedding night as she expects to see the body of a Hercules under the King's robes but instead finds an old, fat man who is impotent. To further complicate matters, Catherine lied to Norfolk about her virginity; and she soon falls into the arms of Henry's assistant Thomas Culpepper (Bates). The two young lovers are found out by Norfolk, who betrays Catherine to the King, setting up both her and Culpepper's executions.

Bates in *Trilby*

Much like his role in *The Caesars*, Bates' role in the highly acclaimed *The Six Wives of Henry VIII* helped to further enhance his visibility with the critics and the viewing public. The series was picked up in America in 1972, first by commercial television station CBS and later replayed as part of the PBS series *Masterpiece Theater*. Bates, dressed in royal attire and with his dashing good looks, was well cast as the young romantic attraction of Catherine Howard. His character is seen throughout much of the episode, but two scenes stand out in particular. One scene is when Culpepper, drunk with wine on Henry VIII's wedding night, confesses to Norfolk that he is bored with the lack of excitement and longs for a Crusade. Bates convincingly does this scene with drooping eyes and slurred words as he tries to steady himself on a table. The other standout scene concerns Bates' last appearance as Culpepper, bloodied, beaten and chained to the rack beside Francis Dereham, who also was tied romantically to the Queen. The two doomed men lament their situation with Culpepper calling for God's mercy and realizing that, despite his calling Catherine evil, he will still be thinking of her when his fate is handed down. Angela Pleasence, who played Catherine in the episode, mentioned that, "Ralph was a joy to work with as an actor. In person I found him to be wonderfully sensitive and amusing." [58]

The next production of 1970 for Bates would be another appearance in the series *ITV Playhouse*. Bates this time played three different roles in *Would You Look at Them Smashing all Those Lovely Windows?*, a dramatic reenactment of the Easter Rebellion of 1916 in Ireland, during which Irish republicans sought to break free of British rule and become independent. This production would be a family affair for Bates, as also starring in the cast was his then father-in-law André van Gyseghem. He had made his acting debut in 1927 in a theatrical tour of *The Constant Nymph* at the Theatre Royal in Bognor and would remain in theater for the majority of his career, although by the 1960s had taken on roles in various television programs. Besides acting, André van Gyseghem was also a long time theater director starting in 1930 with a production of the Agatha Christie play *Black Coffee* at the Embassy Theatre in Hampstead, London. He was influenced by his time spent in Russian theater and with the Workers Theatre Movement and so became known for taking on left-wing plays that dealt with the trials and tribulations of the working class. [59] It would not be the first time that Bates had worked with a member of then wife Joanna's family; he had previously acted with her cousin Ellen Sheean in a theater production of *Tom Jones*. [60]

A Ralph Bates publicity "headshot," circa 1967

One of Bates' most notorious roles was the character of Louis Staunton in the 1970 drama series *Wicked Women*. The series dramatized actual real life Victorian crime cases, often with morbid details. In the episode *Alice Rhodes*, Bates' character Louis is a lowly auctioneer's clerk, a charismatic schemer who marries a shy and naïve older woman named Harriet Richardson, who just happens to come from a very wealthy family. What Harriet does not know is that her new husband Louis is actually the lover of her cousin Alice Rhodes, who has orchestrated their sham of a marriage just to get access to her money. As expected, the relationship between Harriet and Louis quickly changes once the ceremony is over. After purchasing a country farmhouse, Louis and Alice proceed to carry on their own relationship after locking up Harriet in the loft under the guise they are protecting her from her overbearing mother. Harriet is left to basically

Ralph Bates

rot in squalid conditions with no food, eventually resulting in her death and the arrest and punishment of the guilty parties.

While the plot of *Alice Rhodes* was a cruel and brutal look at how greed leads to true evil, it was all the more shocking due to it being based on real events. The production was based on the 1877 case in which Louis, Alice and Louis' brother Patrick and his wife Elizabeth were all found guilty of the murder by starvation of Harriet Staunton. The case, called the Penge Mystery, captured the nation's attention for the horrid details of Harriet's last hours and for the court of appeal process, which based on medical evidence, led to the change of a death sentence to penal servitude for life for the guilty party—with the exception of Alice Rhodes, who wound up being pardoned and released. The real Louis Staunton served 20 years at Dartmoor prison before being released, after which he married Alice Rhodes.

Looks are cast between Bates and Jean Anderson in *Alice Rhodes* (1970).

Bates' character of Louis Staunton, sporting 1877-style long sideburns and hair, is an unsympathetic figure, much like his real life counterpart. Even though when he later feels remorse over the horrible condition Harriet is in, he still goes along with Alice in trying to cover up their crime, which speeds along Harriet's demise. Bates' best scene comes when Harriet's suspicious mother comes for a visit after their wedding. Looking suitably bored in his fake marriage, Bates' Louis does not take long to start a psychological tug of war over Harriet with her mother. As the two suitors for Harriet's attention hurl insults at each other, Louis makes the knockout blow by convincing Harriet she will be forever alone if he leaves her. Harriet's mother leaves, and Harriet's fate is sealed.

The Yorkshire Television produced drama series *Kate*, running from 1970-1972 on ITV, was a production made for actress Phyllis Calvert. With a career stretching back to 1927, Calvert was one of the most popular film actresses in Britain in the 1940s, before turning to more theater work in the 1960s and television in the 1970s. In the series *Kate*, Calvert played Kate Graham, a no-nonsense agony aunt and single mother who writes an advice column under the title "Dear Monica." Each episode had Graham becoming personally involved with the people who write in to her in order to solve their problems. Bates starred as Richard Best in the episode, *A Good Spec*, during the series' first season.

One of Bates' bigger television roles of 1970 is also missing, due to the BBC policy of erasing their old taped programs to save money and reuse the videotapes. In 1970, the BBC adapted the 1887 Thomas Hardy novel *The Woodlanders*. The four-episode drama was filmed at the BBC Television Centre. Among the cast was Felicity Kendal, who had worked with Bates previously on the *Boy Meets Girl* episode *Love With a Few Hairs*, and Angela Thorne, who worked with Bates again in the series she would star in, *Farrington*. Bates played Kendal's would-be perfect husband, Edgar Fitzpiers.

In the story set in a small village, a young woman named Grace Melbury (Felicity Kendal) plans to marry her childhood sweetheart, Giles Winterborne. However, Grace's father (Michael Goodliffe) has other plans for his daughter, who he provided to have a good education while Giles remained a simple woodsman. A new suitor, a young and handsome doctor named Edgar Fitzpiers (Bates), takes an interest in Grace and her father convinces her that he is suitable to be her husband. But not long after the honeymoon, their perfect marriage begins to fall apart when Fitzpiers begins an affair with a wealthy widow and Grace's attempt to reconcile with Giles ends up in vain.

Felicity Kendal filled in her memories of the lost production of *The Woodlanders*: "*The Woodlanders* was a great job with a brilliant cast. As I remember, Ralph played a not too sympathetic character. We filmed the production on location in Dorset and we all got on extremely well. It was of course a wonderful series made from a great book, and all the parts were gifts to we young actors and it was certainly one of the best parts I was offered during those early years. It was a very tragic story that we captured well. I don't remember the reviews, but I think it was certainly a successful series and I know that I got a lot of work from it. I was very proud of the production. I think it was acted and directed very well indeed, and also looked amazing. It featured a very strong cast and crew and it was also typical of the costume dramas that the BBC did so well in those days.

"Ralph was excellent in the production and I seem to remember him being very serious about the whole thing, whereas some of us fooled around a bit. During downtime on *The Woodlanders*, we all spent time eating far too many cream teas in Dorset and some of the actors had to have their jackets let out; not Ralph, though, as he was always skinny. On the set he was quiet and kept to himself more than some actors, who wanted to be the life and soul of the party and tell jokes and have a laugh. I thought Ralph was very sweet, gentle and professional and I really enjoyed working with him; it was a very happy time. Ralph and I did not keep in touch, as with so many acting jobs, you get very close and then move on, although we would meet now and again at theatrical events. I have fond memories, though, of working twice with Ralph, who was a lovely man." [61]

Chapter 3
"The supreme prince of darkness …"

By mid-1970, Bates' career would take a new turn as he was hired by Hammer Film Productions to appear in and star in several of their horror films. The production company was started in 1934 by comedian and businessman William Hinds (the name Hammer was based on Hinds' professional name of Will Hammer). Hammer produced many various types of films, but in 1955, they hit upon what would be their niche in the horror genre starting with *The Quatermass Xperiment*. The studio, then run by James Carreras and William Hinds' son Anthony, decided to remake the old Universal horror films but update them in color. The two most popular horror characters, Dracula and Frankenstein, would prove very lucrative to Hammer and they went on to produce a series of films for each character. The lead actors who starred in the two series, Peter Cushing and Christopher Lee, both became famous around the world for their roles, which while keeping them employed, also typecast them as horror film actors. By 1970, Hammer was already 12 years removed from their first *Dracula* film (1958) and was looking to figuratively inject some new blood into the series for their next installment of the series. Their answer was to bring in a fresh face for audiences—and that face belonged to Ralph Bates.

In the wonderful luridly titled *Taste the Blood of Dracula*, a merchant traveling through Karlsburg happens across a recently dispatched Dracula. He collects Dracula's cape, signet ring, clasp and dried blood and returns to London. Meanwhile, a trio of wealthy men has grown tired of its monthly ribald escapades and yearns for a new thrill. The opportunity arises when they meet young Lord Courtley (Bates), an arrogant debonair aristocrat who was disowned from his family for practicing the black mass in the family chapel. Courtley convinces the men to buy the remains of Dracula from the dealer to conduct a special ceremony for the ultimate pleasure. When the mass goes wrong and Courtley begs for their help, the men kill him and flee. With Courtley's corpse as a host, Dracula returns in physical form and begins to enact revenge for the killing of his servant.

As Cushing and Lee were getting older, Hammer started seeking out younger actors, who they felt would appeal to the current young audience filling the theaters. They also began bringing in other directors besides Hammer mainstay Terence Fisher, who was responsible for helming most

Ralph Bates as Lord Courtley performs a blood ritual in *Taste the Blood of Dracula*.

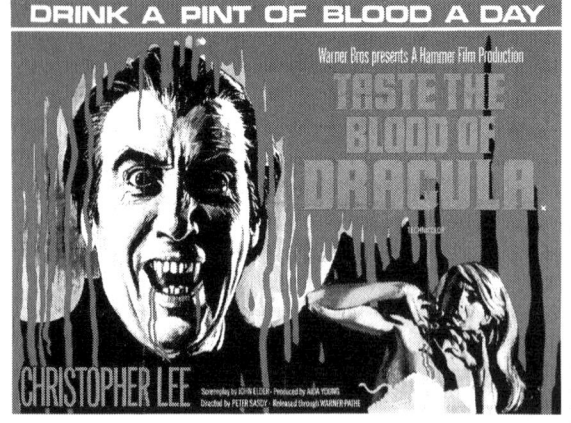

of the company's Gothic horror films. New directors such as Peter Sasdy, Brian Clemens and Roy Ward Baker were brought on board to bring a fresh look to Hammer's horrors in order to appeal to new audiences. Among the new actors in the Hammer stable were Shane Briant, Ingrid Pitt, Valerie Leon and Linda Hayden. Bates, who was now a name actor due to his powerful performances on television productions like *The Caesars*, was the cream of the crop; a young actor who could hold his own with the veteran Hammer actors and even play the lead in productions. Sasdy, who had recently finished up directing the BBC adaptation of the Henry James novel *The Spoils of Poynton*, was already aware of Bates' BBC work and brought him in to Hammer. These new additions allowed for Hammer in the early 1970s to attempt to take their *Dracula* and *Frankenstein* series in new directions and even to try new horror stories altogether. The results, while innovative and a much-needed change of pace, unfortunately would not pan out financially, and the company made its last film (before the 2008 revival) in 1979 with a remake of *The Lady Vanishes*.

As for Bates' role in the film, his performance as Lord Courtley certainly was one of the highlights of the production. Playing Courtley with a sense of flash and bravado allowed Bates to hold equal footing with the three wealthy ne'er-do-wells, played by Geoffrey Keen, John Carson and Peter Sallis. The plot of *Taste the Blood of Dracula* could be defined as a power struggle between the young generation and their elders—with Dracula waiting in the shadows to prey on them all. In this situation, Bates gives Courtley a quality that evens the playing field against the corrupted upper class: his derring-do and power of persuasion. When he realizes the three town elders are susceptible to their vices, Bates almost cannot contain Courtley's inner glee as he proposes, "Would you be willing to sell your souls to the devil?" When questioned why, Bates simply continues to lure them on … promising their experiences would be extended to infinity. Bates does not let up on Courtley's hold over the elders, holding rank over them in the Church and demanding they drink his blood-infused concoction to revive the master. When the elders cowardly balk at bottoms up, Bates flies into an enraged spittle-flying tirade how they will insult the master if they do not comply with his wishes. Trying to lead by example, Bates downs the goblet which does not end well for him—he writhes in crippling pain on the floor as the elders proceed to boot him like a rugby ball, with some whacks from their canes added for good measure. In another actor's hands, Courtley might have been a throwaway role, but Bates brings a confidence in his acting that made his performance stand out and shine.

Bates also knew how to utilize props to highlight a scene or his character's motives. In the Church scene where Bates presides over a black mass to resurrect Dracula, he handles the vial containing Dracula's ashes with a sense of power, slowly pouring some into his goblet before dispersing the rest in those of the three town elders, sizing them up with his eyes to let them know who is really in charge. Another prop Bates makes good use of is the dagger

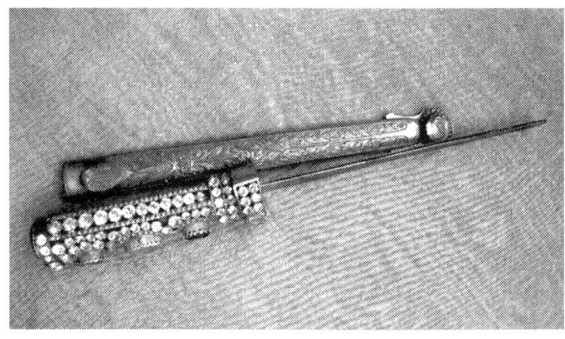

The actual dagger Bates used in *Taste the Blood of Dracula*

used in the ceremony. Bates thrusts it high in the air over his head before quickly pulling it from its sheath, and then he lets the sheath clank loudly against the floor as he drops it for added effect, in the eerily quiet church. After slicing his palm, Bates ever so carefully squeezes his bright red blood upon Dracula's ashes in the goblets, with an almost orgasmic look upon his face. One would imagine that years of appearing in various stage plays had given Bates the experience and know-how to use a prop to make a statement for an audience.

Director Peter Sasdy and Bates would work together again later on the film *I Don't Want to be Born* and they became good friends. Bates described his experience making *Taste the Blood of Dracula*: "I liked the film very much; I think it was the best of the five Hammer films I did. It was so Gothic and well done, in sharp contrast with the most appalling film I've had anything to do with, *Lust for a* Vampire. I never met Christopher Lee; I never had a scene with him in it. I thought John Carson was excellent, a fine actor indeed. Aida Young was an extremely good producer in that she was intensely interested in things that a producer usually does not notice, like clothes and make-up. The director Peter Sasdy has his Hungarian flair, which I think is a breath of fresh air. I enjoyed working with him very much. However it was my first big film and I wasn't too sure about the medium, but Peter helped me a great deal. I only had five days of work on that picture over the six week schedule." 62

In another interview with Carlos Aguilar, Bates reflected on how his acting background influenced his performance in *Taste the Blood of Dracula*: "When I left University I joined a theater company that performed a play every two weeks. It took a lot of getting used to because we would be doing rehearsals in the morning for a stage production that night. When I got into film I was conditioned by this experience. As I didn't know anything

Bates presides over a black mass to resurrect Dracula, handling the vial containing Dracula's ashes with a sense of power in *Taste the Blood of Dracula*.

A Biography

Lord Courtley comes to a bloody end far too early in *Taste the Blood of Dracula.*

about cinematic technique, it was inevitable that my early performances were more dramatic in the theatrical sense than cinematographic. What's more, some directors, instead of correcting me, rather encouraged me to continue my approach saying they liked that form. Peter Sasdy in *Taste the Blood of Dracula* was one of them." [63]

Peter Sasdy elaborated on his working relationship with Bates: "Looking back on our working relationship, I've always felt a kind of responsibility for the direction his film career blossomed throughout the years, having introduced him to Hammer by casting him in his first feature film, *Taste the Blood of Dracula*. There has been a lot of talk through the years that he was brought in as a possible next Dracula to replace Christopher Lee. I'm pleased to put on record that I've cast Ralph for the part he has played and there were no future plans behind it.

"Ralph was very nervous on the first day of filming, when he had a long dialogue scene opposite three well established and experienced actors: Geoffrey Keen, John Carson and Peter Sallis. After a number of hours and unusual number of takes, it became obvious that because of Ralph's 'drying'—not remembering his text—we would not finish the scene on schedule. I decided to let the three other actors go—having finished shooting their scenes and letting Ralph *read* his lines off camera. After a short chat we continued with me reading the text of the three actors, while the camera was facing Ralph. What I've hoped for actually happened: Ralph was word-perfect all the way through ... never a 'dry' and I had a splendid performance. For the rest of the next six weeks of filming he was as word-perfect as all the other experienced actors, and I think our friendship was established." [64]

While *Taste the Blood of Dracula* marked Christopher Lee's fourth performance as the Lord of the Undead for Hammer (not counting the Jess Franco version *El Conde Dracula* made the same year), he was not originally planned to star in the film. Anthony Hinds had written a script without Dracula in order to save the rising fees for hiring Lee. The original plan was for Bates' character Lord Courtley to be the main villain in *Taste the Blood of Dracula*; he would have become a vampire following the ceremony and terrorized the men and their families. Hammer had successfully done a Dracula film before without Lee when David Peel played the main vampire in *Brides of Dracula* (1960), which was the first sequel to the original Hammer *Dracula* film. However, when the studio presented their script to Warner Bros., who would distribute the film, the demand was made to use Christopher Lee as he was the recognizable face of Dracula to the fans and the studio deemed it would then be a more profitable film. So a rewrite of the script was done and Lee's Dracula was inserted back into the storyline. [65] However, it leaves an interesting *what if* scenario had Bates been allowed to carry the film; from his standout performance in the smaller role he was given and recent success playing a lead role in *The Caesars*, there is little doubt that he could have certainly played the lead to great effect in *Taste the Blood of Dracula*.

Linda Hayden, who played one of the daughters of the men being sought out by Dracula, shared her memories of Bates: "I was involved in two films with the lovely Ralph Bates, *Taste the Blood of Dracula* and later on, *Minder on the Orient Express* (1985). I actually never had any scenes with him in either movie, and *Minder* in particular, as my filming only took four days. I did see Ralph around Elstree Studios a lot during the shoot for *Taste the Blood of Dracula*. Ralph was a charming man, very warm and engaging, and lovely to be around. I was very sad when the news of his cancer came to light. The industry lost a very special person when Ralph passed away." [66]

Bates' performance in *Taste the Blood of Dracula* must have impressed Hammer producers enough for them to give him the lead role in his next film for the company, *The Horror of Frankenstein*. In this new version for 1970, series regular Peter Cushing was out as the Baron and Bates was put in his place, becoming a younger version of the Baron during his university days. Young Victor Frankenstein is an arrogant but brilliant scientist whose drive to create new life will let nothing and no one stand in his way. He disposes of his father to take over the family estate and start his own personal lab to push the boundaries of life and death. Along with fellow student Wilhelm Kassner as his assistant, Frankenstein sets about collecting body parts with the aid of a cheerfully enthusiastic grave robber. When his efforts succeed in creating life, this results reanimating a mute creature with a penchant for murder. When a local villager is killed and people start speaking of a huge monster that came from the direction of the castle, Frankenstein comes under suspicion by the Lieutenant of Police, but the Baron remains as determined as ever to continue his work.

In an interview, director Jimmy Sangster explained the choice of Bates portraying Frankenstein. "After a dozen Frankenstein films in 39 years, there aren't many more permutations to be made on the story. Our latest is based on the original story. Peter Cushing obviously couldn't take the role of a young man in his teens, so Hammer looked around for someone who could. We didn't have far to look. We had been enormously impressed with Ralph Bates, who appeared in *Taste the Blood of Dracula* as the Count's disciple. He has a kind of ruthless charm, which is ideal for the part of Frankenstein." [67]

Bates, in his lab, plays Victor Frankenstein in 1970's *The Horror of Frankenstein*.

Had *The Horror of Frankenstein* been a greater success for Hammer, then perhaps audiences might have seen Bates' version of Baron Frankenstein escaping his situation to create something new in the lab in a following sequel. In an interview with Pip Evans, Bates mentioned he would be up for another turn as the Baron. "I am very pleased to be taking on the role of Frankenstein. Quite a number of very good actors have played the part before me and I naturally felt pleased that I should be given the chance to add my name to that list. I've been asked if I will play the part again in subsequent films. The answer is, I just don't know. As yet there has been no suggestion of further films from either side, but if I get offered another and the script is as good as this one, then I shall be very happy to do it." [68] Apparently not afraid of typecasting, Bates shared his philosophy with interviewer Margaret Pride: "Peter Cushing played this role five times, and he gets plenty of other work, because he is such a fine actor. You don't become a better actor by turning things

Bates with Jon Finch (Lt. Becker) in *The Horror of Frankenstein*

down, and you don't become any richer, either." [69]

But this was not the case, and Hammer brought back Peter Cushing for their next and final entry in their Frankenstein series, *Frankenstein and the Monster from Hell* (1973). Part of the issue with *The Horror of Frankenstein* was that it stood outside the Hammer Frankenstein series in that it had a different Baron and it also featured generous amounts of black humor, such as when Frankenstein reanimates an arm to give the two finger salute or his suggestion for a new experiment: "Something harmless like splitting the atom perhaps." Originally the producers had envisioned *The Horror of Frankenstein* as a reboot of the series, something then uncommon but not so for recent reboots of film series such as *Spiderman* (2012) or *Superman* (2013). Director Jimmy Sangster decided that he did not want to essentially remake *The Curse of Frankenstein* and so made rewrites to the script to include the black humor. Original screenplay writer Jeremy Burnham explained his take on the situation. "I only met Ralph Bates once for a fleeting moment, at the studios where they were filming *The Horror of Frankenstein*. The only thing I can say about the screenplay is that my brief was to return to the original story. But when Jimmy Sangster, who was also the director, got his hands on it, he put in a lot of unfunny jokes, and the end result was, in my opinion, a mess. I prefer my 'horror' to be red in tooth and claw, but as I wasn't there through most of the shoot, I had no say in it." [70]

Victor takes a break from his work, relaxing with Alys (Kate O'Mara) his maid, in The Horror of Frankenstein.

Hammer certainly did their best to promote the new *The Horror of Frankenstein*, including a behind-the-scenes mini documentary at the Elstree set, in which Peter Cushing did an interview alongside Bates that could be viewed as his handing over the Frankenstein character to the younger performer. Cushing explained that when he first played the character, the operations provided an interesting what-if scenario, but with the latest advances in modern science, Bates' character would be doing operations that could be done today. When asked by the interviewer if he has to believe in the Frankenstein character to play

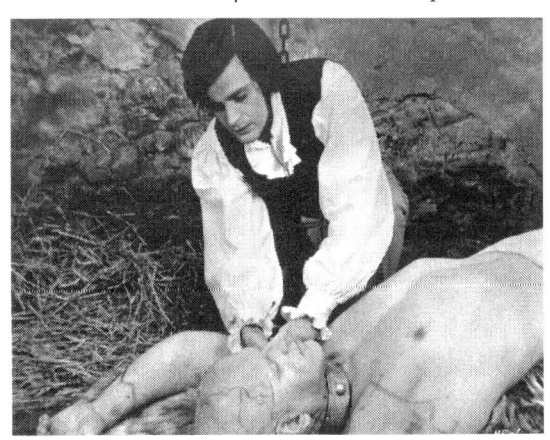

Bates attending to his Monster (Dave Prowse) in The Horror of Frankenstein

A Biography

him effectively, Bates answered, "Oh utterly yes. The nearest thing to it is playing pantomime. Within that convention of pantomime you've got to believe because the kids are the first ones to notice it. This is fantasy but it must be played with conviction".[71]

David Prowse, who played the latest creation by Bates' Frankenstein, as well as the next incarnation in *Frankenstein and the Monster from Hell*, shared his thoughts about his co-worker. "Although my association with Ralph on *The Horror of Frankenstein* was very brief, I did greatly enjoy the couple of weeks we had working together at Elstree Studios. He was a good actor and a genuinely nice person."[72]

"When I first think of Ralph, I think of his lovely, warm outgoing personality," stated Veronica Carlson. "He has a sense of mischief and I smile at the memory as I am snickering now as I write this. I remember him almost collapsing at the knees, while he had to carry me at some point in *The Horror of Frankenstein* (poor chap!). I weighed about 125 pounds at the time, but my abundant, beautiful costume, including boots, corsets and all, made me into a most cumbersome bundle. Kate O'Mara was stifling (and failing) giggles. After the shoot, we all collapsed to our knees with uncontrollable laughter.

"He was a wonderfully generous actor to work with, deeply conscientious and sympathetic. I so coveted Kate's role in this film as she had such a strong role and more screen time with Ralph!

"While working on this film, Ralph and Jimmy Sangster became as brothers. Their sense of fun was boundless, their lust for life insatiable. Their combined company was intoxicating—and I was so fortunate to share some of these moments. Although I felt the film itself was somewhat trivialized by the humor within it, I would not have missed one single second of any of it. I met and worked with a fine actor, who had a glorious future ahead of him. How perfect—it just felt so right."[73]

Even though the new film was separate from the rest of the Hammer *Frankenstein* cannon of films, comparisons of Cushing and Bates in the role were of course made. Both actors did a phenomenal job in their performances as the Baron with subtle differences in how he was portrayed. Cushing's Frankenstein was brilliant but flawed in that he was intolerant of a society that never understood him. He was willing to break the natural laws of science and even put others at risk during his experiments. As an actor, Cushing strived for perfection in his roles as evidenced by the amount of research he would invest to make his character more believable. Audiences appreciated his efforts and Cushing became synonymous with the character of

Bates plays Victor Frankenstein with a healthy dose of sarcasm.

Baron Frankenstein. However, by 1970 Cushing was 57 years old, and Hammer felt they needed to adapt to the new "youth" market flooding the theaters. Bates, then 30 years old with dark and handsome looks, would fit the bill nicely for the production company.

Bates' Frankenstein was similar in intellect and desire, though Hammer's new approach to attract the lucrative youth market of the 1970s had his character also equally interested in the opposite sex, whether a fellow pretty student, the Dean's daughter or his father's mistress. The film's trailer played this up as it announced, "Prepare yourself ... for a new Frankenstein ... searing the screen with excitement ... a young Frankenstein ... experimenting with the forbidden secret of life itself." Another difference was Bates' Frankenstein's immorality

Bates and Veronica Carlson (Elizabeth) in *The Horror of Frankenstein*

and ruthlessness; he was perfectly at ease using his creature as a killing machine and also eliminating anyone he felt may hinder his work. Cushing's Frankenstein also displayed this feature to a degree but Bates' cold-blooded characterization took it much further. One example would be when Bates' Frankenstein sets up his innocent former schoolmate and now personal cook to take the blame for a murder done by his creature. Bates further exemplifies this cynical and ruthless quality in the murder of his own father, a highwayman, and a local professor, even his associate's pet tortoise—though to be fair he does revive it. Perhaps what Bates best delivers that really sets his character apart is his sense of sarcasm. When his maid, played by Kate O'Mara, bows down to show Frankenstein why she was kept employed, despite her lousy cooking, Bates coolly remarks, "You've gained weight in a couple of places." Bates did seek to set his Frankenstein apart, and to that extent he succeeds. In fact, his Baron was more of a villain than Hammer's previous presentation of the character, with Peter Cushing becoming more of a misguided scientist. Overall, there were obviously necessary similarities in Mary Shelley's character but

Another shot of Bates on set with Veronica Carlson

Bates' turn in the role seemed a natural updating for the times in Hammer's attempt to reboot the series. Unfortunately, audiences were so used to Cushing's portrayal of Frankenstein that it was an uphill battle for Bates to take the series in a new direction.

In addition, Hammer did not get the financial return they expected with the fresh approach of *The Horror of Frankenstein* and so it was decided to bring Cushing back in as the title character for a return to the better-established original series in their next outing. It was not a total loss for Bates though, as he made three other films for Hammer and the experience for him was quite enjoyable as he told Sam Irvin. "Everybody hated that film but we had such a good time making it. I really thought it was quite funny, you see. I think we probably had too good a time making it. Jimmy Sangster is probably one of my closest friends; I starred in the first three films he ever directed. He knows the business inside out and is an excellent producer. He can knock screenplays off like they were nothing; he's a very talented writer in that he can practically do a script in a week. I enjoyed making that film probably more than any other actor. I am usually a very reluctant actor, but on this film I could not wait to get to work. I hated to go home at night." [74]

Ralph Bates with good friend Jimmy Sangster on the set of *The Horror of Frankenstein*

Part of Bates' good experiences working on the film was no doubt due to the crew and Bates was very appreciative of such seasoned professionals. "People like Neil Binney, the camera operator, and Moray Grant and Arthur Grant (cinematographers) always had time to explain things, even though it was a very tight schedule. Technical things. I used to perform parts to the camera every morning with Neil Binney. As far as that was concerned, it was tremendous and I learned an awful lot." [75]

Joanna Van Gyseghem confirmed Bates' relationship with Jimmy Sangster: "Jimmy Sangster was such a good friend of Ralph's and we used to go over to France together, because Ralph's family was French and there was this lovely house that his aunt owned,

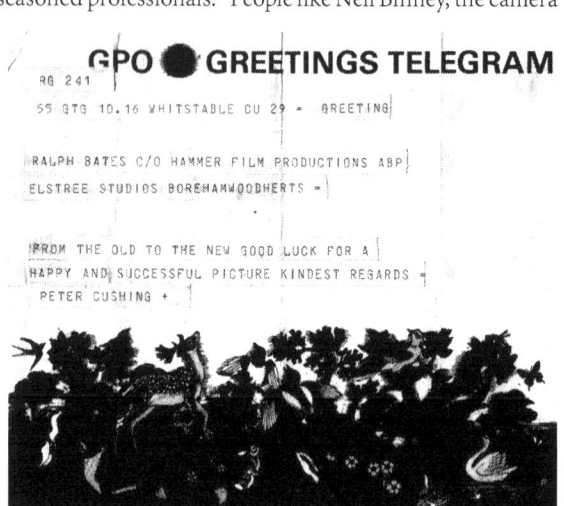

A friendly telegram from Peter Cushing to Ralph Bates, wishing Bates luck.

Hammer's two Frankensteins—Peter Cushing and Ralph Bates—face off.

north of Caen. We were lucky enough to be able to have little parties there on our own, as no one was living in the house at the time. Jimmy had various different girlfriends in those days and sometimes we would all go over to France together and live sort of casually in a grand manner. Jimmy was a really good friend to Ralph.

"Ralph really enjoyed the Hammer films. He was obviously very nervous. But Jimmy was always around. Ralph had a good time doing the Hammer films and I remember the actors from Hammer coming around to our house and we all sort of got everything together. The [acting] work was sort of where you would not really get worried about your motivation. You'd find your marks and stand on them and say your lines." [76]

Another perspective of Ralph was shared by Phil Campbell, who worked for Hammer Film Productions as a runner on several of their films, including *The Horror of Frankenstein*: "The first time I saw Ralph he was on the set for various make-up tests. Both Ralph and Veronica Carlson did some tests to make themselves look younger for when the Baron was at University in the beginning of the film. They were being made up to look around my age of 18, which we joked about. Ralph was generally quiet to start with as it must have been a daunting task to carry a whole film, but this changed within the first week when he clicked with Jimmy Sangster, as they shared a similar sense of humor. From then on he was more relaxed and he was always quite charming and easy to get on with.

"Hammer must have had a lot of faith in Ralph doing *The Horror of Frankenstein*; along with *Scars of Dracula*, these were the first two films that were financed completely by British money. Previous films at the studio had always been partly financed by America, as the films

A Biography

Bates and Graham James examine a decapitated head in *The Horror of Frankenstein*.

would also get an overseas release for their markets. So this was quite an achievement for Hammer to reach the stage where no outside finances were needed. For the crew on the set of *The Horror of Frankenstein* it felt a bit out of the ordinary, as it was a quite different production from the previous Hammer Frankenstein films. It seemed to be a strange script as it was quite light-hearted. I think a lot of people on the film were not exactly sure what to make of it as a result. There was not the usual blood and guts storyline, but [instead it had] a jokey feel to it.

"Jimmy and Ralph would often joke around a bit. Ralph was certainly appreciative of someone who had a good sense of humor on the set. One particular time I remember involved a close-up shot of Ralph as Baron Frankenstein for a scene in the film in which he was cutting something off-camera, which was supposed to be a body. As Ralph was 'cutting,' he used his arm to wipe sweat off his brow, leaving a bloody smear. In actuality, off-screen Ralph was cutting into bits of foam rubber to substitute for the body. But when Jimmy called cut for the scene to end, Ralph kept on going, tossing bits of foam rubber while kidding, "That's a bit of flesh, that's a bit of bone."

"On the production of *The Horror of Frankenstein*, one of the jobs I had to do as a runner was to fundraise money from the cast and crew for the Variety Club of Great Britain, with which Hammer was closely linked at the time. Variety Club was a large worldwide organization that raised funds to help children with disabilities or special needs. It was connected with many big names in the entertainment business, and James Carreras was very prominent and interested in the group and its cause. One of the activities of the Variety Club was the Sunshine [train] Coaches, which were used for taking the children on various types of trips they otherwise would not be able to attend. So, Carreras decided to fundraise for a train coach, of which you could buy individual parts, anything from the engine that cost around 40 or 50 pounds, right on down to the nuts on the wheels, which cost around 25 pence. All these parts of the coach were listed and I had to go around the whole unit asking everyone if they would like to buy a part of the Variety Club coach for charity. I felt a bit awkward about asking all the crew, because some of them felt it was a bit like blackmail, as if by not buying anything they might be looked down upon by the head office. But when I came to Ralph, he just said, "Yes, I will buy something" and he wound up purchasing a part of the engine which was quite expensive, being around 25 pounds. I said to Ralph, "Wow that is very generous," and he replied, "Well, when you make a donation to charity, it has to hurt a bit to make it worth doing, otherwise what is the point?" Considering what happened to Ralph later in his life, I now think back on how poignant his reply was." [77]

Sandwiched between two of his Hammer films, Bates took on the role of Joe Larson for the first episode of a new 1970 television drama series entitled *Grady*. In the episode, *Somebody*

Else's War, Charles Grady is a trade unionist newly released from prison, who returns to his home town. There he soon becomes involved with a group calling for a strike at a local factory. The Yorkshire Television production starred Anthony Bate as the titular Grady and was actually a spin-off from the series *The Main Chance*, in which he first played the character in the 1969 episode *The Professional*. However, the new series *Grady* only lasted three episodes.

Bates' next role for Hammer happened through chance, as he was a last minute replacement for Peter Cushing in their sequel to *The Vampire Lovers* (1970). The film in question, *Lust for a Vampire* (1971), continued the story of the Carmilla Karnstein (now under the anagram Mircalla in this sequel), which was based on the characters by Sheridan Le Fanu. In 1830, 40 years after the Karnstein family's vampire curse threatened the village surrounding their castle, the family uses a village girl's blood to revive Mircalla. Once again walking the earth, the beautiful Mircalla soon sets her eyes on a recently opened girls finishing school. Under the guise of a being a new student at the school, Mircalla immediately catches the attention of everyone, including the headmaster Giles Barton (Bates) and Richard LeStrange, a writer visiting the village to work on his next book about vampires and the occult. Both men fall under the spell of Mircalla's deadly beauty as a number of students and local village girls go missing. LeStrange finally becomes convinced that the stories of the Karnstein family are true, and that his love for Mircalla may cost him his life.

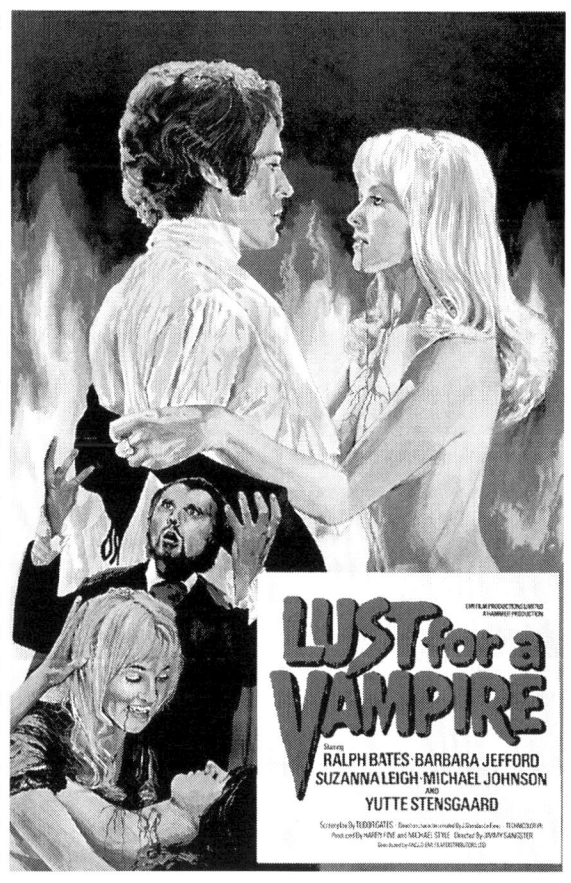

Hammer may have felt they would have a big hit with a sequel to *The Vampire Lovers*, their first foray into vampire lesbianism and eroticism, which fit in with the more overt direction their films were taking in the 1970s. Looking to strike while the iron was hot, Hammer quickly started the follow-up soon after wrapping up *The Vampire Lovers*. For the new film, originally titled *To Love a Vampire*, Hammer began assembling a number of the usual company stalwarts. However, most of the main people slated to be involved did not appear for various reasons, which should have been a warning sign for Hammer. When Ingrid Pitt, who starred as Carmilla Karnstein in the first film, read the script, she felt it was poorly done and turned down the role. Hammer responded by replacing her with Yutte Stensgaard, an attractive Danish blonde, who had appeared in a handful of small film and television roles. Terence Fisher, who

Bates plays headmaster Giles Barton in Hammer's *Lust for a Vampire*.

directed many Gothic Hammer films and was scheduled to direct *Lust for a Vampire*, also dropped out due to a broken leg and Jimmy Sangster was brought in to direct his second film for the studio. Bernard Robinson, who had designed the sets for many well-known Hammer films, including *The Curse of Frankenstein*, *Dracula*, and *The Curse of the Werewolf*, died only hours after being hired to work on *Lust for a Vampire*. Peter Cushing was originally set to play the headmaster Giles Barton, but dropped out of the film at the last minute because his wife Helen had gotten very ill and would pass away not long afterwards. Jimmy Sangster then contacted Bates to replace Cushing for the film.

The resulting film, while not horrible, was certainly not on a par with *The Vampire Lovers* or the third film in the series, *Twins of Evil*. One of the issues with the film was some policy error. The biggest gaffe was the inclusion of the pop song "Strange Love" sung by the singer Tracy during a love-making scene, with LeStrange and Mircalla. It was the first time Hammer had tried this approach of including modern music in a period piece, and it would be the last as well. Another issue was the botching of Mike Raven's role as Count Karnstein. Raven, previously known as a Radio 1 DJ who specialized in blues music, made his film debut in *Lust for a Vampire* with not much success, although it was not completely his fault since Hammer had his voice dubbed by Valentine Dyall and included close-ups of Christopher Lee's blood red eyes substituting for his own during the resurrection scene. But probably the biggest issue with *Lust for a Vampire* was the lack of character development. Richard LeStrange, who is the protagonist of the story, does not seem very heroic at all. Yutte Stensgaard, although quite easy on the eyes, seemed quite wooden as Mircalla and thus was a poor replacement for the vibrant Ingrid Pitt. Lastly, Bates' character of the headmaster Giles Barton was not written for him, and so he had to make do with the role as

Jimmy Sangster directs the cast of *Lust for a Vampire*.

written in the script. Barton is described in the film on more than one occasion as a nasty little man who enjoys watching the girls dancing or getting undressed; not exactly a plum role in the story. He is an expert on the Karnstein family history, which proves useful to the storyline, though when Barton finally deduces Mircalla is really Carmilla, he only begs her to be a servant to the devil and is drained of blood and left to die for his efforts. It was a familiar situation, much better done in *Taste the Blood of Dracula*.

One plus for Bates, although it must have felt like a double-edged sword, was that he was given top billing in the film. Judy Matheson, who played Amanda McBride, one of Giles Barton's students at the school, recalled about Bates: "I have only good memories of working with Ralph. He was fun, witty, intelligent and extremely professional; he and Michael Johnson would giggle a lot with us girls in between takes, but on 'action,' he was the consummate professional." [78]

Bates himself shared his feelings about the film with Sam Irvin: "Peter Cushing's wife was very ill and he backed out of the production, just as it was about to roll. Jim (Sangster) rang me up one afternoon and I was filming the next day. I did it as a favor to him. I thought it was a tasteless film and I regret having anything to do with it. But again, Jim is a close, close friend and so is Peter; so as a friend I was happy to get them out of a very unhappy situation. I mean really, what is more important? In that sense I was happy to do the film. The part was written for a much older person obviously, so I simply acted it as an eccentric, without a great deal of thought. I thought the casting of Yutte Stensgaard was bad. She was certainly no replacement for Ingrid Pitt, who had been so good in *The Vampire Lovers*. If they couldn't have Ingrid, they could have

Bates and Yutte Stensgaard being directed by Jimmy Sangster, who sent Bates the photo with a little constructive criticism add-on as a joke.

Bates checks his script sitting alongside Judy Matheson on the set of *Lust for a Vampire*.

A Biography 67

at least gotten someone with a little more bravura. I thought the whole thing was a disaster. The film was trying to cash in on the success of *The Vampire Lovers,* which was a much better film. This is what has gone wrong with Hammer; they have gotten too greedy. I took Jimmy Sangster to see it, as he hadn't seen the finished version. When that awful vocal song "Strange Love" appeared, I had to pull Jim off the floor to make him watch it. The whole audience was laughing and throwing cups and boxes up in the air. Everybody thought it was hilarious." [79]

Another production for Yorkshire Television followed *Lust for a Vampire*, in which Bates appeared in the episode *Hilda* for the series *The Ten Commandments*. The series, as one could imagine, focused on each of the biblical Ten Commandments, although updated into a contemporary setting. The episode *Hilda* dealt with adultery as the title character, although in a good marriage, finds herself falling for the attractive and French Louis Briquet, played by Ralph Bates. Here, Bates' French background and good looks served him quite well for the role. Actress Mary Peach, who played Hilda, would eventually marry Bates' good friend from Hammer, Jimmy Sangster. Also in the cast as Hilda's husband Tom was James Cossins, who played the dean in *The Horror of Frankenstein* and the doctor in *Fear in the Night*.

Bates' next Hammer film was a clever reworking of Robert Louis Stevenson's classic horror tale, *The Strange Case of Dr. Jekyll and Mr. Hyde*. In keeping with their 1970s approach to trending to the more risqué and showing more female flesh, Hammer scriptwriter Brian Clemens adapted Stevenson's story for their 1971 film as the variation, *Dr. Jekyll and Sister Hyde*. In the story, Dr. Henry Jekyll (Bates) works to combat diseases with a universal anti-virus that will help mankind. However, as Jekyll's friend Professor Robertson points out to him, it would take more than a lifetime to perfect his anti-virus. This switches Jekyll's research to finding an elixir of life in order to continue his work. After early testing using female hormones, Jekyll uses the anti-aging serum on himself, which brings on the unexpected side effect of turning him into a woman, who becomes known as his sister, Hyde (Martine Beswick). Jekyll realizes the unintended effects of his anti-aging serum and tries to find a way to prevent his transformation into Hyde. But when his supply of body parts runs out from two local body snatchers who get caught, Jekyll develops a Machiavellian view and begins taking lives for the good of science.

Robertson and the police soon start following him so Jekyll enlists the help of Hyde to continue his work, although she becomes stronger and fights for control of their body.

The film was quite unique for Hammer and Bates had once again been cast in the lead, evidence that he was certainly being groomed by the company to be one of their new stars, alongside stalwarts Peter Cushing and Christopher Lee. This time, however, Cushing or Lee would not overshadow Bates, as neither played the title character in Hammer's two previous versions of Robert Louis Stevenson's story, *The Ugly Duckling* (1959) and *The Two Face of Dr. Jekyll* (1960). In fact, of all of Bates' Hammer roles, it was Dr. Jekyll that he truly made his own. Bates gives Jekyll a tortured dilemma because he has found a way to extend his life to continue his scientific research, but in doing so, he has unleashed an inner evil that seeks to consume him and anyone around him. With this in mind, Bates plays his character with a serious conflict—he is working against time and also trying to protect his love interest who lives upstairs, neighbor Susan, the woman that Sister Hyde would like nothing more than to dispose of.

A publicity portrait of Bates and Martine Beswick for *Dr. Jekyll and Sister Hyde*

The film's tagline in the U.S. boldly declared that: "The sexual transformation of a man into a woman will actually take place before your very eyes!" This was certainly not an easy task for special effects men of the 1970s, and Hammer had to use technique, camera angles and quick cuts to complete the illusion. Without modern make-up or special effects, Bates does his most to create his transformation into Sister Hyde.

Bates in a promotional advertisement for Hammer's *Dr. Jekyll and Sister Hyde*

A Biography

Contorting his facial features and body, Bates makes the change from Jekyll to Hyde a seemingly seamless process, helped by Martine Beswick's similar facial features and an added mole. In one transformation Bates slumps into a chair and faces a full-length mirror, after taking the elixir, and with his eyes rolling back into his head and covering his tortured face, Sister Hyde emerges. Bates and Beswick also switched arms in shots to depict the merging of the sexes. Dr. Jekyll was truly a perfect role for Bates, and it allowed him to draw a comparison with his parents' footsteps into the medical field. In an interview with *ABC Film Review*, Bates revealed his appreciation for the work that went into making films for Hammer. "When I made my first Hammer horror, *Taste the Blood of Dracula*, I thought it would be pretty simple stuff that I could knock off with no trouble at all.

Bates in another publicity portrait for *Dr. Jekyll and Sister Hyde*

How wrong I was! You've got to make it believable or the whole thing will become a send-up and destroy the illusion."[80]

The film's publicity also drew on Bates' connection to medicine and Dr. Jekyll because of the link between Louis Pasteur and his parents. Bates even mentioned his parents' reaction to his starring in horror films: "As a matter of fact, they declared the films were a good form of psychiatric therapy in certain aspects and in no way harmful at all."[81] In another interview with Ton Paans, Bates explained how his family connection in the medical field assisted him in his portrayal of Dr. Jekyll. "I went down to my father's old teaching hospital for that one, and they took me into the museum. They have the most amazing medical museum and they showed me how to use old instruments and stuff."[82]

Another point brought up during publicity for *Dr. Jekyll and Sister Hyde* was that of typecasting. By this point Bates had already starred in three Hammer Horrors and all signs seemed to indicate the studio was quite interested in having him do many more. Giving some good thought to the issue, Bates responded with his philosophy, which kept him both content with his career and paying the bills. "That's always a problem and one that all actors have to face. If I'm doing this in 10 or 20 years I'll be delighted, as long as I'm doing something else in between."[83]

Bates showed his sense of humor about the film in an interview with Sam Irvin: "At first I wanted to play both parts, doing the female part in drag. I am glad that they did get Martine Beswick because she is much prettier than me. I did not love the film, but I did not by any means hate it. I could have been much better in that film; I thought Martine was smashing." [84] In addition, "Looking back, *Dr. Jekyll and Sister Hyde* has a terrific look to it and likewise brings back some wonderful sentimental memories for me, as I met my [current] wife Virginia on the set. I do recall that in the middle of filming, the great Roy Ward Baker came to me and said, "You know, Ralph, the producers watched the rushes and told me that the production is going very well and that they are very satisfied." I answered "Wonderful!" and Roy responded back angrily, "What the hell do they know!" [85]

Dr. Jekyll (Bates) pours a drink as Susan Spencer (Susan Brodrick) looks on in *Dr. Jekyll and Sister Hyde*.

Martine Beswick looked back at her time working with Bates on the film reflecting: "I had not met Ralph before working with him on *Dr. Jekyll and Sister Hyde*, as I was working in the States. Upon getting to know Ralph during our six-week shoot, I would describe him as a terrific actor, who could be very intense when the scene called for it. We worked closely together for the film and Ralph was also quite a generous actor to me in how we related to the characters. In the mornings and evenings Ralph and I were picked up together by car, so we would have time to talk about what we were filming that day or the next. There was a lot of giggling going on about what we had to do or what we had done. For example, in the story it called for Jekyll and Sister Hyde to leave their bodies and Ralph had to put his hand on my breast, which was supposed to be mine transforming back to Jekyll. While the scene was quite serious in the film, we giggled like crazy offset at the comic moments like this and other ones, in which we had to handle each other's bodies. But when the cameras were rolling, we both were completely serious in our roles. There was also a running gag between us: "Who shall I murder today?" Ralph just had such a great sense of humor and was mischievous, as I also was, so we worked very well together on that level. He was really lovely and I wish that I had gotten to know him for a longer amount of time." [86]

Brian Reynolds, who like Phil Campbell, was a runner for Hammer Film Productions, remembered a job Bates requested of him, which did not go according to plan. "I only met Ralph a couple of times as being a production runner required me

Dr. Jekyll faces himself in *Dr. Jekyll and Sister Hyde*.

Dr. Jekyll passes by his own wanted poster in *Dr. Jekyll and Sister Hyde.*

to leave the set to run various errands, and besides working on *Dr. Jekyll and Sister Hyde*, Hammer also had me working in another feature being filmed at the same time, *On the Buses*. I was introduced to Ralph when he was in the make-up chair for his character and the make-up artist explained to me that Ralph was the star of the production. Ralph was just a nice guy; he always struck me as the sort of chap who was very much like Peter Cushing, well-mannered, kind, calm and friendly. When he spoke to you he made you feel like he knew you all his life. I remember one time in particular during the end of filming of *Dr. Jekyll and Sister Hyde*, Ralph asked me to get him various bottles of liquor to bring onto the set, so he could share them with the crew. This happened on a Friday during when I was extremely busy with the call sheets, so by the time I got back to the set with an armful of gin, vodka and whisky, it was late and only the electricians were still around. So unfortunately I spoiled it for Ralph, and when I eventually caught up with him I was so sorry and apologized for being late, but he was fine. You could tell he was disappointed but he didn't rip into me and told me not to worry about it, which made me feel even worse because he was so nice and I could not deliver the drinks on time. Ralph was so pleasant and was the type of guy that everybody liked. I enjoyed watching Ralph in various television series years later and was shocked when I heard he passed away, as he was so young and on the brink of much success with *Dear John*." [87]

Besides writing duties, Brian Clemens also co-produced *Dr. Jekyll and Sister Hyde* and had a long association as the writer and producer of the fast-paced, action-packed show *The Avengers*. This influence showed through in the film as he seamlessly blended the stories of Dr. Jekyll and Mr. Hyde, Burke and Hare, and Jack the Ripper all into one. The result was an interesting and quickly paced film highlighted by the performances of Bates and Martine Beswick. As previously mentioned, Bates and Beswick shared a similar facial look enhanced by added moles on their right cheek, thus making Dr. Jekyll's transformation into Sister Hyde more believable. An interesting plot point was then added in which a sister and brother living upstairs from Dr. Jekyll's flat each fancy one of his personalities. Sister Hyde, although described as evil and harmful by Jekyll, is not really a villain in the classical sense. When she is created, she seems mostly curious about herself, almost as if she were a young child. But upon each transformation back into Hyde, she becomes more aware of her persona and has a desire to remain in control, as evidenced by the dresses she orders, much to Jekyll's embarrassment and horror. This inner struggle for dominance does not prevent Hyde from helping Jekyll when he needs her assistance filling in for him in obtaining more organs.

Clemens, who became friends with Bates during the production of *Dr. Jekyll and Sister Hyde*, shared his memories: "I think that Ralph was an excellent actor and was very professional. He was getting better all the time and his early death robbed us of seeing his true potential realized. His comedy touch was briefly displayed in the British series, *Dear John*. It was later canceled because it was cheaper to buy and import the American version of the same thing. That series too was okay, but it lacked the peculiar Britishness of the humor.

"In person Ralph was difficult to get to know. I think that secretly he was a shy man (yes actors *can* be shy!). He was never unpleasant or demanding, he simply got on with the job in hand—brilliantly, I might add.

Ralph Bates and Martine Beswick make a fine pair, with matching moles on their faces, in this publicity shot in *Dr. Jekyll and Sister Hyde*.

"On the set of *Dr. Jekyll and Sister Hyde* I saw Ralph every day. He made use of his own locked up persona (except when a pretty girl was around!) and played the role in a close-to-the-chest, secretive performance that exactly suited it. Ralph never pontificated or went 'all method' about the role; he just slipped into it with a natural grace and determination. His scenes with another fine actor, Gerry Sim, were a delight; they struck sparks off each other to our benefit. It helped too that Ralph and Martine Beswick shared a more than superficial likeness.

"I'm sure you have already heard Virginia Bates say, 'The first time I met Ralph, and he tore my clothes off and stabbed me to death!' They were married soon after they met for the first time on *Dr. Jekyll and Sister Hyde*, a marriage that survived until his death and even after. I guess that I was the matchmaker, having cast them both!" [88]

As Clemens mentioned, one of the best aspects of filming *Dr. Jekyll and Sister Hyde* for Bates had to be meeting his future wife Virginia Wetherell, who played Betsy, one of the victims. During Bates' tenure with Hammer he was also going through a trying time, as he was undergoing a divorce from his first wife, Joanna Van Gyseghem. This event in Bates' life would help shape his performances as a divorcee in future productions, including *Second Chance* and *Dear John*. In an interview with Ian Woodward during the latter production, Bates looked back on his personal experience. "There wasn't any bitterness when Joanna and I split up; it was a mutual agreement to part. We are still good friends. I suppose, looking back, it was a help we didn't have any children. There was none of the heartbreak that takes place over who has custody.

"However, I was still shattered and felt the same kind of loneliness John [in *Dear John*] does. You can't just shrug off eight years of marriage. My way of getting over it was to keep moving. I had a mini-bus in which I lived when I took it all over Europe and visited my mother's family in France. Then I traveled round America." [89]

In effect, Hammer would provide Bates with a release from his loneliness and another chance at happiness. Virginia Wetherell, the future love of Bates' life, was born in 1943 in Farnham, Surrey. She spent some of her childhood on the island of Mauritius, before her parents brought her back to England at age 12 to attend boarding school. One of Virginia's early introductions into the acting business was being selected as one of the original Cadbury's Flake girls. Harboring an independent spirit, Virginia gravitated toward a theatrical career and by 1963 was getting bit roles in various television productions. She received her first big break playing the alien Thal character Dyoni in the *Doctor Who* serial *The Daleks*, which introduced the classic villains to audiences for the very first time. Following that role, Virginia had an ongoing role as Julie Serres in the BBC drama series *The Troubleshooters*. Roles for Virginia continued through the 1960s and, like her future husband, she appeared in a couple of horror films, including *Curse of the Crimson Altar* (1968), in which she acted with Boris Karloff and Christopher Lee. Following their meeting in *Dr. Jekyll and Sister Hyde*, Virginia appeared in Stanley Kubrick's classic *A Clockwork Orange* (1971) and in another film for Hammer, *Demons of the Mind* (1972). While acting in films, Virginia would often collect antique clothing and furniture from local shops; in May of 1971 she turned her obsession into another career and opened her very own antique clothing store, located on Portland Road in London, and suitably named *Virginia*. In an interview with *TV Times* years later, Virginia explained how the store got started. "It happened by chance when I had to get rid of a garage full of junk, which belonged to my parents. I took this place, paying £40 rent in advance, and my stepfather lent me half of it. I sell Victoriana, lace, art nouveau and masses of bathroom fittings. I enjoyed the experience and I've been here ever since." [90] Future clients of Virginia's shop would include Jill Townsend, Sarah Miles, Princess Michael of Kent, Helena Christensen, Naomi Campbell and John Galliano.

Bates explained to Ian Woodward what attracted him to Virginia, "What appealed to me so much about Virginia was that she was such a very down-to-earth person, and she laughed a lot. She saw an element of fun in things in general, and I didn't in particular. I always see the gloomy side and Virginia sees the bright side. It was springtime when we were courting, and I used to give her lots of daffodils. I'd buy a hundred and fill up her antique shop. She liked that." [91]

In *Dr. Jekyll and Sister Hyde*, Jekyll spots Betsy in the street at night outside a pub and later picks up her fallen handkerchief to give her. Their first cinematic exchange follows.

Betsy: "Thank you kind sir, you are a gentleman"
Dr. Jekyll: "May I escort you?"
Betsy: "I knew you were a gentleman. I'm very popular with real gentlemen on account of the fact that I speak fluent French"

Although sounding like a nice start, Betsy soon becomes Jekyll's very first victim as she is viciously stabbed to death. In speaking to Sam Irvin, both Bates and Virginia shared their memories meeting each other and a showing of the film:

Virginia: "I met Ralph on *Dr. Jekyll and Sister Hyde*. We had briefly met on the set and at the day's end I asked him if he would mind dropping me off at the station and, of course, being the proper gentleman that he is, he gave me a lift. That is how we met. We eventually went to see the film together one night at an all-night horror program. What a nightmare! It was at the most disgusting theater you can ever imagine. You see you pay a pound and you get to see all these films, plus you get a package meal. So every bum in London was there because it was too cold outside to sleep in the gutter and this was the cheapest place open at that time of night."

Ralph: "Oh it was terrible. Junkies, drunks, the whole lot!"

Virginia: "The smell when you walked in was just unbelievable. I refused to sit in any of the seats."

Ralph: "So we had to sit on the floor."

Virginia: "Yes! So here are the two stars of the film sitting on the floor." [92]

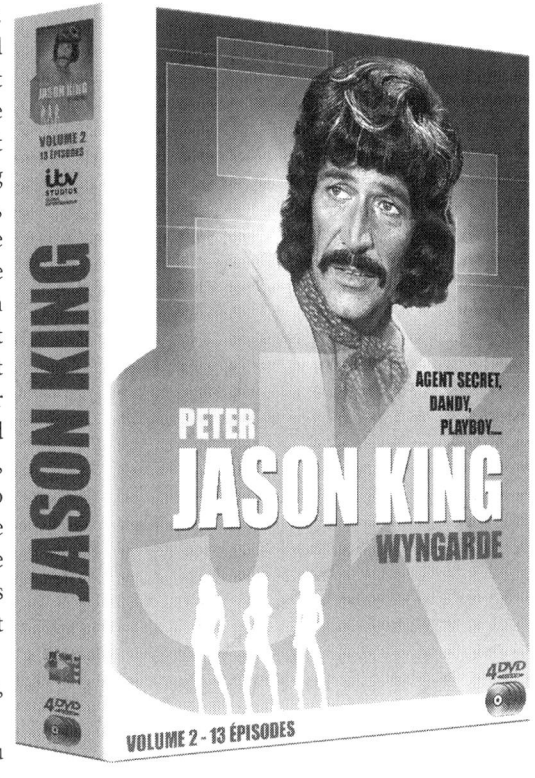

Following Bates' role in Hammer's *Dr. Jekyll and Sister Hyde*, he returned to television for a couple of parts. First up was a spot on the popular series, *Jason King*. The series starred Peter Wyngarde, who was then at the height of his popularity. Wyngarde had first come into the public spotlight for his role in the successful 1969 ITV spy series *Department S*, in which he played author/agent Jason King. Along with two other agents Stewart Sullivan and Annabelle Hurst, they were part of a special department of Interpol (hence the "S" of the title *Department S*). Wyngarde's character was a fashionable trendsetter and also quite the womanizer: Actor Mike Myers credited him for his own spy character in the *Austin Powers* film series. After becoming the dominant character of *Department S*, it was not long before a spin-off series was commissioned, focusing on Wyngarde's character and simply named *Jason King*. The new series focused on King and was a send up of the popular spy genre on television including *The Avengers* and *The Saint*. The premise of the series had King leaving Department S to become a full time writer of his Mark Caine adventure novels. While traveling the world doing research however, he often got entangled in various cases and even returned to working for the British government on occasion to help in international matters.

In the 1971 episode *Variations on a Theme*, King travels to Vienna to help Alan Keeble (Bates), an old friend who is a British agent presumed dead but instead very much alive and

A Biography

being pursued for his black book of names. While meeting with Keeble's girlfriend, the Russians latch onto King in their pursuit of Keeble. King turns for help to a British intelligence officer John (Julian Glover), in an attempt to get Keeble to safety in exchange for his book. Keeble's girlfriend is suspicious of the whole deal, however, and John may or may not have ulterior motives.

Bates fared well in the episode, as by this time he was no longer a novice acting in both television and films. Like other episodes of *Jason King*, some of the scenes in *Variations on a Theme* were shot on location, this time in Vienna (including marvelous shots of the famous Zentralfriedhof cemetery) and the episode also featured Alexandra Bastedo and Eric Pohlmann as guest stars. Julian Glover, who played John, the British intelligence officer, shared his memories of Bates: "I remember my time working with Ralph on *Jason King* as one of the most wonderful times of my career. He was such a versatile actor, a very quietly spoken chap, who got along with everyone involved in the production. He had a very distinguished presence and was delightful in every way and was a true gentleman. The movie and TV industry lost an actor of the highest caliber when Ralph sadly left us. He's so very sadly missed by all". [93]

Although *Dr. Jekyll and Sister Hyde* is the film where Bates would meet his future wife, they only shared one scene together. But in their next production together, the BBC 1971 *Play for Today* episode *Thank You Very Much*, Bates and Virginia got plenty of screen time together, playing members of an advertising agency in playwright N. F. Simpson's satire on the advertising profession. Simpson, along with other playwrights including Harold Pinter, was associated with the Theatre of the Absurd, which delves into the exploration of human existence.

Virginia explains their role together and how a comment made led to her nickname for her future husband: "*Thank You Very Much* was a very prestigious teleplay because *Play for Today* featured stories by very established writers, and this one was an N. F. Simpson play. It was about two rival advertisement agencies and their competition to be number one. One agency was based on the prestigious J. Walter Thompson Company, which coincidentally Ralph's ex-wife Joanna was in (though at that point they were still married). Ralph and I were both cast to be part of the new rival agency, which was sort of very hip and cool. This production was unique in that we were together in every scene. At the opening of the episode I had the very first line of the recording with Ralph and myself together on set. We were in the same shot and it was almost like a live production, as everyone was watching it on the BBC on Sunday night. Ralph and I were sitting side by side before taping began and I knew that I had the first line so I was getting really nervous as the five-minute countdown was announced. So I mentioned to Ralph, 'I'm dying to go to the loo. Do you think that I have time?' Ralph in his mischievous way said, 'Depends whether you need to do biggies or not!' which caused me to burst into hysterical laughter. After that occasion, I used to call Ralph 'Biggies' which got shortened to 'Bigs' and he became known to all our friends as 'Bigs.' And that is the story of how I nicknamed Ralph." [94]

Bates continued the year with a role in the short-lived action series *The Persuaders!* starring Roger Moore and Tony Curtis. In the series, Moore (also a co-producer of the show) played

English Lord Brett Sinclair while Curtis played American Danny Wilde. The two characters were like oil and water in personality, Sinclair being an upper-class gentleman with dry humor and Wilde, much like his name, the more unpredictable. However, both men shared being wealthy, along with a love of women, the good life and adventure. As a result they became friends and teamed up to solve crimes, which baffled the police. When the series was eventually cancelled, Moore would go on to play his most famous role in the *James Bond* film series.

In the episode *Nuisance Value*, Bates played Michel, a mysterious Frenchman who is not quite what he seems. At first he is seen in a Spanish hotel calling Lisa Zorakin (Viviane Ventura), the daughter of a wealthy businessman, and she has fallen for him. He then quickly reveals to a partner his intentions of kidnapping Lisa for half a million dollars ransom. Wilde unknowingly tries to set up a double date for him and Sinclair, with Lisa and her assistant Mary, but things go awry quickly when Michel grabs Lisa, and Wilde is blamed for the kidnapping. When Sinclair finally tracks down and disarms Michel, Lisa explains that they were to be married and wanted the ransom money to start a life together away from her demanding father. Things go from bad to worse as Zorakin sends his henchmen after Sinclair and Wilde; Lisa escapes from them to free a locked up Michel, who then double crosses her and takes off with the money to meet his real partner in a race for the border.

The role of Michel was a typical sinister Frenchman, complete with accent from Bates. At first Michel seems like an obvious villain but that view changes when Lisa begs to let him go as she loves him and they plan to elope. Bates does a formidable job passing off Michel as a poor writer, who wants to win Lisa's hand in marriage. The double cross then is especially shocking, as Bates coldly brushes a weeping Lisa aside and takes off with the money in Sinclair's 1969 Aston-Martin DBS. There is one great moment as he sits in a hotel room by the Spanish border and, while counting his money, calls room service for champagne. He specifies French champagne but is unimpressed, making a look of disdain after tasting it.

Viviane Ventura shared her memories of Bates. "I was very young with not a lot of experience when I filmed *The Persuaders!* episode with Ralph, but I remember him to be very helpful with advice for me and I will always cherish that. The character that Ralph played was every mother's worst nightmare for their daughter, a double-crossing liar and swindler! But I'm glad to say that Ralph was completely the opposite in person. He was a total gentleman on the set, was always on time and knew his lines.

A Biography

"Another point about Ralph's performance in the episode was his French accent. When an actor who is English has to play a Frenchman, they usually make the accent so pronounced that you know it is phony and it becomes almost a farce. But Ralph did not do that and his slight accent made it very plausible for his character, and I believe it helped demonstrate his good acting ability." [95]

Another leading role came Bates' way following his last Hammer film in the long running ATV romantic drama series, *Love Story*. Bates starred as the romantic interest Purves in the 1972 episode *Alice*, alongside Lois Baxter. It serves as an example that Bates could appeal, as not only villains but also as romantic types, and sometimes even a mix of the two. Although a number of episodes from *Love Story* were lost, *Alice* still remains (although the only copies existing have burnt-in subtitles).

Nest for Bates was another ATV production entitled *Crime of Passion*. The British courtroom drama was set in France and similar to *Wicked Women*; its stories were based on real life French criminal trials of murderers who committed crimes of passion. In the 1972 episode *Lina*, Bates played a character involved with the title woman. Creator Ted Willis was also responsible for the *Mrs. Thursday* series, in which Bates had his second television role. Two Hammer connections from *Crime of Passion* came from series regulars Anthony Newlands, who had starred in the 1965 psychological thriller *Hysteria*, and John Phillips, who appeared in 1967's *The Mummy's Shroud*.

A real coup for Bates came in the summer of 1972 when he was cast opposite American actress Mia Farrow in a theatrical revival of J.M. Barrie's play *Mary Rose*. In the story, taking place shortly after the First World War, Mary Rose (Farrow) disappears as a child during a family vacation on a remote island in the Scottish Outer Hebrides. Her father leads a search for her to no avail, but she reappears 30 days later in the same spot where she vanished, with no memory of the lost time. Years later, Mary Rose is now a young wife and mother and she convinces her husband Simon (Bates) to take her back to the island she visited in her youth. After vacationing on the island, Mary Rose disappears once again right before they are set to leave. Another search is conducted but there is no trace of Mary Rose. Twenty-five years later Mary Rose, who has not aged at all, finally is found back on the island and is brought back home. Just as the first time she disappeared, Mary Rose does not remember what happened. During

Bates with Mia Farrow in *Mary Rose*

this long gap of time, Mary Rose's son Harry (Bates) has grown into an adult, joined the Navy, and is now physically older than his mother. The two meet and a resolution is made regarding Mary Rose.

Essentially a ghost story, *Mary Rose* draws some comparisons to J.M. Barrie's most famous work, *Peter Pan, or The Boy Who Wouldn't Grow Up*. Like the character Peter Pan, Mary Rose remains childlike and innocent, although not of her own choice. There is much mystery in the play, which is left to interpretation, such as what the island stands for. One of the play's most well-known admirers was no stranger to mysteries himself, Alfred Hitchcock. The famous director saw the original 1920 theater production and made it his lifelong dream to try to make a film version. Hitchcock even purchased the story rights to *Mary Rose* in 1963 to film as *The Island That Wants to be Visited*, with Tippi Hedren in the lead role, but for various reasons was never able to get Universal Studios' backing to make his project. The 1972 London theater production with Farrow and Bates turned out to be a big success, which revived the push for a film version. Screenwriter Jay Presson Allen unsuccessfully tried to buy the rights from Hitchcock and have Farrow replay her role and reunite her with Roman Polanski, her director in *Rosemary's Baby* (1968), the film that originally brought her to fame. [96]

A letter from Peter Cushing to Ralph Bates concerning Bates' appearance in *Mary Rose*

As for the 1972 production, stage rehearsals by the Manchester 69 Theatre Company started on April 24 and were held at Manchester University Theatre. Braham Murray directed the play but by 1976 had become one of the artistic directors at Manchester, a position he had held longer than any other at the University when he retired in 2012. Besides Farrow and Bates, the play also starred Carmel McSharry, Lee Fox, Oliver Ford-Davies, Roy Sampson and Ann Way. The production began as a short tour before settling in on July 13th at the Shaw Theatre in London for a five-week limited run. As *Mary Rose* was Farrow's introduction to British theater, there was a lot of press for the production. Braham Murray had great praise for Farrow in his autobiography, *The Worst It Can Be is a Disaster*, and stated that she was born to play Mary Rose. He also revealed that among the opening night guests for the London showing were Katherine Hepburn and Noel Coward. Bates was given the unique opportunity to play dual roles in the production; certainly something he did not get the chance to repeat in his career. As the husband, Bates was dressed in a naval captain's uniform with his jet-black hair dyed gray for the aging of his character. As the son, Bates regained his dark locks with a youthful preppy look of a sweater worn over a collared shirt.

Director Braham Murray revealed some insight into his play *Mary Rose*: "*Mary Rose* had a very distinguished cast. Mia Farrow was huge at the time, a very big star and it was quite an accomplishment to get her. Mia and I shared the same agent and she wanted to appear on the stage. My agent asked if I would fly out to see her, as she was doing the film *Docteur Popaul* for director Claude Chabrol, in Bordeaux. Shortly before leaving, I was having dinner in London with a company manager who had been with us for years and she suddenly started singing "Mary Rose." I asked her what that tune was and she said it is from a wonderful play and she didn't know why she started singing it. So I inquired more about the play and she explained it to me, and two nights before I flew out, I got a copy of the play and read it and went over to Bordeaux and told Mia, 'This is going to be very strange to you but I just got this strange message that we should be doing this play.' And Mia read it and said, "I love it, I'll do it." And so that was the start of putting *Mary Rose* together.

"Ralph's agent John Miller recommended the actor to me. So I went to see *Dr. Jekyll and Sister Hyde*, which was playing at the theater, and I thought Ralph was rather wonderful in it, and then afterwards we met in person. I thought Ralph was ideal for the dual parts because he was a very kind and gentle person who could also do something quite strong and powerful when he needed to. So I cast Ralph and he was absolutely wonderful with Mia Farrow in *Mary Rose*. Ralph played both the characters in the production marvelously because he could do the Australian one very strongly and he could do the more tormented and gentle one beautifully. The connection between Ralph and Mia onstage worked terribly well. Afterwards Ralph and I became very good friends. One time I was directing a show in Paris and he came to see it and we spent some time together. Ralph was just a wonderful person and the shock when he died was enormous. I was very fond of Ralph; he was sympathetic and intelligent and a lovely fellow." [97]

Bates' co-star, Mia Farrow, shared her thoughts of working with him in the production: "Ralph played my husband and my son in the production of *Mary Rose*, a play as odd as its author, J.M. Barrie. I had recently moved to England to join my husband, André Previn (conductor of the London Symphony Orchestra). I had wanted to return to the theater and when this play was offered me, I agreed to do it. We began the production at the 69 Theatre Company in Manchester, then doing Brighton before opening in London. Ralph was cast soon after I joined the production. I can say that Ralph was superb in both roles. He was all the things a great actor is, but without a trace of selfishness. The reality he brought to each scene, of course, made my job easier and a joy. He was also the kindest of people. After the play ended, we went our ways and I never saw him again. As I look back, I see only beautiful times with Ralph, both on stage and backstage. A lovely man; a lovely actor." [98]

Following *Mary Rose*, Bates returned in what would be his last film for Hammer, *Fear in the Night*. This time he was teamed up with Peter Cushing for the studio's 1972 psychological thriller. In the story, Peggy Heller (Judy Geeson), a young newlywed schoolteacher, is set to join her husband Robert (Bates) at his new job at a secluded boys' school in the country. But before she leaves, a stranger with a prosthetic arm tries to strangle her. When she comes to, she tries convincing her landlady and husband about the attack but, having had a nervous breakdown previously, has a difficulty being believed. At the school, Peggy meets the headmaster Michael Carmichael (Peter Cushing) and his young wife Molly (Joan Collins). Although the setting of the school is peaceful, Peggy is soon attacked once again by the stranger in her new home on the campus. Not being able to convince her husband once again, Peggy is left alone with a shotgun, as he goes off to attend a school conference. As day turns to night, Peggy faces her worst fears; secrets are revealed, and a deadly surprise awaits.

Bates obviously relished the chance to work with Cushing, as he related to author Ton Paans: "He's the master, isn't he? Terrific! He was very good to me. I had met him before we did *Fear in the Night* on the set of *The Horror of Frankenstein*. We became friendly and I used to meet him at 'Browns.' He's a very wise man. When I was working on a play, *Mary Rose*, and Peter was shooting at night, he bothered to come down on a matinee, just to give me a bit of support, and then he'd go back to London to shoot again." [99]

Fear in the Night was the third film directed by Jimmy Sangster, who also wrote and produced it. In fact, Sangster was responsible for writing most of the Hammer psychological thrillers, starting with 1961's *Taste of Fear*. These films were all loosely based on the 1955 classic French psychological thriller *Les Diaboliques*, in which the wife of a cruel headmaster and his mistress plot to murder him. *Fear in the Night* had a long genesis from Sangster's original 1963 script to the eventual 1971 film. During these years it went through three title changes. It was originally called *Brainstorm* in 1963, it was retitled *The Claw* in 1967 and then finally it was filmed and released as *Fear in the Night*. The plot location was also changed from a houseboat to a school setting. In *Fear in the Night* the small cast of four main characters narrowed down the culprit before the finale, but the built-up suspense and twist ending, practically a required staple in the psychological horrors, are well done. Among the supporting cast was Joan Collins, who appeared in a number of horror and thriller films in the 1970s, including another film with Bates entitled *I Don't Want to be Born*. When Collins' career became red hot with her role as Alexis Carrington Colby in the 1980's television drama *Dynasty*, it led production companies to retitle *Fear in the Night* to *Dynasty of Fear* for VHS releases, to cash in on Collins' success. Bates expressed his admiration for the film along with a humble look into his acting, in a conversation with Sam Irvin. "I liked doing *Fear in the Night* very much, particularly because I am a very good friend of Judy Geeson and Peter Cushing. I am not as good an actor as I would like. I can't wait until I get much older, because then I feel I can put on a little weight and do some character acting." [100]

It did seem a bit unusual to see Bates in modern clothes, as all his other Hammer films had him in period dress. However, his performance in *Fear in the Night* was perfectly suitable and his character's change from the charming and caring husband into a frustrated and crazed man on a rampage was reminiscent of a *Dr. Jekyll*-type personality change. Bates' best scenes come after Judy Geeson's character has supposedly killed the headmaster Carmichael, only to find the body missing. Robert, thinking all had gone according to plan, dances carefully around the issue of where the headmaster might be, but as he spots blood stains on the floor and his wife denies doing anything to Carmichael, he slowly starts to unravel and loses control. Here Bates plays Robert, trying by any means possible to get the truth out of Peggy, promising, lying, even telling the truth, but finally threatening when all else fails.

Bates and Judy Geeson keep warm (right) on the set of *Fear in the Night*.

In publicity for *Fear in the Night*, Bates provided some insight into his personal life and interests. Hinting at his mother's French influence, Bates stated that he adored French

The cast and crew of *Fear in the Night*: On the couch in front is Ralph Bates, Jimmy Sangster and Judy Geeson

food, especially the best of Burgundian cookery with cream from Normandy. While confirming his interest in the sport of cricket, Bates revealed that he often played with his friend and fellow actor Gerald Harper on a showbiz cricket team. Harper, like Bates, had early aspirations to pursue a career in medicine before turning to acting. Also like Bates, Harper appeared in a Hammer film, the 1979 remake of *The Lady Vanishes*, their last production before their 2008 revival. Bates also professed a love of playing squash and enjoying swimming. For music, he mentions that while he admired the work of Carole King, Virginia was the

Judy Geeson and Bates receive direction by Jimmy Sangster on the set of *Fear in the Night*.

musical one of the family, something she would pass on to their son William, who would become an award winning composer and founder of the group Fall On Your Sword. Among the directors Bates admired, the top three included Federico Fellini, Luis Bunuel, and Joseph Losey, who also had a Hammer connection in that he directed the productions of *A Man on the Beach* (1955) and *These are the Damned* (1963), and co-directed (uncredited) *X-The Unknown* (1956). Among Bates' ultimate ambitions was to gather a small band of like-minded fellow actors who could do progressive work in the manner of the old style stock companies.
101

Had Hammer continued to thrive as they did in the late 1950s through the 1960s, there is little doubt that Bates would have been featured in more of their films, as they were actively promoting him. When Sam Irvin broached this subject and asked what Bates felt about possibly replacing Peter Cushing and Christopher Lee as the next "King of Horror," Bates replied, "I had never heard that before, but now that you say it, I can see that it is probably exactly what Hammer was trying to do with me. But, I think those days of typecasting are gone. I really don't think audiences will create another Peter Cushing and Christopher Lee. I think that era is past. There is not that volume of work being done. The only way anyone could become a new King of Horror, as you call it, is for a company like Hammer to take an actor and put him in 10 major roles in remakes of the classic horror films. I only did two. Peter Cushing and Christopher Lee were not made Kings of Horror by

Bates and Judy Geeson clown around on set.

A Biography

83

Hammer, but by the audiences, and nowadays the audiences like new faces as much, if not more, than old established ones. As much as I respect Peter, I would not want to be another Peter Cushing or any of the others. I want to be Ralph Bates." [102]

Among the many people Bates met while working for Hammer was fellow former Trinity alumnus Shane Briant. Like Bates, Briant was also being groomed by Hammer to become one of their future stars and he appeared in several of their productions including *Straight on Till Morning* (1972), which was on the double-bill with *Fear in the Night*; *Demons of the Mind* (1972); *Frankenstein and the Monster from Hell* (1973) and *Captain Kronos—Vampire Hunter* (1974). Briant shared his memories of Ralph Bates: "I can't remember exactly when Ralphie came into my life, but I can say this, he added such a happy glow to my life. I can't conjure up an image of Ralphie in which he is not smiling, nor an occasion where we met and he wasn't radiating *joie de vivre* and happiness. I must have come to know him through Virginia and Jimmy Sangster, while I was under contract to Hammer Films at Elstree. Wendy, my wife, and I saw a great deal of Virginia and Ralph, and the high spot of each year was being invited to their home in Barrowgate Road to spend Christmas Day. The Bates made it their business to think of all those who didn't really have a jolly family to spend Christmas with, and asked them to join them. There were usually 12 or so around the table and all were kind of showbiz people—musicians, writers, actors etc. It was the best fun. I remember Ralphie's son William was a child then and would be glued to the TV screen and constantly calling out—"Can't see!"—if anyone obscured his view. Daisy was the sweetest little girl. We all had a small task. Mine was to make bread sauce. It was before the dreary old days of watching one's cholesterol, so I always made a rich sauce with extra butter cream and onions. Everyone seemed to like it. On one occasion years later, in 1981, Wendy and I were asked to the premier of a film called *Roar* about lions, starring Tippi Hedren. Virginia and Ralph

Ralph Bates (with facial hair) and Shane Briant, along with wives Virginia (blonde) and Wendy

Ralph and Virginia, with Babette sitting on the bench, in the Johnson family garden, 1974

came with us and Tippi asked us if we could chaperone her young daughter, Melanie Griffith! She was a shy sweetheart!" [103]

Following Bates' last Hammer film, he returned to television where he got a supporting role in the 1973 BBC drama series, *A Picture of Katherine Mansfield*. Bates appeared as the character Robert in the fourth episode of the series, named for him. Also in the episode, as a chambermaid, was Fiona Gaunt, who would go on later that year with Bates to star in the science fiction series *Moonbase 3*. The series was based on the real life of modernist writer Katherine Mansfield, while also recreating some of her stories for television. Each of the six episodes was broken into three parts with the first segment entitled "The Life," which delved into Mansfield's background, and the other two segments being adaptations of her short stories. Vanessa Redgrave played Mansfield and Jeremy Brett played fellow writer John Middleton Murry, her second husband. Eleven years later Brett would start his run as one of the most admired performers in the role of Sherlock Holmes. Bates would also have a Holmes connection, playing the character Windibank in the 1990 BBC audio drama, *The Adventures of Sherlock Holmes*.

Bates as Michel Lebrun in *Moonbase 3*

In the summer of 1973, Bates had landed a role as Frenchman Michel Lebrun, the Deputy Director, on the BBC space drama series *Moonbase 3*. Created by two veterans of *Doctor Who*, producer Barry Letts and script editor Terrance Dicks, the series was to be a realistic and serious attempt to envision the future of the space program. To that end, James Burke, the BBC science journalist who reported on the NASA program, was brought in as the science advisor for *Moonbase 3* to make sure that everything depicted was scientifically possible. The resulting series was quite remarkable in its scientific theories and based in plausible reality. Unlike *Doctor Who*, which featured outlandish space monsters on a weekly basis, the closest *Moonbase 3* ever came to featuring a menacing creature was in the episode *Behemoth*; and it turned out to be a limited shifting layer of permafrost. The series was almost lost forever when the BBC wiped the master tapes. This was their standard practice at the time to make room for newer shows and save money on tape. It took until 1993 for NTSC copies to be discovered in co-producer Fox's archives, which were then restored and released to the public.

The title of the series referred to Europe's Moonbase, situated in between the other nations' bases: America was Moonbase 1, Russia was Moonbase 2, China was Moonbase 4, and

A Biography

Brazil was Moonbase 5. Set 30 years in the future during 2003, Europe's Moonbase 3 was afforded a limited operating budget and a demanding group of administrators who expected results from the scientists stationed there. As the actual series itself had a limited budget, this worked quite well for the stories. The spacesuits were quite convincing, as was the base, although at times the lunar surface gave away its illusion as the actors bounced on it during scenes. Unlike later big budget science fiction fare with fancy special effects, *Moonbase 3* focused on the crew and their interaction, which made for a fascinating character study.

Bates (left) and cast members of *Moonbase 3*

Although Bates' character appeared in all episodes of *Moonbase 3*, there were three episodes in particular in which Michel was heavily featured and played a crucial role. In the first episode, *Departure and Arrival*, Michel's insistence of going by the book and ignoring Dr. Helen Smith's advice of not letting pilot Harry Sanders fly a mission results in an accident, which causes the death of Base Director Tony Ransome. The fallout from the incident has the Director General of the European space program choosing a new Director to investigate Ransome's death. While Michel feels he should be chosen as he is next in command, the panel of advisors agrees, but the Director General passes over him in favor of David Caulder, a scientist turned civil servant. As a result, Michel almost resigns in anger and this sets up his unease with the new Director, leading to a testing of the wills in a later episode. Bates' first appearance as Michel shows him as not on the same page as his colleagues, and he does this extremely well in his authoritarian role when he is challenged by Dr. Helen Smith's hunch that something is awry with Sanders. While Michel is part of the crew, Bates almost makes him seem alone in his approach to dealing with people and situations.

The second standout role for Bates is in the fifth episode, *Castor and Pollux*. Head technician Tom Hill gets trapped in his spacecraft and faces a life or death situation. Caulder is willing to do anything to save Tom, even going against the Russian Director and using a man to risk his life to save Tom. Michel sees this as a huge mistake and goes head-to-head with Caulder. The Director General relieves Caulder of his duties and places Michel in charge. Once given total power, Michel rethinks his stance and decides the logical choice would be to let the Russian cosmonaut continue in his attempt to save Tom. What particularly stands out in Bates' performance is how his growing disapproval of Caulder now finally emerges and he takes a stand against him. The ending shows that Michel is not as inflexible as he presents himself, once he is given the opportunity to think of all the possible outcomes.

The third standout role for Bates is in the very last episode of the series, *View of a Dead Planet*. A sense of doom and desperation fills Moonbase 3 as visiting celebrity scientist Sir Benjamin

Bates (back right) looks intense in *Moonbase 3*.

Dyce (Michael Gough) announces that his Arctic Sun Project is going to have an unintended consequence, the destruction of the Earth itself. While the crew initially dismisses Dyce's declaration, when all contact is lost from Earth following the project's initiation and a cloud encompasses the planet, everyone's hopes fade rapidly. Michel volunteers to take a solo craft back to Earth in a last ditch effort for humanity, while plans are being made at the base to euthanize the crew. Bates really shines in this episode as Michel finally breaks out of his shell joking about the horrible-tasting synthetic wine he is drinking on Bastille Day. Up until this point Michel did not seem to have a sense of humor, as his main concern was following all the rules by the book and making logical decisions; this fits the mold made by Spock on the Starship Enterprise. However, *View of a Dead Planet* allowed Bates' character to show further humanity, such as his desire to have the final say in his own fate, taking the lone trip back to Earth with the possibility of a doomed ending for all of mankind.

Garrick Hagon, who played scientist Bruno Ponti in three of the episodes of *Moonbase 3*, shared some of his memories of Bates and the production: "I admired Ralph as an actor, in his thoroughness of preparation, his charisma, his affability, his generosity and his calm. One moment during the shooting of *View of a Deadly Planet* I remember well. Toward the end of a long day wonderful actor Michael Gough had a long and difficult speech involving lots of technical language. He was tired, as we all were, and was having some trouble keeping his lines on track. Somehow the rest of we actors in the long scene thought we could give some psychic support, and so we, being full of hippy enthusiasm, gathered around Michael and, while he was in full flow, we sent out waves of mental encouragement to him. It worked. Michael mastered the scene. Whether he was grateful to us remains unrecorded." [104]

Bates' involvement in *Moonbase 3* also coincided with a happy event in his life. As Virginia explained, "We got married in 1973, while Ralph was in the middle of filming *Moonbase 3*. On September 14 we went down to the registry office in Kensington to get married and then had our reception at Julie's Restaurant, which is opposite my shop on Portland Road. It was actually one of the first wedding receptions they ever had there. Gerald Harper, who was very well known at the time, was our Best Man. Ralph and I didn't go on honeymoon until after he was finished filming, and at that time we went to Tras Talloires in France. I was just at the beginning of my pregnancy and unfortunately had terrible morning sickness and I threw up all the time while in Talloires and felt quite dreadful, but at least we got to get away!" [105]

Gerald Harper reflected on his first meeting with Bates and their common love of cricket: "I first met Ralph on the set of *The Caesars*; I had a small part as Lucius Vitellius and shared just one scene with Ralph, that took place on a huge flight of stairs. On the take I marched up to him, bowed low and unwittingly stood on his toga, so that he was trapped, unable to move throughout the scene. Anyone else would be white with anger, but afterwards he just roared with laughter and we were friends for the rest of his life.

"Ralph was the gentlest, kindest man I ever knew with a great talent as an actor, but he had an even greater talent for friendship. He also had a smile that you could never forget. He therefore had a wider circle of friends than anybody I have known. Actors, singers, musicians, boxers and taxi drivers—they all came under his spell—and our joint love of cricket helped. We were both members of the MCC (Marylebone Cricket Club) and we shared a locker in the Lord's pavilion, where we kept our gear, including a venerable old cricket bat that we christened HARBAT. We had practice at Lords, bowled at by the ground staff. We played for a team run by the well-known bandleader Vic Lewis. He was a terrible cricketer but a lovely man, who collected a team with actors including Oliver Reed and a couple of professional cricketers, to give us firepower.

"I met the great Edward Dexter (aka Lord Ted) when he was the captain of England's team, and I struck a deal with him in which I gave him tickets to a play I was in and took him out to dinner. In return he would give me a net practice at Lords. Who would love [to share] this opportunity the most? Obviously Ralph, and I invited Harold Pinter as well, who turned up with the most expensive set of gear I had ever seen. Pinter, however, was so overwhelmed by meeting the great man that he never said a word. To crown it all, Ralph, who was a very good slow bowler, would have had Dexter caught in the slips, if there had been the opportunity.

"I remember Ralph taking me out to dinner to meet his new girlfriend, the wonderful Vig, and was thrilled when he said I was the most responsible person that he knew and would I be his Best Man. So Ralph spent the night before his wedding with me in my flat in Ladbroke Grove. Unfortunately, and to my eternal shame, I timed it all wrong, and we had to run the last half mile to get to the wedding on time! Having been unable to have a child with his first wife, it came as a bit of a surprise later on when Ralph came round to tell everyone that he and Vig were having a baby, and I found out at the same time that Joanna was also pregnant.

"Only two years before his death, we were told that court (aka Royal) tennis was a game you could play into old age, and as Lords has one of the few courts in existence, Ralph and I started to take lessons together. From the day Ralph died I have been unable to go onto that curious Medieval court again ... I miss my good friend." [106]

The Protectors was a popular ITC production created by Gerry Anderson, who was most known for his science-fiction series made using his Supermarionation technique. After a decade of creating futuristic stories using marionette puppets for such series as *Thunderbirds* and *Captain Scarlet and the Mysterons*, Anderson took a break from the genre to develop a live action adventure series involving three wealthy international private detectives, who belong to an organization to protect the innocent. The three leads were played by Robert Vaughn as Harry Rule, Nyree Dawn Porter as Contessa Caroline di Contini and Tony Anholt as Paul Buchet. In the 1973 episode of *The Protectors* entitled *Petard*, Rule is contacted by the owner of a cleaning products firm, which has had its last product idea stolen by a rival competitor. Rule goes undercover in their company as a consultant with the Contessa as his secretary. Among the suspects as a possible insider spy is David Lee (Bates), a company executive with great ambitions. With the aid of a telecommunications expert, Rule sets a trap to out the guilty party and turn the tables on their industrial espionage.

An American one sheet for *I Don't Want to be Born*, here retitled *The Devil Within Her*

Bates, dressed in a business suit and wearing thick-rimmed glasses under his neatly combed hair, serves as a red herring as the potential spy in *Petard*. He shoots a concerned glance at a colleague upon meeting Rule, appears nervous when his boss asks about the company's financial losses and grills the Contessa on information about Rule. However, Bates does get to show off some of his charisma and charm when his character convinces the Contessa to let him take her out to dinner. As the Contessa explains to Rule afterwards, "He is bright and carries his ambition like a torch." Iain Cuthbertson, who played Lee's boss Wyatt in the episode, would work again years later with Bates in the *Storyboard* drama *Lytton's Diary*, in which he played Lytton's editor and Bates played a politician.

Bates returned to film in May of 1975, after his string of previous Hammer horrors, in another horror yarn, this time involving a killer infant. Known by a slew of different titles including *The Devil Within Her* and *Sharon's Baby*, the plot for *I Don't Want to be Born* was seemingly inspired by two of the biggest horror blockbusters of the time, *Rosemary's Baby* (1968)

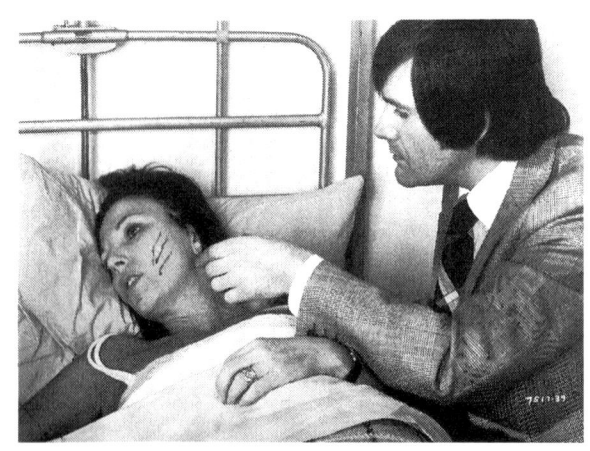

Gino Carlesi (Bates) examines the scratches on his wife's (Joan Collins) face in *I Don't Want to be Born*.

and *The Exorcist* (1973), both of which opened a floodgate of similar films in the 1970s concerning the Devil's influence on infants, children or adults. A number of articles reported on this phenomenon in movies with one example declaring, "If you care about the welfare of films, of women and little boys, these movies, to say nothing of the dozens of sequels already planned, represent a long step sideways onto the soft shoulders of puerility."[107] As a result, similarly themed horror films of the decade eventually faded away in favor of the new slasher film genre, although there were still some notable exceptions like *I Don't Want to be Born* making the rounds.

In *I Don't Want to be Born*, Lucy Carlesi (Joan Collins) experiences a difficult birth that produces a rather large and strong baby boy. Her attempts to bond with the baby are unsuccessful, as the baby immediately scratches her face and sucks blood from his fingers. Lucy's husband Gino (Ralph Bates) discusses this with Dr. Finch (Donald Pleasence) and is told that it is nothing more than the baby's survival instinct. But additional mishaps with the baby convince Lucy otherwise; she confides in her friend Mandy (Caroline Munro) that while previously working as a stripper in a seedy strip club, she was cursed by a dwarf named Hercules for spurning his sexual advances. Gino's sister Albana (Dame Eileen Atkins), a nun, comes to London to visit the new baby and believes evil exists within him. A plan is made with Dr. Finch to take the baby for observation to the hospital, but things take an unexpected turn when the possessed baby begins a violent and deadly string of attacks on everyone who comes into contact with him.

The tone of the film is set in the opening scene with Lucy in the throes of a difficult labor and a puzzled Dr. Finch telling his nurse, "This one doesn't want to be born." From then on there is plenty of footage of 1970s English locales, along with a funky jazz film score. While somewhat campy, *I Don't Want to be Born* does have its creepy moments, such as when Lucy realizes that her own baby may be out to kill her. Eerie synthesizer music and quick film cuts aid in giving the baby a demonic presence. The plot involving the Devil, a curse, strippers and a dwarf is certainly exploitative and failed to impress the critics, one who wrote, "The film is a smear to dwarfs everywhere."[108] Bates likely took the role as his friend Peter Sasdy was directing the production. However, it might have made better sense to have changed the nationality of Lucy's husband to that of an Englishman or Frenchman, as Bates seems to struggle with Gino Carlesi's Italian accent. His character is not given much to do other than provide some comfort to Lucy and introduce his sister Albana, who plays a more important role in the story, before the baby kills him. Bates' appearance in the film, however, did give him the opportunity to work with Dame Eileen Atkins and popular character actor Donald Pleasence, who had a long association playing various villains in many thrillers and horror movies.

In an interview with Ton Paans, Bates told a story regarding his death scene from the film. "You remember me at the end of *Fear in the Night* hanging from a tree? Well, I had a similar scene in *I Don't Want to be Born* and it was the last shot before lunch. Gradually the rope got tighter around my neck and the harness got tighter and I was actually blacking out. The last thing I can remember was Sasdy saying, "Shoot it, looks good, quick shoot it!" And they let me down as I passed out on the floor. It was really hairy. Things like that have to be done properly. Now this is the difference: The Hammer people knew exactly how to do it, but the other people on this production weren't the same people and see what happens. This is just to illustrate what superb technicians Hammer employed." [109]

Susan Richards, Joan Collins and Bates in *I Don't Want to be Born*

Director Peter Sasdy, who reunited with Bates for the film, shared an embarrassing moment on the set: "A number of years later, and by then Ralph was well established as a leading actor in films and television, we had a chance of working together again, this time for the Rank Organization on the feature film *I Don't Want To Be Born (The Devil Within Her*, U.S.A.) playing opposite *Joan Collins*. This time he was very confident on the set. It was interesting for me to see the difference, but also he had remained a good mate to the crew ... never playing the part of a *star*. I know he much enjoyed working with Eileen Atkins and Donald Pleasence, actors he had respected and learned from. However, near the end of our shooting schedule, our dear Ralph slightly over-relaxed and, while waiting for the next shot, he just happened to sit on a very special antique glass table and broke it! Panic on the set ... we've already photographed it a number of times, so we must have the same table for the final scene. Ralph is suddenly as nervous as he was on the *first* day—maybe today it's his *last*?—as we managed to change the schedule for the rest of the day. Our magnificent art department during the night created a look-a-like glass table and next morning we've completed the shoot. Of course Ralph was keeping a safe distance from the table ..." [110]

Renée Glynne, who did continuity for *I Don't Want to be Born*, shared her memories of Bates: "I first encountered Ralph at Virginia's shop, as I used to pass by quite often. He charmed me but was also suspicious of me, as I'd known Virginia since childhood having worked with and been a great friend of her mother. It was not until Peter Sasdy's *I Don't Want to be Born* that I really got to know him. He was gorgeous to work with and talk to at the end of the day in the Pinewood Bar, where the cast and crew would meet up. I'd fled from Hammer after *The Quatermass Xperiment* and so missed out on Ralph's great body of work, although recently, seated with Virginia, I saw and much enjoyed his performance in *Dr. Jekyll and Sister Hyde,* shown in Leicester at a Hammer Film Festival."[111]

Following *I Don't Want to be Born*, Bates got a role in the popular BBC long-running police drama *Z Cars*. Set in the fictional northern English town of Newtown, the series was a gritty and realistic look at police dealing with various social issues, cases and criminals. In this respect it was a breakaway from the previous televised offerings depicting police as glorified heroes, exemplified in another long-running BBC drama, *Dixon of Dock Green*. Bates appeared as Roy Hurst in the 1975 episode, *Distance*. Bates' character was teamed with Joanne Hurst, played by Lois Baxter, who previously acted with him in the 1972 *Love Story* episode *Alice*. Also in the episode *Distance* was actor Ian Cullen, who played popular recurring character Detective Constable Skinner. Cullen, a prolific writer as well as actor, would go on to write for the 1981 drama series *The House on the Hill*, in which Bates starred in the episode *Man of Straw*.

Before signing on to appear in what would be his last film, Bates appeared in an episode of the popular suspense television series *Thriller*. Not to be confused with the same titled 1960s horror anthology series narrated by Boris Karloff, this series was a British creation and ran from 1973-1976. If the episode, *Murder Motel* (1975) sounds like a takeoff on Alfred Hitchcock's *Psycho* (1960), it certainly paid homage to it. Series creator and writer Brian Clemens (who had been the scriptwriter for *Dr. Jekyll and Sister Hyde*) starts the episode with a murder taking place in a shower, although the victim is a businessman and his death is at the hands of two other men. The story involves a business recently stolen from, and the Woodheath Motel, which has deadly connections thanks to its greedy owner and his two hired killers. Bates played Michael Spencer, an accountant who discovers that the money is missing. He nervously arrives at the hotel with his sister, planning on secretly taping a meeting there with his boss. But Spencer becomes the next victim at the hotel, and his sister too. Although it was a small role for Bates, he makes the most of it and portrays Spencer as a man already feeling doomed by what he thinks is a set-up by his boss. He was right, although the set-up turned out not to be caused by his boss and worse than he ever imagined.

Anne Rutter, who played the sister of Bates' character in *Murder Motel*, reflected back on the production: "Although I only worked with Ralph that one time, I remember it vividly because it was directed by my late husband, Malcolm Taylor, who had already directed another episode in the same series called *A Killer in Every Corner*, featuring Joanna Pettit. The script was unbelievably *ropey* and so Malcolm thought the only way to make it halfway credible was to employ reliable actor friends, who would do their best to make a silk purse out of a sow's ear! We had a long night shoot somewhere in Bucks, I think; it was very cold, the techies sat around mentally counting their overtime, and the rest of us got very giggly, not least because the final touch was a shoot-out by the police in which the neon lit name of the motel Woodheath (entirely invented by my husband) was damaged to read … D-EATH MOTEL. I remember that Ralph was as excellent as the script allowed, a very nice person to work with, and hey, we all had to eat!" [112]

The British film industry would take a downturn in the 1970s due to a combination of a loss of overseas Hollywood investments, and in 1975, it saw the end of government subsidies for domestic films, under the Conservative Party led by Margaret Thatcher. [113] Being a niche with a select audience, British horror films would suffer badly during this decade. Hollywood by now was bypassing the British horror film industry and producing bigger budget genre films such as *The Exorcist* and *Rosemary's Baby*. Hammer Film Productions and their main competitor Amicus Films would barely last until the mid-1970s. In spite of this drastic change in the industry, a new independent British company decided to take a stab at the horror genre. Film producer Kevin Francis and his director/cinematographer father Freddie (who had previously directed both Hammer and Amicus films) created Tyburn Films. The first feature production from Tyburn was the psychological thriller *Persecution* (aka *The Terror of Sheba*), filmed at the home of Harry Saltzman, the producer of the *James Bond* films. Like Hammer who got former Hollywood star Bette Davis to star in two psychological thrillers, Tyburn reached out and hired former Hollywood star, Lana Turner. Although Turner had only one horror genre connection with *Dr. Jekyll and Mr. Hyde* (1941), her performance in *Persecution* was enthralling. Her character mentally tortures her son (Bates) by strictly controlling his every move, while showing even more affection to her cat named Sheba.

Bates gives it his all as the tortured and unhinged son, David Masters. Repeatedly exposed to his mother's put downs and controlling demeanor, the viewers can practically see the inner turmoil of Bates' character as he is wound to the point of breaking. Carrie

A Biography

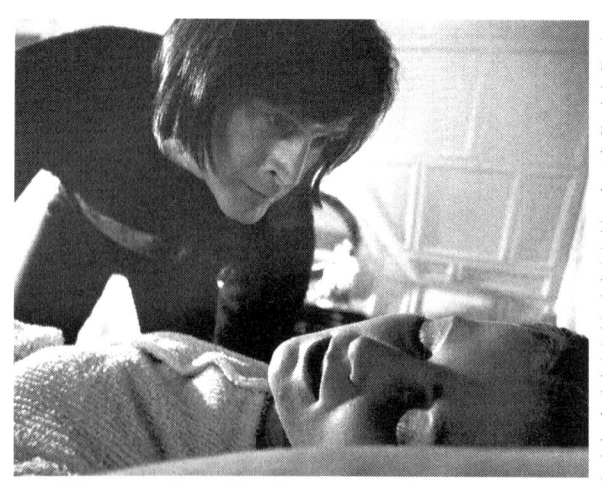

David Masters (Bates) lurches over another person in *Persecution* **(aka** *Sheba***).**

Masters' constant psychological abuse results in young David killing her beloved cat Sheba in an act of revenge, only to have it be replaced by another one with the same name. On top of the feline issue, his mother keeps David in the dark about who his mysterious father really is. This bizarre control over David's life even continues into his adulthood when his new wife Janie comes to live with him at the family house. David's new marriage is doomed from the start with the Lana Turner character pulling all the strings. After a devious plot by his mother involving a paid off nurse and the death of Janie, his baby and his real father, David is left with nothing but the hatred he dishes out to his mother.

The film is really worth seeing only for the performances of Lana Turner and Bates. *Persecution* turned out to be one of Turner's last films, but she was still in strong form and dominated her scenes. In fact, Lana Turner received a Best Actress award for her role as Carrie Masters at the Sitges International Film Festival held in Spain. Bates played David Masters as a tortured soul and elicits a lot of sympathy throughout. The struggle of wills between the mother and son is gripping and powerful and lifts the film above other low-budget genre fare of the time. In an interview with Ton Paans, Bates revealed an embarrassing story from his first meeting with Turner: "She was a legend. She used to go home at three o'clock and I was left to do a lot of close-ups with the continuity lady. The first day I met her I had this temporary cap on my teeth. We were introduced and I shook hands with her and, as I bit my tooth, it flew out and hit her on the chest. Not really knowing what to say, I said, 'Well, I so much wanted to make an impression on you …'"

David Masters tries to maintain his sanity in *Persecution***.**

94   **Ralph Bates**

'I'll never forget *you*,' was her reply.

"She was pretty extraordinary!"[114]

Bates revealed to Sam Irvin his own thoughts on making *Persecution*, as well as hinting that he made his dislike over *Lust for a Vampire* well-known to the Hammer executives: "I like that film as well. It was Tyburn Production's first film. Kevin Francis heads the new company. He is the famous director Freddie Francis' son. He is only about 24 years old, a whizz kid. I liked him very very much; he's very funny. I got paid very well for that film, which is what paid for all the furniture around my house. Lana Turner is a sweet lady, she really is. There was a slight problem with her, but it all boils down to the fact that she is not offered as much as she used to be and I think this must be depressing. I really loved her, though, and I feel very sad whenever I think of her. She has been quite battered by life. Kevin has got a lot of pizzazz. He is at a stage where Hammer was say 20 years ago and he will do very well, I'm sure. I am not so sure about Hammer. I don't think I will ever work for Hammer again and I think the feeling is mutual. I think the coming years lie in the hands of Kevin and perhaps Amicus Productions. I was offered a part in Amicus' *Tales from the Crypt* but I turned it down because I was busy with other things, but I really thought the script was poorly written to begin with. I understand that some of their other films are quite good and I hope they offer me another part next time from a good script."[115]

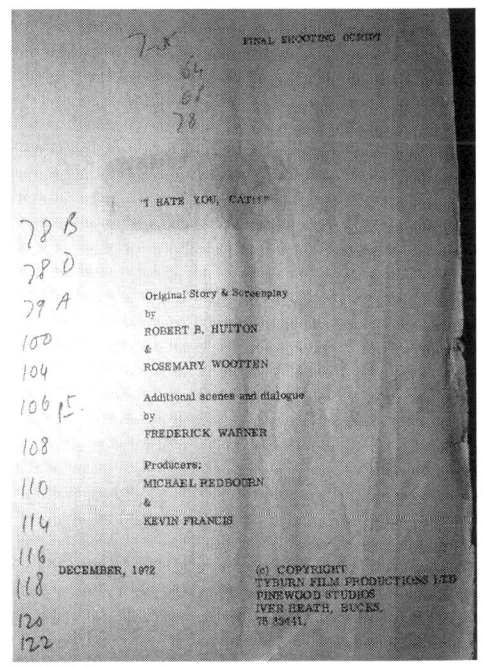

Bates with the cursed feline in *Persecution*

Title page of the screenplay for *Persecution*, with its original shooting title *I Hate You, Cat!*

While Bates would have no way of knowing at the time, his theatrical film career would be in limbo for 16 years following the 1974 production of *Persecution*. Producers who had turned to Bates to play dark and brooding characters in horror and thriller films no longer had a market to support such film genres. Years later Bates looked back on this point in his career. "There was a consequence to

A Biography 95

my typecasting in genre films. I had only made fantasy films and I loved to make them. Then when these types of films stopped being made, producers stopped calling me. I don't know. Perhaps if I had combined my film career playing fantasy films with other genres, when Hammer and other companies making genre films went out of business, I may have been offered roles in other types of films. But it didn't turn out this way and, after *Persecution*, I worked mostly on the stage and television."[116]

Although his film career was virtually over, there was one quite happy event for the Bates family that occurred on January 5 of that year as Virginia gave birth to their first child, a daughter they named Daisy. Growing up with her father involved in the acting profession would eventually convince young Daisy to follow in her father's footsteps. She made her television debut at the young age of 15 in the ITV drama *Forever Green* and would go on to appear in other series, such as *Kavanagh QC*, and also films, including *Harry Potter and the Chamber of Secrets*.

Daisy recounted growing up in the Bates' household, and her memories of her dad: "My dad was pretty wonderful and he was very much loved. He just wanted a house full of friends and family. Often times he would be cooking these fantastic Sunday lunches for tons of people. He had a fantastic sense of humor, playing the spoons after dinner and pretending to be French when the police caught us breaking into parks; it was fun.

"He was a dad who really embraced fatherhood—funny, worldly and ready to have fun. I remember him as this real positive force, who was always ready to piss about. He was inventive as well. I had a friend over from school one time when I was around eight. Dad dressed up as a waiter when we came home from school and turned the kitchen into a restaurant. He had written out the menu on a board and kept bowing to us like Manuel from *Fawlty Towers*. It was so much fun, especially as he shook the tomato ketchup that didn't have a lid on and it exploded all over the room!

"He was always looking out for the underdog and inviting people into our home. He was open and generous in a way that was pretty extraordinary. He would regularly drive the great Tommy Cooper (a prop comedian and magician, who lived on our road) to the hospital toward the end of his life. I remember Tommy and his wife Gwen sitting at our kitchen table well into the night chatting with my family. I'd get my rabbit out of her hutch and literally put her on Tommy's lap, waiting for him to do some magic.

"Although I followed in my father's footsteps to pursue a career in acting, my dad didn't really help me audition much because he didn't want either of us to do it. Perhaps there was a side of him that was disillusioned with the business or maybe he was so terrified of it, but he definitely wanted me to have a proper job like a barrister or doctor. Something less precarious than being an actor, everything he wasn't I guess." [117]

Bates' return to television in 1975 was a recurring role in the Granada Television series *Crown Court*. The popular dramatic series, which began in 1972, delved into the legal cases in the fictional town of Fulchester. Each case would usually be played out over three episodes shown consecutively Tuesday through Thursday at lunchtime. While professional actors played the prosecution, defense and foreman, the actual jury was picked from the public and so the actors would not know the outcome of the actual case they were involved in. Therefore, separate endings had to be planned in advance, depending on the jury's verdict. Bates appeared in the three-story arc *Two in the Mind of One*, in which he played George Ross, an architect in the middle of a messy affair. He also made later appearances in the episodes *In the Heat of the Moment* and *Inside Story*, in which he provided a memorable performance as Anthony Mills, a career criminal who has an issue speaking the Queen's English.

Working with a set television schedule allowed Bates to make another return to the theater, this time in a 1975 revival of the Noel Coward play *Private Lives*. Here, the play's director Gareth Jones shared his memories of the production and Bates: "Ralph was such a wonderful and beautiful man in every sense of the word, very handsome, loving and fun. He was always great company and a tremendous family man. In addition, Ralph was a brilliant actor, which made working with him a joy. He was just one of those early departures which should never have happened. It was a terrible shock when I heard the news, as we did spend time together and I was a guest at their house and had known Virginia and had held Daisy as a baby. So it was terribly sad to know that he had gone. In ones twenties life has to move on very fast, therefore my connection with the family was for that limited time and then I found myself working in other parts of the country, and not just in London anymore.

"I was an exceptionally young theater director in those days and was only about 24 years old when I went out casting. I was not yet out of a traineeship that I had been awarded by Thames Television through a program than benefitted a lot of directors, who have since gone on to great things in television, film and theater. From there I joined Prospect Theatre Company for two years as a trainee director and barely a few months in I formed my own touring subsidiary aimed at taking slightly less capacious work to more modest venues, and we called it Wider Circuit. *Private Lives* was very clearly a magnificent four-hander and it fitted the bill for our company absolutely. My casting here was probably far removed from the company I was serving. The Prospect Theatre Company already boasted the meteoric talent of Ian McKellen, Derek Jacobi and Timothy West, who were the founding members. I was a late arrival to the Company in 1974. The Prospect Theatre Company was based on a sort of acting school, which at the time was very modern and dedicated to new interpretations of Shakespeare.

"Ralph did not exactly come from that same sort of professional background and so the cast that I put together as a very untried theater director at 24 raised a certain number of eyebrows because there were none of the old hands (who were still rather young at the time) present. There was a certain repertory around Prospect Theatre Company, but I went out in search of slightly different actors who were not Oxford educated.

"I knew that Ralph had already made a name for himself in film, and that was quite unusual in those days because the crossover between film and theater was extremely limited. I think that it raised eyebrows among my superiors, not particularly the casting of Ralph as everyone, of course, liked him, but my casting policy which involved bringing fresh blood into the Company. Ralph most certainly rose to the challenge. I do remember Ralph telling me with his characteristic generosity, 'You know, I really don't mind which of the male roles you give me, I just would like to be involved.' Of course there is a very substantial difference between the two male roles in *Private Lives*. Noel Coward took the lion's share in the original production, and the secondary role was allocated to Laurence Olivier. You could say that Ralph was being very clever, because he knew that you could shine and indeed come off very handsomely even in the lesser role, and since he was so gracious, that was the role that I gave him. I think that I was correct in doing so because he was miraculously funny in the part. He brought it to life with an understanding of the period and a comprehension of the erotic duel going on, and he was well aware of the limited intellect of the character he was playing, which made him an absolute joy to work with. It's always quite a challenge as an actor to represent truthfully and wittily a character that is less intelligent than he is. But this aspect Ralph was able to do with great flair, enormous good humor and great charm.

"The tour was a great success and our audiences liked it. Audiences were amused; it raised many laughs and was stylish. In fact it was quite funny from beginning to end. We had to stop ourselves from being run over from too many giggles and laughs in rehearsal. I think our show arrived at an important point for Ralph. I think it was a point where out of his early film career something else started to develop that he was more than up to taking on. He was a great star in the production, and a bit like Laurence Olivier, who played the same part all those decades earlier, and Ralph went on to continue making very good use of those skills in theater. He had a great sense of comic timing that was quite amazing. He was a natural. Of truthful characterization expressed through good timing, his reaction to the audience was quite miraculous. I think that his comic sensitivity has sort of gone missing in today's generation of performers. There seems to be very little now between totally straight acting being apparently unaware of the audience on the one hand and rather ungracious and indeed possibly extreme mercenary buttering up audiences on the other. Ralph held the stage in the middle of those two extremes quite brilliantly, and he never gave himself away. I was thrilled to have been able to offer him a choice role in our theater production. It was quite a good stable to join. For me of course it was an undreamed of windfall that it started my career. Ralph was a constantly supportive member of the cast. He was an endlessly entertaining and witty actor on stage and in rehearsal. And he was a very dear friend whom I have missed now for many decades."[118]

Another person working on *Private Lives* was Shelagh Bourke, Bates' dresser. "I met Ralph Bates when I was a student at Warwick University in the spring of 1976. He was appearing in *Private Lives* as Elyot in the newly built Warwick Arts Centre. I was obsessed with theater and studying it along with French and managed to grab a job as a dresser. As anyone who has been a dresser will know, it's a strange role, as you're close to the action and meet everyone, but never actually get to see any of the production. Nevertheless we all wanted to work backstage. I remember Ralph Bates walking into his dressing room where I was introduced to him. He was slight in stature and very handsome and charming and I felt very shy when I first met him. That soon passed though as he gave me a hug! He was warm, funny, lovely and very popular with the rest of the cast—I remember a lot of laughter. He was very interested in what I was studying and oddly never ever appeared to be the slightest bit nervous of playing such an iconic role. He just seemed to breeze onto the stage with an air of calm. I had to make sure he looked smart in his formal evening suit, black tie etc. This was a look that really suited him. It was a lovely week and just about the time when he became known on television in *Poldark*. If it came on when I was at my parents' house, my dad would shout "Poldark, Poldark!" and we'd all rush in to watch Ralph. They were really proud that I'd met him, and so was I." [119]

During the theater run of *Private Lives*, a young fan had a chance encounter with Bates that would leave an indelible mark on him, and eventually lead to a lifelong friendship. Writer Tim Goode reflected back on his first meeting Bates in 1975: "I first met Ralph in the 1970s. I was a big fan of Hammer, like many young kids were at the time. I used to go get autographs from the actors at my local theater in Bath. I would catch the bus and then not always see the productions, but if I knew there was someone in the play from a Hammer film, I would hang out by the stage door and meet them afterwards. One of the greatest

Bates as George Warleggan in *Poldark*

prizes was when Ralph showed up in a theater production of *Private Lives*. I thought this was wonderful as Ralph was always a particular favorite actor of mine. By hanging around I actually bumped into him in the street. I introduced myself as a fan, and to my amazement he said, "Why don't you come for a drink? We aren't on stage for an hour." So we went to a local pub—I was underage though he didn't realize it—and Ralph was wonderful and he signed my photos. He also showed interest in my wish to become a film student, and I remember him mentioning that Jimmy Sangster was actually staying at the family's home." [120]

As he had landed his part in *The Caesars*, so now another television production would propel Bates back into the spotlight after his film career dried up. In 1975 he was cast as George Warleggan in the BBC adaptation of *Poldark*. The novels by Winston Graham fueled the 18th-century historical drama series. Spread through 12 novels, the story featured Ross Poldark (played by Robin Ellis), a British army officer who fought in the American Revolution and who returns home to Cornwall only to have his life take many unexpected twists and turns in love and fortune. His fiancée Elizabeth (Jill Townsend), thinking he died, married his cousin Francis. The Poldark family owned tin mines in Cornwall, which Ross works to reopen to restore his

A Biography

fortunes and help the local townspeople, who depended on the mines for their livelihood. Meanwhile, George Warleggan also returns to Cornwall and, along with his banker father, seeks to upstage and drive away Ross, whom he sees as a threat to his own success. Ross eventually finds love again with Demelza Carne (Angharad Rees), a servant girl with an independent spirit. After letting go of family bickering and on the verge of a new venture, things take a turn for the worse as Francis dies and Elizabeth, needing someone to support her, marries George Warleggan, ripping open old wounds and setting in motion more conflict and loss on both sides.

Winston Graham wrote the first of his novels *Ross Poldark* (*The Renegade* in the U.S.) in 1945 and by 1975 he had completed three additional novels, including, *Demelza*, *Jeremy Poldark*, and *Warleggan*. The BBC acquired the rights and filmed the series for eight weeks on location in Cornwall. Shown on Sunday nights beginning on October 5, 1975, the series proved immensely popular, attracting audiences of up to 15 million people. The series successfully sold around the globe, and in America was featured as part of *Masterpiece Theatre*, hosted by Alistair Cooke. Consequently, the BBC then acquired the rights to three additional novels by Graham entitled, *The Black Moon*, *The Four Swans*, and *The Angry Tide* and a second series was completed for the fall of 1977. Reviews were favorable, one example being from the *Sunday Times*: "The flair Mr. Graham has always shown for making his people seem to think and behave in a convincingly period fashion."[121] *Poldark* marked a highpoint for the costume dramas that the BBC had specialized in and would return to with equal success many years later with *Downton Abbey*. The original series' popularity continued with a 1996 stand-alone television production by ITV based on Graham's eighth novel, *The Stranger from the Sea*, and a remake of *Poldark* aired in 2015, with Aidan Turner as Poldark and Jack Farthing in Bates' original role as George Warleggan.

Bates' first appearance as the character George Warleggan would occur in the sixth episode of the first season, and he would appear in almost all episodes of the continuing first season, as well as the entire second season. Bates' introduction set the tone for his character, as it is already revealed that the Warleggans look to corner the market on copper mines, and Ross Poldark makes known he despises everything their clan stands for. The character of George Warleggan would also continue to get more screen time become the main antagonist to Ross Poldark. The scheming George Warleggan and his father Nicholas weekly plagued the heroic Poldark. As described by Graham in his novels, George Warleggan was one of a new class of industrialists, who, while impeccably dressed and capable of excellent manners, is considered an upstart by the aristocracy, which is part of the feud between Ross Poldark and him. This role involved depth and development, which Bates duly took advantage, making the character his own. *Poldark* also marked a *Fear in the Night* connection, as Judy Geeson played Caroline Penvenen, the love interest to Ross' friend Dr. Dwight Enys. Among the many episodes featuring Bates as Warleggan, there are a few which stand above the rest.

By the ninth episode of the first season, Warleggan's good gestures are completely washed away and his villainous nature is finally revealed in his scheme to have Poldark set up for the rioting. The episode ends with an embarrassment for George, as Elizabeth's husband Francis exposes him for the scandalous fliers that he dumps into the fireplace at a guildhall reception. George has one of his henchmen bribing witnesses and has fliers made and posted around town to defame Poldark. Bates acted opposite Nicholas Selby who played the Warleggan patriarch (Selby would be replaced by actor Alan Tilvern in the second season). The two generations of the Warleggan clan were shown to have different viewpoints on a similar goal. While Nicholas Warleggan is content to stay behind the scenes, plotting with fellow investors to try to take over Poldark's business and drive him away, George Warleggan plays a much more active role in confronting Poldark and getting involved in trying to have Poldark hanged, even to the point of putting himself at risk. Bates portrays George as being disgusted by his father's gluttonous eating and ogling pretty women, while he focuses on business.

On the cover of the DVD collection of *Poldark*, Ralph Bates appears second from the right.

Things go from bad to worse by the 12th episode when George has his men attack and seemingly murder Judd Painter, who reneged on his deal to speak against Poldark in court. Nicholas Warleggan is infuriated that his son has stooped to this violent level for a meager 15 guineas. When Ross and Francis go into business together to reopen their Wheal Grace copper mine, George realizes the danger of underestimating his enemy. This episode features one of the big fight scenes between George and Ross, which shows Bates in one of the most physically demanding scenes of his career. George blocks Ross' way out of a tavern with his cane, which is quickly thrust back against George's throat. After Ross attempts to dress him down, George jumps up repeatedly striking back with his cane and the pair practically tear down the tavern around them in their explosive confrontation. The two men brawl back and forth until Ross finally gets the upper hand, leaving George floundering on the floor as he walks out telling him, "Give my regards to your tailor, George."

In the last episode of the first series, George has struck back at Ross by marrying his first love Elizabeth, whose husband died in a mine accident. To add insult to injury, George takes over Trenwith, the old Poldark estate, and drives out the villagers on the land

Ralph Bates as George Warleggan in *Poldark*

before enclosing his new property with a fence and henchmen to keep everyone away. After George loses a lawsuit against him, Ross attempts to reason with George but comes away with the realization that: "George is a man at war with everyone around him—war against the defenseless, those you despise, those you envy." Bates conveys this quality of George Warleggan with a steadfast temper and a burning desire to get revenge on those he believes wronged him. This episode also features the second fight between George and Ross, only broken up by the angry mob of villagers, who are intent in burning down Trenwith and killing George for kicking them out of their homes. The episode ends with Ross saving George's life from a thrusted axe, before putting Elizabeth and him on horses to escape, George remembering he owes Ross his life.

In the fifth episode of the second season, George's hatred of Ross has only intensified over his thinking that he caused the villagers to rise up against him. This episode features Bates showing George under two different lights. One side of George is shown but not previously displayed—fear when his new baby with Elizabeth is diagnosed with rickets. While Elizabeth usually shies away from confrontation with George, she finally stands up to him over their child's care, causing him to back down and admit that he does not know what to do. While this revelation that George cannot handle everything is revealed, his penchant for revenge is thrust back to the forefront in the culmination of his power struggle with Aunt Agatha, whose home they live in while Trenwith is being rebuilt. Seeing George for whom he really is, Aunt Agatha does not miss a chance to put him in his place, which only causes George to boil with anger. When Agatha announces her plans for a grand celebration on her 100th birthday, George sees a way to get his revenge as he cancels the party and announces, due to his research of the family Bible, that Agatha is actually turning 98, crushing her spirit. Bates and Eileen Way, who played Aunt Agatha, have a powerful scene in which George refuses to let Agatha have her moment in the spotlight, only for her, in return, to curse his baby and let on that Ross may be the real father, which quickly spirals out of control as George goes into a rage and shakes Agatha to death.

On December 4, 1977, the last episode of the second series brought the battle between George and Ross to a climax. Elizabeth, pregnant with George's child, seeks a way to cause a premature birth to convince George that their first child, Valentine, was his and not sired by Ross. She finds a doctor who gives her a medication with a horrible trade off; she gives birth prematurely (at eight months) to a girl who soon afterwards loses her sight and becomes gravely ill. When Elizabeth refuses to tell Dr. Enys in front of George what medication she took, this results in her death. George's fears are confirmed about Ross' involvement. The episode ends with George alone in his giant mansion, with his deceased wife in a coffin, with the wind blowing the drapes. Valentine watches his father who, after cursing Aunt Agatha, ignores him as he walks out of the room, a powerful scene that Bates carries out with a feeling of malevolence.

Although the BBC wished to continue *Poldark* for another season, when scriptwriter Martin Worth approached Winston Graham about contributing to new scripts, the novelist flatly refused, which led to the sudden end of the series. For Bates, appearing as George Warleggan in *Poldark* brought him to new fame; viewers now saw him as a solid television actor as well as a stage actor. This helped guide the rest of his acting career. Much as with his role as Caligula, it was television which made producers stand up and notice how adaptable Bates was in creating characters that truly came alive. During the course of filming, Bates made long-standing friends with many in the cast. Robin Ellis mentions that, "Ralph was a fine actor, a worthy enemy in *Poldark* and a cherished and wise friend. He once calmed a very agitated me down before a recording of *Poldark*, saying, "Robin—it's only a play!" [122]

Jill Townsend, who played Elizabeth, the eventual wife of George Warleggan, revealed that, "Working with Ralph was bliss! Not only did he have a great sense of humor, but he was also a very intelligent and elegant man. For me, it was a challenge getting through a scene with him, as he could make me laugh quicker than anyone … We spent much of *Poldark* making each other laugh off camera. Ralph was brilliant and a joy to spend time with.

"As an actor, Ralph was a natural … Everything seemed effortless, natural … I am sure it was *not* effortless, yet he made it seem that way. Everything about him was authentic. We were all nervous as we were taping the series … When we were filming on location, we had the ability to re-do something that went wrong. When taping, we don't … so I think we were all nervous at the start of the taping, yet Ralph never made a big deal of it. He was very conscious of other people, not wanting to create problems for others and always very thoughtful of them. As far as I am aware, the success of *Poldark* never went to his head … he was always Ralph; generous, funny, a good man … who loved his wife and children … a joy to be with. We spent a lot of time together … I was so fond of Virginia and Daisy, although I never got to know William very well. We were always in each other's houses. How can I possibly pick one memory? I do have one regret, though, and that is that I never got to go on a driving trip through France with them, buying things for Virginia's shop. Virginia practically furnished my home with goodies from her shop!" [123]

Hugh Dickson, who played Dr. Behenna, the family physician for the Warleggans, shared his memories: "I and one or two others joined *Poldark* for the second series. It is not always easy for new actors to be integrated into an established cast. I knew Robin Ellis from the television mini-series *Elizabeth R*, but I had never met Ralph before. His straightforward friendly professionalism made things easy. Ralph, though an established leading man, had no side, no self-importance. A special memory I have involved another production that I was rehearsing at the same time, in the same building as *Poldark*, about the life of Marie Curie. As Curie was a naturalized French physicist, I naturally persuaded Ralph to talk about the French scientific tradition and the Pasteur and the Jura mountains (which I confused with the Vosges). We were never very close, but it was a pleasure a year or so later to meet him on Chiswick High Road, both of us with our families." [124]

Jean Gates accompanied her son Stefan onto the set of *Poldark* as he played Geoffrey Charles Poldark, the child of Elizabeth and Francis Poldark. "I have very fond memories of

Ralph as he was very kind to both Stefan and me. As you know, he played Stefan's father in the series; he was always ready to answer Stefan's endless questions (Stefan was six at the time of the first series and was interested in everything, from why the men wore such large hats when they were riding their horses, to how the gunpowder for the guns was made, to why everyone seemed to have maids doing all the work for them!). Ralph was always lovely to Stefan and always took a real interest in what he was doing and always listened to what he was saying. Stefan was very proud to walk around the set with him, especially when they were both dressed in costume and were ready for filming." [125]

David Delve played Sam Carne, the devout Methodist brother of Ross' wife Demelza. "I do remember Ralph as a charming, gentle man, appearing reserved, but with an impish sense of humor and a dry wit. Playing 'the baddie' is always a treat for an actor, and he relished it, as a total contrast to himself, so he was a joy to play opposite. At a cabaret we did at the end of filming he performed a silent act involving a raincoat and magic—totally off the wall! I recall cheery nights in Julie's, a restaurant near Virginia's shop on Holland Park. Apart from the official photographs of shooting days, I have a typical snapshot of Ralph sound asleep in costume on a chair in a field, awaiting a call-to-film; another late night?" [126]

While Bates' run on the popular series *Poldark* continued, he also took on roles in other television series. The first, during 1976, was a recurring role on the six-part political spy thriller, *Dangerous Knowledge*. The story revolved around Bill Kirby (John Gregson), a former British intelligence agent, now an insurance salesman, who may or may not be more than what he seems. On a ferry to Southampton, Kirby removes a briefcase from the trunk of a car whose driver had been shot dead inside. Fearing he may be noticed, Kirby quickly befriends a young woman named Laura Marshall (Prunella Ransome) and tags along with her to avoid suspicion. But Kirby's fears are proven true when a well-dressed man named Sanders (Bates) notices him and begins pursuing Kirby in his Ford Capri. In taking the briefcase, Kirby has become a wanted man by Sanders' boss Roger Fane (Patrick Allen), a senior civil servant for the British government. As Sanders closes in, Kirby manages to stay one step ahead with the aid of his ex-wife, son Robin and Laura, who is torn between him and her stepfather, who just happens to be Fane. But when Kirby's connection in France turns up dead, his thoughts of an easy commercial deal to make some quick money vanish and things take a decidedly dangerous turn. As Kirby's situation seems to spiral out of control, the intrigue deepens with members of the French Resistance of World War II, the KGB and CIA; information that may or may not expose a national security threat to Britain's government come into play.

Dangerous Knowledge was written by Southampton native N.J. Crisp for Southern TV and shown on the ITV network. Director and producer Alan Gibson, like Bates, was also no stranger to Hammer Film Productions, having helmed their first foray into television with the *Journey to the Unknown* series, the psychological thriller *Crescendo*, two of their later *Dracula* films and finally two television episodes for *Hammer's House of Horror* series. John Gregson was a very popular British film actor in the 1950s, appearing in numerous dramas and comedies, most notably *Genevieve* (1953). *Dangerous Knowledge* would be his swansong, however, as he passed away unexpectedly in 1975 and the program was broadcast posthumously. The series, with its exterior shots done on film and interior on video, provided viewers with much intrigue throughout its six episodes. Bates added to the tension of the series with his portrayal of Sanders, a cool-as-a-cucumber agent whose loyalties make him even more dangerous than perceived. Sporting stylish wire-rimmed sunglasses and initially a pink shirt under a dark suit, Bates looks like a suave 1970s fashion model, although his quick hand with a pistol proves otherwise. Unlike Kirby who thinks more with his heart, Sanders seems devoid of emotion and is clinical in his job. He trails Kirby like a bloodhound by land, sea or air and displays some rather aggressive driving skills in a 1976 Ford Capri Mark II. After Kirby deduces that Sanders killed Madame Lafois, he tells him, "Quite a little hit man, aren't you?" Old and new guard face off as Kirby and Sanders hunt one another among the dunes, on a windy Normandy beach.

In a busy time between Bates' key roles in *Poldark* and *Penmarric* were four appearances in other series. In the episode *Rich* from the Yorkshire Television drama series *Forget Me Not* (1976), Bates played Henri Teliot, the husband of the character played by actress Stephanie Beacham, who had a Hammer connection with *Dracula A.D. 1972,* as well as appearing in an episode of the *Hammer House of Mystery and Suspense.* Following that role was an appearance in the long-running police drama, *Softly Softly: Task Force,* in which Bates played Frenchman Pierre Mandel in the episode, *The Visitor*. The series was a continuation of the original 1969 *Softly Softly* series, which itself was a spin-off from a previous long-running police drama, *Z-Cars*. One of Bates' fellow actors in *The Visitor* was Anthony Bailey, who worked with him previously in the *Z-Cars* episode that Bates appeared in. Bates also appeared as a guest star in *It's Childsplay*, a set of short plays written entirely by young people under 16 and, in what must have been a thrill for Bates, introduced by comedy greats Eric Morecambe and Ernie Wise. In the summer of 1977 Bates appeared on the Granada Television production of *Here I Stand*, in the episode *Margaret Clitherow*. The story was based on the real-life case of Margaret Clitherow, who became a martyr of the Roman Catholic Church. Bates played Sheriff Roland Fawcett, who sought her arrest for sheltering a Roman Catholic priest during the reign of Queen Elizabeth I. Among Bates' castmates on *Margaret Clitherow* was Donald Douglas, who played Captain Malcolm McNeil on *Poldark*. Douglas stated, "Although we were both in *Poldark*, we were not in the same storyline and so did not get to work together. However, I knew Ralph socially and he was a charming and easy going fellow actor." [127]

During a busy television year, 1977 also marked the birth of Virginia's second child, William. Jimmy Sangster from Ralph's Hammer days was chosen to be William's godfather. Like his older sister Daisy, William (Will or Wills as his parents called him) would give acting a try, appearing as John Lacey's son Toby in *Dear John*, with Bates portraying John. Will appeared in three episodes of the John Sullivan television comedy, but Will had other interests and gravitated towards music, training to become a saxophonist. Today Will is an award-winning composer and the co-founder, along with Phil Mossman, of the music group Fall On

A Biography 105

Your Sword. Besides performing live shows, Fall On Your Sword is responsible for numerous film soundtracks including *Lola Verses*, *We Steal Secrets: The Story of WikiLeaks* and *Going Clear: Scientology*.

Will remembered his childhood and also his dad's involvement in the Hammer horror films. "My dad was the funniest, warmest, kindest and most worried man I ever knew. Like most little boys, I hero-worshiped my dad; all I ever wanted to do was make him proud of me. He could be so funny, so incredibly witty and dry, but he was also extraordinarily kind and generous. He could sometimes get stressed out with the job. Things could get pretty intense when he was preparing for a role. But I remember that if he ever yelled at me for any reason, he would always find a way to fix it. He was very honest and self-aware. that way.

"He was around less than my mum was when I was growing up. He toured a lot and even when he was working in London on a play or a TV show, his hours wouldn't necessarily line up with the school run. But whenever he could he'd make himself available. If something were going on at school that I needed help with, he'd be there for me; he'd want to be very involved with fixing things. He'd always somehow have time to help me with my homework, as long as I tested him on his lines.

"As in any artistic career, the highs are very high and the lows are very low. At the end of any job he would assume that he'd never work again, but of course he always would. It became something of a joke actually. 'Worried of Chiswick,' as John Sullivan used to call him. I recognize a lot of that anxiety now. It is part of the job, and having that self-belief is so important. I think he struggled with that a bit.

"Thinking back to my dad's horror films for Hammer, it was all pretty normal in our house. Although, of course, I watched my dad die in every way imaginable before I'd hit the age of 10. He was pushed down a well, hanged from a tree, fell off a roof. I mean, he killed my mum on their first date! Sounds very macabre, but I was always aware of the make-believe aspect of those movies. Hammer was in the past by the time I came along, and it was treated as this fun thing that my parents did before I was born. It really wasn't taken that seriously.

"I think I was about eight, and we were watching *Lust for a Vampire* in the kitchen at home. My godfather, Jimmy Sangster, was there while my mum was cooking us all supper, and the telly was on in the background. I noticed that I could see Jimmy reflected in the side of one of the horse drawn carriages in a scene. My dad made me rewind and pause the machine on that scene and there he was, and you could just make him out behind the camera with his long hippie hair. Dad didn't let him hear the end of that one. Poor Jimmy!

"As I've gotten older Hammer has become more of a source of pride. I love that my parents have this legacy. Those movies are so amazing now, but I think that one of the things that makes them so amazing is the fact that all these incredibly talented people were having so much fun making them." [128]

In an interview with Ian Woodward years later, Bates provided his thoughts on his children: "Actually, I'm quite happy on my own, as long as I know my family is near. I delight in my children's company. I do understand people living through their children. I often think that, if I won the pools, I'd actually like to just sit and watch Daisy and Wills. We cleared one of the rooms upstairs yesterday and found little things that Daisy used to wear. Time goes quickly; I wish we could just hang on to it. Actually, I always think of myself as 30 pushing 17! The eternal adolescent." [129]

Bates mixed the year 1978 with television and theater. In the BBC Two documentary *A Woman's Place?*, the issue of women entering the workforce was examined through interviews and a story involving Kay (Anna Calder-Marshall), a woman married to Derek (Bates), who is trying to balance her married life, being a mother, and also trying to be accepted as a working woman. Bates made another return to the theater in 1978 for the two-act modern thriller *Double Edge*, directed by Anthony Sharp. He starred alongside Richard Todd and Hildegard Neil, and the touring play appeared at locations such as the Kings Theatre in Southsea and the Theatre Royal at Newcastle upon Tyne.

August 28 of 1978 marked a personal loss for Bates, as his father Ralph Marshall Bates passed away at the family home in Colchester. The British Medical Journal listed his accomplishments in the medical field. He was well known for his high level organization and administration at Royal Eastern Counties Hospital in Colchester, where he was the medical superintendent; psychiatrists from overseas would come to visit the hospital to learn from Bates, Sr. how he had set everything up, and in 1961 he received the Most Excellent Order of the British Empire (O.B.E.) for his work in the medical field. Of his private life, the Journal wrote: "He was essentially a family man with deep religious feelings, devoted to duty and a staunch friend for those in adversity. He had a full and busy professional life but found time and relaxation in painting in oils and in gardening, where he specialized in orchids and daffodils. His large and beautiful garden delighted many who enjoyed his warm hospitality." [130] Bates' father no doubt had a great influence on him, as he too was always willing to help those in need.

The beginning of 1979 saw Bates appearing in two episodes of the ITV Granada television drama *House of Caradus*. The series dramatized a family who own an auction house located in Chester, England. The once successful business is run by Victor Caradus (Robert Grange), who enlists the help of his cousins Helena (Sarah Bullen) and Lionel (Anthony Smee) to turn things around. With the House of Caradus in financial despair and on the verge of bankruptcy, the family must struggle with competing auction houses, forged art treasures and a variety of clients from all walks of life. Bates played Luke Hussey in the episodes *Venus Disturbed* and *Long Shadow*, his character being employed at the House of Caradus and put in charge of organizing a picture sale.

In the October 1979 BBC period drama *Penmarric*, Bates got the chance to play a more sympathetic character. Based on the best selling novel by Susan Howatch, *Penmarric* was an almost Shakespearean tragedy in telling the tale of the loves and hatreds of three generations of a Cornish family and their obsession with the Penmarric mansion and surrounding lands. Howatch's novels often tended to involve family chronicles in great detail over lengthy periods of time, and *Penmarric* was a perfect representation of her work. The BBC production, filmed on location in Cornwall, was hailed for its attention to detail, its costumes and its lavish settings. The Flete House at Holbeton, in the South Hams district of Devon, stood in for Penmarric mansion.

The story of *Penmarric* begins when Maud Penmar's father tells her that she will not inherit his mansion, as it must go to a man, and his only son died in an accident. Maud falls in love with her cousin Giles and wishes to marry him, but when they go to her father for his blessing, she is told she will marry Laurence Castallack (Bates). Their marriage does not last long and they separate after having a child, Mark. Giles manages to win the blessing of Maud's father and adopts the name Penmar, thereby giving him rights to Penmarric mansion. Young Mark is affected by his mother's constant battle with Giles over Penmarric, so much so that he becomes jaded and turns against her when Giles reluctantly names Mark (Thomas Ellice) his heir, after his own son dies. Upon a visit with his father, Mark happens across an attractive older widow named Janna (Annabel Leventon), with whom he quickly becomes infatuated. Although they both harbor secrets, after a series of events, Mark and Janna eventually marry and their relationship, children and Penmarric all become intertwined in a tragedy of permanent consequences for all involved.

Bates' character of Laurence Castallack is one of the few characters in *Penmarric* who maintains his values without becoming too compromised. Giles describes Laurence in the story as one of the few honest men who entered Penmarric house. To this end, Bates infused Laurence with a certain fatherly love and underlying sadness of the events unfolding around him. Laurence's marriage to Maud is doomed from the start over her true love of Giles and her obsession with the Penmarric mansion. His relationship with his son Mark is delicate as he tries to steer him away from the influence of wealth and power. Paul Spurrier, who played young Mark Castallack in the first episode of Penmarric, recalls, "I remember that Ralph Bates was fun to work with. He had a great sense of humor and we had lots of laughs." [131] To show his aging through the storyline, Bates first appears clean-shaven, then with a mustache and finally with a full beard. Although Bates only appears in the first three episodes of the

12-part series, he creates a lasting impression with his performance. Bates appreciated the opportunity to play his *Penmarric* character, which he stated in promotional materials for the stage play *Jet Set*. "I don't usually get the chance to play goodies." [132]

Most of Bates' best scenes as Laurence came opposite Martin Thurley, playing his son Mark, as the two discussed family history and life and its tribulations in general. Laurence offers Mark a different view of life from that of the decadent Penmarric, living a mostly solitary life at the humble Deverill Farm overlooking the mines across the moor. One of the two standout scenes featuring both actors involved Mark telling Laurence that he will inherit Penmarric mansion, something Laurence knows will change his son's innocence forever. The tension among the uneasy quiet following the revelation by Mark hangs in the air like a cloud, before the two can manage to hash out their feelings. The second standout scene involving Bates comes when Laurence finds out through one of Mark's cousins that he has impregnated a girl and sought financial help from Giles rather than come to him for any advice on the matter. It is this scene in which Bates first trembles a bit before exploding in anger over the betrayal by his son, and then blaming himself and walking out. It is a powerful scene especially as Bates has tears welling up in his eyes as he walks away from Mark. Laurence quickly tries to make amends by seeking out his son on a freezing rainy night, which results in his contracting pneumonia and dying, but not before revealing something about Janna that will drive the story forward. Bates' character dies by the end of the second episode, though he turns up again in the third episode through flashbacks of Janna remembering him.

Martin Thurley shared his memories of his fellow actor and friend. "It was great working with Ralph as he was such a consummate actor and a lovely man. He was a great joy to meet because he brought a lot of fun to everything. Ralph could be quiet as well on the set and he didn't suffer fools gladly. He hated any pomposity and all that. He also had a wonderful twinkle about him, which I just adored.

"We shared a similar approach to acting in that we just ... acted, there was *no* Stanislavski angst about things. Ralph really wasn't into all that. He just had fun until the red light was on and then he went out, did his lines as best he could and put in a great performance. That's why I adored him, as he was down to earth.

"Ralph was a real sensitive chap and could sometimes get a bit nervous before filming, depending on the scene, but he covered things up with joking. He didn't make it hard work and he made it good to be around him in acting and in life. We continued a correspondence after doing *Penmarric*. He would pretend as if he were my father as in the production, writing to me as though I was at Penmarric Prep School. And he would always write, "Dear Son, I've heard from Matron (by which he meant the director Tina Wakerell) that you've had to see the Head Master" (who was the producer Ron Craddock). These letters were in reference to the experience we had filming *Penmarric*, which was a bit of a nightmare production to be involved in. I was a bit badly behaved and it was the last thing I ever acted in before I became a full time writer. I sort of lost focus, so, I think, that I was rather difficult to deal with. Ralph and I just used to joke about it really. This stemmed from the producer not really being in charge and we just told whoever was directing what we ought to be doing, which probably was not the best thing. That is how our whole Penmarric Prep School correspondence came about; I was constantly being naughty ... in the letters.

"I remember one evening on the set that Ralph and I were laughing about just the profession in general and people we had come across over the years; people we loathed and people we loved. Another memorable evening involved Ralph, actor John Castle (who played

Mark Penmar in the production), a great friend of Ralph and myself. We were all quite drunk in Flete House and were all playing a game called Billiard's Fives in which you use billiard balls and sort of barge each other out of the way. It is a sort of upper class drinking game, though none of us were upper class of course. It was a wonderfully riotous evening.

"He was a great person to be in company with. Ralph was very supportive of me. I saw him later when he did *Dear John*, as I was good friends with John Sullivan as well. And I used to go to Ralph and Virginia's house for parties. They were wonderfully generous and they had an extraordinary house, which Virginia had decorated with all Victorian lace." [133]

Peter Blake played Michael Vincent, the lawyer friend of Mark Castallack and he reflected. "We met in 1979 when I was appearing in *The Rocky Horror Show* at The Comedy Theatre in the West End. Because of these gigs, my hair was very long, dyed magenta in color, cut very spiky on top. Make-up had to hide it under a short wig for the filming of *Penmarric*. Ralph honed in on me almost immediately—I suppose I didn't look like an actor in a period drama! His charm and ability to make whoever he was talking to feel that he was really interested in them was disarming, to say the least, and I liked him immediately." [134]

Secret Army was a very fine drama co-produced by the BBC and the Belgian National Broadcaster. Created in 1979 by John Leslie "Gerard" Glaister, the World War II drama involved a Belgian resistance movement that secretly smuggled Allied pilots, the ones shot down, back to Britain. Bernard Hepton starred as Albert Foiret, owner of the Café Candide, the location where the resistance group called Lifeline runs its operations. Complicating matters for the group is the arrival of Sturmbannführer Ludwig Kessler, who comes to aid Major Brandt locate and stop Lifeline. The tension mounts as Lifeline faces increasing risks to rescue, hide and assist the Allied pilots, all while under close surveillance and investigations by the Germans. The series had a realistic historical quality to it, no doubt thanks to Glaister's personal experience during World War II as a member of the Royal Air Force. It also was a big hit for the BBC and very popular with the public. *Secret Army* was so ingrained in the viewers' minds for its serious look into the war that it became ripe for a parody, and in 1982 David Croft and Jeremy Lloyd created the hilarious BBC series *'Allo 'Allo!*

Bates first appeared in a recurring guest star role as the Communist Paul Vercors, in the first episode of the third season of *Secret Army*. In *The Last Run*, the plotline was set up for the final run of the series, which was set during the end of the German occupation of Brussels. Bates' character was a tie-in to the previous season, when Max, a member of the Communist Resistance, challenges Albert, who is trying to take over Lifeline. The second season ends with Albert tipping off the police about Max and his group, which results in them being killed. Paul Vercors is the only member of the Communist cell who survives, and when he appears during the last 10 minutes of *The Last Run* blackmailing Inspector Benet (Richard Beale) to find out who betrayed them, the viewers knew this was a character that would cause major problems for Lifeline. This was due to the raw intensity Bates brought to his performance as Vercors, which was reminiscent of his turn as Caligula in *The Caesars*.

Vercors' plan of revenge begins in the episode suitably titled *Revenge*, in which he informs Benet he will require his help again. When Benet questions being involved, he is informed by Vercors, "Albert Foiret has been sentenced to death. When and how is left to me." The scene is set at the Café Candide and, while Albert and his staff expect an attack, they do not know by whom or when it will come. As each patron comes into the restaurant, the rising suspense builds, and though Benet aids in the removal of a trio that Albert thinks may be the Communists, he is also the one sent by Vercors and arrests Albert outside the café. In the following episode viewers learn that Vercors has lodged an accusation with the authorities that Albert murdered his wife.

In the following six episodes, Albert deals with his arrest and Bates' character is not seen as he is rebuilding his group. When Albert gets off from a trumped-up murder charge and is finally released in the episode *Collaborator*, Bates' character is back as Vercors and is determined to take matters into his own hands, eliminating his old enemy. The timing works out perfectly for Vercors, as the Germans are retreating from Brussels in the face of advancing Allied armies. Bursting into the Candide with his men and guns drawn, Vercors verbally and physically abuses Albert, his staff and Major Reinhardt, who planned on surrendering to the Allies. It is the episode *Collaborator* in which Bates has his strongest presence in the series *Secret Army*. Bates makes his character Vercors a sheer terror in his quest, hell bent on revenge and blind to the facts. He is downright scary in the Candide, brutally hitting Albert who tries to reason with him and Major Reinhardt, who also tries to explain the facts to him. With his machine gun in hand, Bates' character sneers as he calls Albert an informer, black market operator and collaborator, and he even spits in his face. It is a powerful scene that ends abruptly, leading into the next episode, *Day of Judgement*.

At the beginning of *Day of Judgement*, Vercors takes Albert and his other captives to a hideout where he plans on hanging all of them. He almost succeeds, but he is interrupted by the sudden arrival of Albert's barmaid Natalie, who brings a British general with her. Vercors manages to push Albert off a platform to hang, while he makes his escape taking Albert's mistress Monique as a hostage. Later in the episode he appears again at another café and coldly brushes off Natalie's pleading to know the whereabouts of Monique, who he handed over to the Communist resistance. Again, Bates provides a strong performance for a conflicted character that sees his brutality as a necessary part of his loyalty to friends, who died fighting for the resistance. This takes Bates' characterization above the average villain to create a more three-dimensional persona, which only adds to the suspense that Vercors provides in the series. The only let down is that his character does not crop up again in the final two episodes, presumably having to leave Brussels once the Allies liberated it.

Michael Briant who directed Bates in the episodes *The Last Run* and *Collaborator* comments commented: "I liked and admired Ralph very much and I thought that his presence in *Secret Army* was a great bonus toward the end of the series. He was a clever and intelligent actor and seemed to be a very nice person indeed. The episodes that I directed him in were sort of a build up to the later episodes, in which he featured more importantly, so I did not really get a chance to know him better, as that was the only time I worked with him. Our contact was brief and pleasurable as Ralph was an actor I had longed to work with and I was sorry not having a chance to work with him again." [135]

Bates joined the cast of the N.J. Crisp 1979 theater production *The Jet Set*. The production, staged at the Theatre Royal in Bath, also starred John Moulder Brown, Ewan Solon, Norma Streader and Hilary Tindall, all under the direction of Hugh Goldie. Streader had previously worked with Bates on *Poldark*, playing Francis Poldark's sister Verity. Like Bates, Solon also had a Hammer connection, appearing in a number of their early productions including *Hound of the Baskervilles*, *The Terror of the Tongs* and *Curse of the Werewolf*. This successful stage appearance ended a busy and varied decade in Bates' life.

Chapter 4
"Excuse me my dear, I have some work to do"

A romantic Valentine's Day gesture in early 1980 by Bates to his wife Virginia provided a prime example of the old adage, "No good deed goes unpunished." As Virginia recalled, "On the evening before Valentine's Day I casually mentioned to Ralph that if he was going to give me any flowers, I only wanted pink tulips. Typical of Ralph, he immediately wanted to grant my wish and quietly slipped out of the house to head to the florist. A couple of hours later, while I was feeding the children, the phone rang and it was Ralph to say that he'd been hit by a car while crossing the road and was in the launderette waiting for an ambulance. He said the nice lady in there had let him use the phone (in the days before mobile phones) in order to call me. I didn't even know that he had left the house so it was quite a shock! I spent the next two hours trying to find which casualty unit he'd been taken to. I then bundled the children into the car and we brought him home. Thankfully the accident wasn't serious. Ralph had four stitches in his forehead and a sore leg, but he was more worried about the six bunches of pink tulips left in the launderette! I did feel guilty about it when I went to pick them up the next day; luckily the nice lady had put them in a bucket of water." [136]

A *Secret Army* reunion of sorts was involved in the 1980 re-staging of playwright Anthony Shaffer's mystery drama, *Sleuth*. The play, about a mystery writer who lures his wife's lover under the guise of a robbery to set him up, was first performed in 1970 at London's St. Martin's Theatre with Anthony Quayle playing the mystery writer, Andrew Wyke and Keith Baxter playing the younger Milo Tindle. The popular play was transferred to Broadway at the Music Box Theater, where it would go on to win a Tony Award. Shaffer sold the film rights, which resulted in the 1972 movie with Laurence Olivier and Michael Caine, respectively playing Wyke and Tindle.

The production involving Bates and Terrence Hardiman (Vercors and Major Reinhardt from *Secret Army*) was staged in Sweden with performances in theaters in both Stockholm and Gothenburg. Hardiman shared his memories of the production: "Although I met Ralph first when working on *Secret Army*, it was only when we went to Sweden to perform in the theater production of *Sleuth* that I got to know him better. *Secret Army* had been a great success when shown on Swedish television,

Bates strikes a pose in his *Sleuth* dressing room (Sweden, 1980).

A Biography 113

and as a result several actors who had been a part of it were invited in the early 1980s to take some English theater to Stockholm and Gothenburg. In the play Ralph played Milo Tindle, the young estate agent and lover of the wife of Andrew Wyke, the detective thriller writer and Wyke was my part. It being a two-hander, we needed to get on well, and we did. He was a generous, amusing and warm-hearted colleague, and an absolute pleasure to work with. We were performing twice a day, first to school children who were studying and practicing English, and in the evening to the regular theater-goers, so it was quite a tiring assignment. The youngsters occasionally rewarded us with sweets thrown at the stage, but we escaped unscathed! In the play's interval Ralph had a complicated make-up change to affect a disguise, which involved false nose, wig and facial hair, an uncomfortable business, but he never complained and approached it with wry amusement and proper professionalism. My association with him was relatively short, but I knew him to be a fine and honest actor, as well as a very good man." [137]

Bates' first television role of the 1980s was a guest part in the ITV comedy drama *Turtle's Progress*. The title character, played by John Landry, had first been seen in the 1975 television drama *The Hanged Man*, both series having been written by Edmund Ward. Turtle, a small time crook in the previous series, has moved on but not by much, now living with his Aunt Ethel and employing a minder known as Razor Eddie (Michael Attwell). They decide to nick a van for some quick income, not realizing that it contained a load of stolen safe-deposit boxes. Each episode of the series would involve them opening one of the boxes, which in turn would lead to some sort of blackmail, reward or underhanded dealings. Always just on their heels but not quite in the know was Superintendant Rafferty, who lent some additional issues for Turtle. Six months after *Turtle's Progress* began airing, the BBC launched a similar style series entitled *Minder*, which would go on to have a much longer run.

In the episode *Box Nine*, Turtle finds a catalogue listing antiques but he has no idea as to what the purpose and value of it is. With a little help from Henry Furniture, the antiques expert, Turtle and Eddie learn exactly what they have on their hands and decide to go into the antique business to make a large profit on the upcoming Rochester Grange auction. Complicating matters is a crooked antique dealers ring that is also very interested in the catalogue and its potential windfall valuations.

Appearing as the Frenchman Pierre Sablon, Bates sported a long tan trench coat and large sunglasses. Playing it up as a high roller, Bates delivers the line to a fellow crook concerning the Rochester auction with aplomb, "There is a great deal of profit to be made ... and I want to make it." His character has several brushes with Superintendant Rafferty, who has been alerted to him by INTERPOL. A definite treat in the episode is hearing Bates exchange some dialogue in French with his henchman, simply known as Corsican (Roger Lloyd-Pack). However, crime never pays and both Sablon and Corsican end the episode knocked flat by Razor Eddie and dragged out by their heels. Also in the episode, playing Henry Furniture, was Michael Ripper, a character actor who had a long association with Hammer, including one in Bates' first film for the company, *Taste the Blood of Dracula*.

Bates followed this production up with the Yorkshire Television six-part drama series, *Second Chance*. In the story, a middle-aged couple, Kate (Susannah York) and Chris Hurst (Bates), have recently divorced. They had been married at a young age and now, 18 years later, their relationship has hit an impassable stumbling block and they mutually decide that a divorce will give them both a second chance. Their problem of trying to adjust to life after marriage is complicated, both parties trying to balance it all out with the needs of their two children, Jill and Martin. Kate finds herself wanting to break free of the rut of an unfulfilling job to feel independent once again, while Chris tries to navigate the nuisances of reentering the dating scene at an older age. Caught in the middle are Jill, graduating from school and desiring to travel and explore before attending college, and Martin, dealing less well with the divorce and harboring some resentments about his situation. Along their post marriage journey, Kate and Chris find themselves encountering friends and acquaintances, who either try to help or take advantage of their status.

Bates and Susannah York in *Second Chance*

Presented in six parts covering different months of a year, *Second Chance* was a series that took on all the hot-button issues that divorced couples had to deal with: needs of the children, dealing with an ex-spouse, dating versus family time, rediscovering oneself, women's lib versus homemakers and questions of remarriage. In this respect, it covered some of the same ground that another series starring Bates, *Dear John*, would cover. However, while *Dear John* presented its topics with a sense of humor to find pathos in the situation, *Second Chance* played it rather straightforward, almost in a documentary way. Another difference between the two series was the relationship of the spouses; the couple presented in *Second Chance* clearly has a better working relationship than the one depicted in *Dear John*, in which the husband is shown as more of a victim, who struggles to maintain a relationship with his child. Written by longtime *Coronation Street* scriptwriter Adele Rose, *Second Chance* was a hit in England and was rebroadcast in other countries where it received favorable reviews, including this one from Australia: "The show makes some quite strong, thoughtful observations." [138]

Bringing in some realism to the production was the fact that the stars, Susannah York and Bates, both were previously divorced. No doubt they took some of what they personally dealt with and infused it into their characters. Indeed, the best scenes of the series often involve Bates and York discussing their separate trials together, sharing mutual understanding they did not have during their marriage. Bates plays Chris Hurst as a man wanting to once again find happiness, but not at the expense of his children or having more kids at his age. He pines over his situation, where he gets to see his children only on Saturdays and Tuesdays, while his coworkers, single and married, try to give him advice as they watch sports on the television at his flat. The

Bates, wife Virginia and Dave Prowse (children Will and Daisy in the background) at the first Hammer Convention in London

relationship between Chris and his son Martin is delicately played out, with the two trying to find a middle ground to communicate. Chris' dating other women complicates his relationship with Martin, who still somehow hopes his parents can work out their issues and come back together. After a tense scene at Martin's birthday when Chris and Kate get into an argument, there is a touching scene with Martin and Chris riding together through a park and starting to build a connection once more. An interesting bit has Jill telling her mother her plans after graduation, including the possibility of taking a Greyhound bus across America to see the country; this is exactly what Bates did in real life when he was younger.

Bates, being a working actor, was often at rehearsals or in productions that meant time away from the family, something not easy with young children at home. In this aspect, Virginia was very helpful by taking on a lot of the home responsibilities, while still also managing her boutique shop. "Being a working wife with a young family has drawbacks but I chose a job which would combine with family life," Virginia told *TV Times*. "I don't have a nanny, so I take my children to and from school everyday. When Ralph is away on tour, or rehearsing, as he was doing recently for a new Yorkshire Television series called *Second Chance*, I am home, so they have a secure family life." [139]

Steve Hackett, a good friend of Bates, created the instrumental main theme to *Second Chance*. The title song was also featured on Hackett's *Bay of Kings* album. Hackett first rose to fame for his guitar work in the progressive rock group Genesis, of which he was a member from 1970 until 1977, when he left to do solo albums. In 1986, he co-founded the group GTR with fellow guitarist Steve Howe, who was a member of both Yes and Asia. Following his work in GTR, Hackett continued to pursue his solo career. Hackett shared his memories of his good friend Ralph Bates: "In the 1970s I was living around the corner from Virginia's shop and I struck up a conversation one day with Ralph, when he was sitting on a chair outside the shop. I believe he offered me a drink. He was immediately open, friendly and very witty. He explained he was an actor. I told him I was a musician. We were interested in each other's professions, and it turned out that we shared the same birthday. He was exactly 10 years older than me to the day.

"He was an extraordinarily good actor, and even though I knew him as a friend, when he was playing a mean part, you could really believe that he was hateful! He told me once that his young daughter Daisy was watching him one time on television hanging somebody. He had mixed feelings about her watching that ... He was equally adept at comedy as straight parts ... truly versatile. I know as an aspiring actor he was impressed with Laurence Olivier. He wanted to be able to play heroes, but he was invariably chosen as a villain, probably because of his Hammer horror successes. I thought he was particularly good in a piece on television called

Man of Straw, where he played a corrupt politician. He had an amazing way of morphing himself into any part he played.

"In person Ralph was friendly and gregarious, the life and soul of any party. He was multi-talented. As well as his acting ability, he was also a brilliant squash player and cook. He was always concerned for the welfare of others. He and Virginia used to take people under their wing. They kept open house for many an out-of-work actor or lonely soul on Sundays, and sometimes even took people in for at least several weeks. They were an extraordinary couple with big hearts and it was lovely to feel part of their extended family, once a week. Sometimes that hearty meal went on into the night ... Ralph was a lovely man and extraordinary friend. He and Virginia often came to my shows and were very complimentary, but I feel he was a national treasure and I always wished personally I could have given him more. I'll never be able to repay his myriad kindnesses. He was even thinking of others at the end of his life in [the] hospital.

Bates is having fun with the goblet from *Taste the Blood of Dracula* at the first Hammer Convention.

"Ralph actually got me the job to do the theme for *Second Chance*. I had a pre-existing melody that I adapted for the television series. I knew of the story and I was trying to come up with something suitably wistful and poignant, a duet for flute and guitar. I distinctly remember recording it on the day Ralph informed me that John Lennon had just been shot. Ralph became a kind of mentor to me. I looked up to him as a man of experience with real substance. He was also extremely funny. Because he once had to put up with a voice constantly shouting out 'Hackett!' at one of my shows, he did a great impression and forever after used to greet me in a very loud whisper with 'Hackett!' He could do a great impression of George Formby, replete with ukulele, and sometimes I found it so funny I ended up in stitches on the floor. He was a particularly special friend and I still talk to him as if he were here still with us. I remain in touch with his wife Virginia and with his son and daughter. They have always been a very talented and warm-natured family. Ralph was a one off and I will always miss him terribly." [140]

Tim Goode first met Bates in 1975 during the *Private Lives* run, and a similar encounter in 1980 resulted in an invitation for dinner. "I was a film student by then at the Royal Polytechnic Institution of Central London and was with a student film crew in the car park of the Middlesex Hospital. We were at the main entrance and—blow me down—Ralph came out! So I ran up to reintroduce myself, but to my surprise he said, 'You're Tim Goode, aren't you?' He actually remembered my name after all those years, just off the top of his head. He and the student crew had a good chat about Mrs. Thatcher, the new Prime Minister; Ralph didn't particularly like Thatcher and nor did we. He invited me for Sunday dinner and from that point on we just kind of hit it off.

After arriving for dinner he asked me to follow him downstairs where he had a storeroom marked D8 in the basement. In it was a large trunk. He said, "I want you to go through that box, it's all my stuff from my career. Put aside anything there you fancy, especially if it doesn't have my name on it." In the trunk were his Hammer scripts, call sheets and the dagger that he cuts his hand with in *Taste the Blood of Dracula*. Any sort of Hammer fan will guess that I couldn't believe I was really awake! There were also handwritten letters to Ralph from Peter Cushing, some addressed from film sets. I'm afraid I can't remember what we ate for dinner. "I want you to come back and sort out all this material, there's too much of it. Come back next weekend," Ralph suggested. It was incredible. I guess now that Ralph knew what the trunk in the basement would do to a fan-boy's head. Well—it did." [141]

Bates poses with props from *Taste the Blood of Dracula* at the first Hammer Convention.

In 1981 Bates would give a riveting performance as career politician Rupert Douglas in the drama *Man of Straw*, which was an episode of the series *The House on the Hill*. The series was made up of six episodes and all took place around a house in Glasgow, from 1878 to the 1980s. In the drama, Douglas has returned to Glasgow with his new wife Aileen, who happens to be related to the new Prime Minister. While his parents are not exactly pleased, as Aileen is an outsider from London, Douglas explains to his campaign manager Leon Campbell (Brian Cox) that sooner or later women will be able to vote and he wants to further his career through his marriage. But upon his welcome back party, Douglas begins to get embroiled in a tight political race dealing with his new proposed land tax, as well as his rubbing against an outspoken press reporter who criticizes his policy. Douglas wins his re-election that seems to overshadow the announcement of Aileen's pregnancy. His success is short lived, however, as a scandal breaks out in which it is revealed that his father was involved with insider trading for a government account he recommended. The result of the scandal is the forced resignation of Douglas, clearing the way for Campbell to make his own run for office. Douglas then realizes the force at work behind his downfall and tries to begin anew.

Man of Straw gave Bates the opportunity to portray a truly flawed individual in what amounted to an in-depth character study of the liberal politician Rupert Douglas. Sporting a mustache and dressed to impress, Bates' interpretation of Douglas starts as a man who is blinded by his political tunnel vision. He marries not for love but for connections, and only seems interested in securing his re-election with the help of his advisor. There are some good conversations between Douglas and Campbell concerning politics and life in general. Brian Cox, who got his start in acting around the same time as Bates, also contributes to the overall quality of the production, which benefits from their strong performances. By the end of the story Bates shows that Douglas has completely lost touch with his family, his wife passes away from childbirth complications and learns that he has a daughter who will not be able to follow him into politics, Douglas simply leaves her behind with his parents as he heads off to try and restart his career. There is one telling scene in the story which sums up Douglas. A doctor tending to a pregnant Aileen sees Douglas for the first time and congratulates him, to which

Douglas quickly says it was a fine result, referring to his political win and not realizing the doctor meant his baby.

Cox shared his memories of working with Bates and of the production: "I did work with Ralph and remember that he was a good friend of Gary Waldhorn, who I was sharing a house with in the early 1970s. I used to see Ralph occasionally, and of course I remember the shop Virginia had in Notting Hill. Ralph was a very sweet man, a very good soul and generous spirited. He did all those wonderful films for Hammer, including *Dr. Jekyll and Sister Hyde*, which was a twist on the original story, [but this time] being about a man who becomes a woman. And then he did that popular John Sullivan series *Dear John*." [142]

The Cleveland Press Dec. 4-11, 1981

TV SHOWTIME

Helen Mirren and Brad Davis in 'Mrs. Reinhardt'

Series writer Ian Cullen remembered: "I met Ralph when I went to the producer's viewing of the episode. At the event we had quite a discussion because I felt that the outer impression of strength and ability of the character had been lost a little, and that Ralph was playing him too weak to have convinced the electorate and his political party of his potential. Only those closest to him were concerned about the character's inner cowardice and lack of commitment. Most people were taken in by his charisma and oratory. Ralph took the point graciously and adjusted his performances to produce a brilliant interpretation, in a subtle and demanding role. He was always impressive and had enormous charm in performance. I found Ralph to be a consummate, versatile actor who had honed his technique to near perfection.

"As a person I found Ralph to be always gracious and with enormous charm. He had great humility but at the same time knew his capabilities and was proud of his standing in the profession. Natural talent such as his was a great gift. He knew this, was suitably grateful and worked hard to keep his talent bright and shining. Although I had only worked with Ralph on *Man of Straw*, I got to know him a little more during my time as Head of Drama at the Elmhurst Ballet school, but his focus was on the future welfare and prospects of his daughter Daisy, who was a student there at the time." [143]

Bates' last television work for 1981 was the BBC2 Playhouse episode *Mrs. Reinhardt*. Adapted for the screen by Irish writer Edna O'Brien from one of her own short stories, the drama told the tale of a betrayed English wife (played by Helen Mirren), who leaves her husband and goes to the country in France to get away. There Mrs. Reinhardt meets an American drifter with

A Biography   119

Bates demonstrates group interaction with the cast of *Instant Enlightenment Plus V.A.T.*

whom she gets romantically involved, until he reveals his true self that brings a new shock to her fragile state of mind. O'Brien's works often tell of women's inner feelings, especially towards men, and *Mrs. Reinhardt* is a prime example of her work.

Playing Harold Reinhardt, Bates' character is shown mostly in flashbacks throughout the production as Mrs. Reinhardt remembers different periods of time in their troubled marriage. The character also provides a bit of a different look for Bates as he grew a full beard for the role. Although the plot centers on Mrs. Reinhardt, played exquisitely by Helen Mirren, Bates does make the most of his role and adds some depth to his character as well. Harold Reinhardt is an art critic whose wife followed him around everywhere. One symbolic item that ties them together is his mother's necklace, which he presents to his wife on her birthday. It is this necklace that Harold tries to get back as his wife leaves him and also which she tries to find after it becomes lost at the hotel where she was staying. Bates has two excellent scenes in the production. One is when in the midst of a heated argument Harold and his wife must work together to herd some stray cows and assist one that had gotten caught in barbed wire. The other scene comes at the conclusion in which Harold makes a surprise visit to his wife to beg for forgiveness and try to reconcile their marriage. Bates' performance was noted in a *New York Times* review, "And Ralph Bates makes the two-dimensional figure of the husband far more convincing than might be thought possible." [144]

While *Mrs. Reinhardt* aired on October 30, Bates was on stage in Andrew Carr's play, *Instant Enlightenment Plus V.A.T.*, at the New Half Moon Theatre in London's East End; it was originally a BBC *Play for Today*. In the theater production Bates took on the role of Malcolm, whom Tim Wylton had played in the television production. In the story, an aggressive American trainer named Max Schreiber (Robin Nedwell) runs a weekend enlightenment seminar in which paying clients are promised that their personal problems will be exorcised. Malcolm (Bates) is a journalist who joins Max's class to do an exposé piece on his Kasna seminar. However, Max's use of ranting insults in his motivational seminar to degrade his clients into submission before "saving" them from their personal issues just may make Malcolm the latest convert. Also among the cast were Joanna Monro and Robin Halstead as Max's principal assistants. The tale of people exposing themselves to cult brainwashing was based in part on real life trainers such as Robert Daubigny, who in the 1970s ran the Exegesis Seminar, which helped create Programmes, Ltd., one of Britain's top sales companies of its time. Writer and director Andrew Carr, who wrote the story based on his actual experience in Exegesis, sought to make his play feel as real as possible by placing his actors among the audience and having Kasna's three trainers on duty in the theater foyer before every performance to neatly label everyone by their first names. *The Stage* newspaper gave *Instant Enlightenment Plus V.A.T.* a positive review, stating the cast (including Ralph Bates) gave "alarmingly authentic performances." [145] An interesting note on the production was that Mary Peach was one of the members of the seminar group, and she was married to Bates' good friend, screenwriter and director Jimmy Sangster.

Joanna Monro spoke of Ralph and the production: "Ralph was what I would call a company actor. There are certain actors who tend to think that the play revolves all around them. But Ralph was the sort of actor who loved working with people. It was really all for one and one for all. This is terribly important in theater to be known as a company member, who can work with a large ensemble to make the piece work. Ralph had a lot of television success and was probably one of the biggest names in the production. But he was one of the most generous, thoughtful and insightful people and was wonderful to have in the company. It didn't matter if it were a first time actor or a big name actor, everyone was treated the same by Ralph. Everybody loved him, the crew and management alike. He would often have us all in hysterics and he used to make us all laugh so much. And he was just a joy to watch. He was a consummate performer. The part of Malcolm was a very difficult part for him or for any actor in general, but Ralph was brilliant in the role. It was a tricky play to do because it was actually based on Andrew Carr's personal experience. Andrew had gone to Exegesis undercover to do an exposé and had been taken up by the movement, which took over his life for a while. This is why he wrote the play. So basically Ralph was playing Andrew in the production. Ralph couldn't therefore hide in the role but had to play it real, and his character has a full breakdown in the play, which he performed every single night.

"Our friendship really started with that show and afterwards we really didn't see each other a lot, but whenever we did it was great fun. We used to follow each other around the country because he would be touring and I would be touring and either I'd follow him into a theater where he was acting in a production or vice versa, and we would leave notes for each other. Robin Nedwell would also join in on the note writing. We all sort of followed each other around the country at various theaters. A funny side note was that until the day he died, Ralph would call me *Joahne* Mingo because, on the play's original poster outside the theater, instead of saying *Joanna* Monro, for some reason they spelled my name *Joahne* Mingo. Now at this point in time I was on television twice a week in a series called *Angels,* about nurses, so my name was regularly in the castings for the *Radio Times* listings. I have no idea how they made me sound like a Nigerian woman. So as a joke whenever I left notes for Ralph in the theaters, I would sign it from *Joahne* Mingo. We thought it was a wonderful, funny bit associated with the play. But to their credit the producer did bring out all new posters with my name spelled properly.

"After rehearsals Ralph used to drive the three of us, since we were somewhere east of London. As he drove us home he would tell us wonderful stories. One time he explained that he had passed his driver's test in Ireland when he was quite young. He said it was great and so easy because all they wanted you to do was drive forwards, backwards, try turning around that corner; good, congratulations, you have passed your test. Another story involved Guinness beer mats, which in those days you would get at the pub to put your pint on. These beer mats happened to be the same size as a tax disc, which was a circular document that had to be displayed in your car to prove you paid your highway tax. Ralph explained that when he was much younger and couldn't afford a tax disc, he used to put a Guinness beer mat in its place and no one would give it a second look, because they automatically assumed it was the tax disc!

"I had previously watched Ralph on television before working with him. Most notable was his role in *Poldark*. He was usually cast as these dark, brooding, handsome beasts, of which he couldn't have been more opposite. So it was a pleasant surprise when he did *Dear John*. To see Ralph playing this wonderful, lovelorn lost soul was a true delight, as the role was probably more him despite the fact that he was incredibly happily married to Virginia. They were a wonderful couple and absolutely adored each other. Ralph was very sweet and his role in *Dear John* was very different from the many roles I had seen him in before, which proved how versatile he was as an actor. He was one of the funniest, kindest, most wonderful people I've ever worked with." [146]

Bates and Toyah Wilcox on the set of *Tales of the Unexpected*

The Roald Dahl-inspired series, *Tales of the Unexpected*, ran from 1979 to 1988 and involved nefarious plots with twist endings, which the noted author was well known for. In 1982 the episode *Blue Marigold* had Bates playing the wealthy love interest to the title character. The story involves Marigold (pop star Toyah Willcox), an actress known for her print ads hawking Blue Marigold cosmetics during 1969. Marigold is eagerly awaiting the upcoming preview of her new commercial, in which she finally gets a speaking role, playing a spy to promote the brand. However, upon seeing the commercial, Marigold is horrified and embarrassed to find out that an unknown actress named Sophie has dubbed her lines.. The indignity of being told she is perfect except until she opens her mouth to speak sends Marigold over the edge, resulting in her driving away her lover Paul Foster (Ralph Bates), losing her job to Sophie and ending up having a mental breakdown. Years later Marigold is out of rehab and runs into Sophie, who is now the fiancée of Paul. Marigold decides to give it one last shot to revive her career and win back Paul, but all is not what it seems.

As the character Paul Foster, Bates provides a grounding influence on Marigold. His down-to-earth logic balances her diva-like behavior. But his influence only extends so far and eventually he comes to his wits end and decides to leave Marigold, which completes her breakdown. Bates does a good job expressing the frustration of trying to convince someone who is lucky enough to be famous and wealthy to stop while they are ahead of the game. His final scene, part of the twist ending, is the straw that breaks the camel's back. Thinking she can edge out Sophie for Paul's affection, Marigold arrives dolled up like it is still 1969, only to find out Paul has been disfigured in a car accident and is now blind. Bates is done up in make-up to contort his face, which looks quite convincing, and his kind welcome serves as a final statement to Marigold, who based her life on looks alone.

Agatha Christie's detective novels have long entertained readers and many have found a home in television productions. She wrote over 60 novels, many of them starring her popular characters Hercule Poirot and Miss Marple, and she remains the best selling novelist of all time. Producers of course adapted many of Christie's stories, starting with the 1929 film *The Passing of Mr. Quin*. 1982 brought two independent television adaptations, *The Spider's Web* and *The Seven Dials Mystery*, besides a full 10-episode series entitled *The Agatha Christie Hour*, produced by Thames Television in England and later shown in the U.S. on the PBS program *Mystery!* The British series featured hour-long adaptations of Christie's short stories and often starred well-known actors in the lead roles. While some of the stories ventured into Christie's crime stories, others were in the romance genre like *Magnolia Blossom*.

The episode *Magnolia Blossom* takes place during the 1920s as Theodora Darrell (Ciaran Madden) is bored, stuck in a marriage of convenience to Richard (Jeremy Clyde). Her life of entertaining at fancy dinner parties is interrupted when she meets Vincent Easton (Bates), an orange grower from the Transvaal of South Africa, who had a business dealing with her husband, an investor. A mutual attraction and shared interests develop into a deep simmering love between the two, and Theo slowly finds herself wanting to choose true love over her loyalty to Richard. But when Theo finally decides to follow her heart and goes with Vincent for a rendezvous by the ocean, she finds herself pulled back to Richard when news of a scandal involving him comes to her attention. She returns to Richard hoping to save their marriage out of her sense of duty, but when she is forced to do the unthinkable to prevent her husband going to prison, she comes to a realization that will set her free. Although perhaps hampered a bit by the typical love triangle and feeling a bit rushed in a one-hour time slot, Agatha Christie manages to put an interesting twist ending on what could otherwise be a mundane story. Solid performances by the leads are another plus. Ciaran Madden, who would go on to appear in two more Christie adaptations, *Miss Marple: The Body in the Library* and *Poirot: The Incredible Theft*, brings a good amount of inner turmoil to her character, one torn between two men. Jeremy Clyde's performance builds to an interesting climax of how far he is willing to use his wife to save himself. Bates, first seen looking quite dapper in a tux with his hair slicked back, creates a character with a deep consuming love, whose hopes rise and fall as he becomes a victim of circumstance. Always excelling at playing a colonial gentleman, Bates as the jilted South African argues with an air of dignified civility, even when losing his lover.

Panorama is one of Britain's longest-running current affairs programs, started by the BBC back in 1953. It was rare for *Panorama* to take a step into drama, but reporting from Poland, now under martial law, was banned. The program had a camera team working in Poland in the days preceding the government crackdown and got out on the last plane to leave the country. *Panorama*'s applications for visas to return to Poland were rejected. [147] A docudrama then seemed the best and only way to tell the story, resulting in *Two Weeks in Winter: How the Army Took Over Poland*. Andrew Carr, who had previously directed Bates in the theater production *Instant Enlightenment Plus V.A.T.*, wrote the script. The 1982 production marked the first anniversary of martial law in Poland; the People's Republic of Poland, using the military had taken control of the government on December 13, 1981 and sought to suppress any opposition in their bid to hold onto power. Under rule by General Wojciech Jaruzelski, the military cracked down on the pro-democracy Solidarity movement formed a few months earlier. Anyone supporting the former government could be arrested and held without any formal charges, and a number of citizens were killed in the protests against the People's Republic. The martial law did not end until July 22, 1983 and conflict between the two groups vying for power in Poland continued until 1986, when general amnesty for political prisoners was granted. The imposition of martial law was called by Jaruzelski to fend off intervention by the then Soviet Union, although there is still some debate about the details of the event. Directed by longtime series producer Christopher Olgiati, the *Panorama* documentary used actual film of confrontations between workers and the new People's Republic. To fill in the rest of the story, actors were brought in to dramatize the events taking place from the workers' point of view, who were helped by a local priest played by Jonathan Pryce. Bates played Tarnowski, the Wujek's Solidarity leader of the coal mine, who vows to resist martial law and is interned along with many of the workers as political prisoners. *Two Weeks in Winter: How the Army Took Over Poland* was repeated in the U.S. and shown on WNET. It was reviewed by the *New York Times* which was quite favorable of the production: "The frail dramatic structure of *Two Weeks in Winter* is more than redeemed in its portrayal of ordinary folk driven by tyranny to heroism, a compelling tribute to Solidarity on this sad anniversary." [148]

Director Christopher Olgiati shared his memories of the production: "I remember Ralph as an extraordinarily charming, kind, funny person who, through a long shoot, made his young director feel better about everything. The project was extremely demanding of all of us: Pittsburgh bizarrely enough stood in for Poland, because it had old mines, a large population of Polish origin who we could use as extras and tanks that could be rented from the National Guard. The film brought together actors and hard-nosed journalists, with me flitting between the two worlds trying to ease frustrations and sometimes blank incomprehension on both sides. Because I came out of current affairs, it took me some time to get used to actors and to understand what they expected from me. The mix was a daunting one, but if ever an anti-director vibe began to spread among the cast, Ralph extinguished it. Despite his phenomenal reputation and long record on the stage he never made me feel I wasn't 'one of us.' In addition to his talents as an actor, he did much to keep up morale despite the daily calamities of film-making ... the paint coming off the Polish tanks ... the snow (foam from airport fire trucks) blowing away in the summer breeze ... us forgetting to run the camera on our most spectacular action scene, involving bombs and fast cars. Throughout it all, he had a sort of luminous, smiling charm which made our disasters seem less and helped unite cast and crew." [149]

Ibsen's *Hedda Gabler* opened on May 17, 1982 in the West End with an all-star cast assembled by Bill Kenwright, which included Susannah York as Hedda, Tom Bell, Tom Baker, Paula Wilcox and the veteran, Irene Handel. The drama passes in Kristiana, Norway in the socially oppressed 1890s, and revolves around Hedda, daughter of the late General Gabler, who has reluctantly married.

With its theme of a powerful tragic woman, the role of Hedda is highly sought after by actors during its many performances down the years. Susannah York started this run off-Broadway and Harris Yulin played the new husband, Tesman. Bates played the role of the scholar. He performed it with a febrile intensity, like an excitable pet of Hedda's, always needing to please his haughty young wife, and always failing. He brought a family heirloom into his performance, a full length coat lined with squirrel fur that belonged to Dr. Adrien Loir, Bates' great-grandfather, also Louis Pasteur's nephew and assistant.

Reception of the London production was somewhat critical as evident by a *Post* critic, although Bates was singled out for his efforts. "Only Ralph Bates shows anything like a sense of character as the ineffectual Tesman, and he is too often weighted down by the turgid atmosphere around him." [150] The production was held back by a degree of friction within the star cast, and rehearsals had been skimped, leaving Ibsen's subtext largely unexplored." [151] However, when at last Hedda's crimes against her friend Lovborg (Tom Bell) came to light, the appalled realization of a scholarly idealist of his wife's cruelty and willfulness, in Bates' hands, seemed to destroy a rarified world.

In between stage plays and television performances, Bates liked to take his family on vacations for some relaxation. Being half-French, Bates often picked the country as the family place to get away. However, due to the nature of his business, everything was usually a little bit impromptu because inevitably he was working in a series or on tour during the holidays. So Bates and Virginia would instead pick up Will and Daisy from school on a Friday afternoon, pile into the car, drive to France and go to Normandy for the weekend, or stay at random hotels near the coast. Occasionally they would drive a little further and go to Paris. If he were unable to get away from work, such as when he was on tour, Bates would invite the family to fly or go on the overnight train to Scotland, or wherever he was performing. Then they would all be able to spend time together during his time off. Another favorite location for family vacations was the island of Ibiza. "My mother had a house there," Virginia explained. "So we would also visit there a lot, which could be fairly chaotic as her house sometimes lost electricity or there would be no running water, so it would turn into an adventure."

Virginia also revealed Ralph's love of the sea and boating. "Ralph bought a boat and we wanted to call the boat Daisy, after our daughter, but there was already a Daisy registered, thus we came up with Sea Daisy, which was pretty cool. Ralph became a prolific sailor and every free moment would be off to Plymouth, where the boat was moored. The only problem with Ralph was that he was fearless and sometimes the sense of adventure would get the better of him. The Coastguard once rescued him after losing the boat's rudder in a gale, and in true Bates fashion, he managed to get towed to a great bar along the coast where he spent the night. Wills often crewed for him and would recount some pretty hairy moments that terrified me. I'm afraid to say Daisy and I avoided going, not liking the cold and suffering from sea sickness!" [152]

Bates' first role of 1983 was in the popular ITV police drama *The Gentle Touch*. The series, which ran from 1980 to 1984 and starred Jill Gascoine as Detective Inspector Maggie Forbes, was notable for breaking barriers and featuring a woman as lead character in a

Bates' boat *The Sea Daisy*

police drama. Shown on Friday nights, *The Gentle Touch* became a huge-ratings hit for ITV and it was not long before other similar-themed shows would follow suit, including the BBC's *Juliet Bravo* and CBS' *Cagney and Lacey*. The series also treated its subject matter with respect and a real life look at how the police had to deal with various issues. This was not a romanticized view of good guys versus bad guys, but instead showed people coping with their own struggles and trying to determine right from wrong in a society that was forever changing.

In the episode *Who's Afraid of Josie Tate*, Mrs. Tate (Paola Dionisotti), an angry woman who has just learned she had inoperable breast cancer, visits Detective Forbes. Mrs. Tate comes to the precinct under the guise of collecting the belongings of her husband (Bates), who is locked up and awaiting trial at Brixton prison for robbing a supermarket. However, Mrs. Tate manages to smuggle two hand grenades into her purse and she steals Forbes' keys to lock themselves together in her office. Then she makes her demands to Forbes that she wants to see her husband and have the case against him dropped. However, the evidence that Mrs. Tate provides to prove her husband's innocence only opens a whole new can of worms for him, and Forbes must then try to cope with an irrational woman who holds the power to take both of their lives.

Bates' role in the episode was that of Wallace Tate, a career criminal with a wandering eye for tarty women, as his wife explains. First seen in the back of a squad car in his leather jacket and sporting a nonchalant demeanor, Bates portrays his character as a tough guy willing to do prison time for robbery with no complaints, but his wife implicates him for murder and, as his cover story is exposed, Bates explodes into an uncontrollable rage, screaming and threatening his wife, as he is dragged away by the police.

Who's Afraid of Josie Tate is also notable in that it is only the second time that Bates would get to work with his wife Virginia. In the episode, Virginia plays Elaine Decker, a nightclub hostess who turns out to be the girlfriend of Wally Tate. Although referred to a few times, she appears in only one scene, in which the police come to interview her about her relationship with Wally and his supposed alibi for the night of the robbery. Interrupted, as she is just about to plunge a needle in her arm, the police threaten her into revealing all she knows about Wally, which leads to his new incrimination. Virginia plays Elaine as a desperate woman, crying with mascara running down her face, as she breaks down in front of the police. Unfortunately, Bates and his real life wife do not get to share any scenes together in the episode.

Written in 1954, *Gigi* was originally a novelette by French author Sidonie-Gabrielle Colette that became her most famous work, and it was soon adapted for the stage, enjoying many revivals. In June 1983, Bates joined a national tour of the play under the direction of Hubert Gregg, produced by the Cambridge Arts Theatre Trust. Billed as "the original straight play," one of the main stops on the tour was the Grand Theatre, Leeds. Deborah Watling played the 19th-century Parisian girl being groomed by her aunt Alicia (Dawn Addams) for a career as a courtesan. The wealthy playboy Gaston (Bates) is unhappy at her transformation, and eventually realizes that he is attracted to her.

During the run Bates and his wife chanced to meet someone he had long been compared to since his time at Trinity College, Louis Jourdan. They all happened to be on the same boat while returning from France. Bates had always admired him and Virginia recalled her first meeting with her husband on the set of *Dr. Jekyll and Sister Hyde*, after which she described him to a friend of hers as being very good looking, quite like Louis Jourdan. Bates and Jourdan, who had played Gaston in the 1958 film version of *Gigi*, hit it off immediately, even speaking French to each other. "My goodness, I've never met an actor who resembled me so closely," Jourdan said over drinks. "Yes, I've been told that," Bates replied, "And at the moment I have the honor of playing your role in *Gigi*." [153]

Storyboard was a series of one-off dramas produced in the 1980s by Thames Television. Some of the dramas proved popular and were green-lighted for their own series, including *Lytton's Diary*, *The Bill* (which had an amazingly long run until 2010), *Ladies in Charge* and *King and Castle*. Bates would guest star on *Lytton's Diary* (1983), which was developed into a series lasting two seasons from 1985-1986. The series was co-created by actor Peter Bowles, who also starred as the title character Neville Lytton. Bowles had a long career in mostly television dating back to 1959. He also played the British chieftain Caractacus in the series *I, Claudius*, which was inspired by *The Caesars*. By the time he devised *Lytton's Diary*, Bowles had carved out a niche for himself playing upper class characters. The series was a good fit for Bowles, playing the suave Lytton, a Fleet Street reporter whose gossip column exposed corruption and the seedy elements of society. He could sometimes be underhanded and his personal life was far from perfect, but he was also devoted to his job at uncovering scandals.

In *Lytton's Diary*, Neville Lytton gets a lead on a hot scandal involving much loved M.P. Jonathan Burridge (Bates), who has supposedly been unfaithful to his wife and is dealing, under the table, with a chemical company with known violations at the same same time he is running the environmental group Earth Peace. But when the story goes to print, it is Lytton who gets the biggest shock, as Burridge declares Lytton's work a complete piece of fabrication and takes steps to sue him and the *Daily News* for libel. Hauled in by his editor, Lytton finds that his only chance to redeem himself is to prove everything he wrote in the article, which becomes quite difficult when his sources start to disappear or change their stories. Lytton knows that something is amiss and he continues to dig deeper until discovering a cover-up even bigger than what he originally thought.

The episode *Lytton's Diary* was a well-written drama, which presented an interesting look at the inner workings of reporters trying to get their stories, so it is not too surprising how it was later developed into a full series. In fact, the story in *Lytton's Diary* was redone as part of the series in the fourth episode, *Tricks of the Trade*, in which Lytton again is involved with an M.P. who is threatening to sue the *Daily News*. Bates had previously played an embattled politician in *Man of Straw*, and in *Lytton's Diary* there are some obvious similarities. The admiration from the public, the quality of being hard-working to a fault and eventually his fall from grace immediately come to mind. Perhaps what makes Bates so compelling in these political roles are a combination of his clean-cut looks, natural charm and an underlying intensity that he could bring to his characters. He certainly seemed like someone who could attract the attention of a political movement. His performance as Jonathan Burridge displays these qualities, as he heads the family dinner, rallies the troops at his Earth Peace organization and tries to explain his difficult decisions to Lytton. *Lytton's Diary* star Peter Bowles summed up Bates succinctly, "Ralph was a lovely man and a very good actor. His death was tragically too early." [154]

"One of my favorite memories of Ralph is from the spring of 1983, when I was making my degree film," Tim Goode recalls. "I think that when actors get to a certain age or a certain level they love the credibility of knocking around with students again. I know that Ralph always enjoyed being a student; Virginia told me he was happiest when she packed a lunch for him and he went off through the front door to do his job, and then back home later. This was not working in an amateur sense but just [working] without the trappings; Ralph loved the craft. I was excited because I was learning and he just enjoyed being himself. I had adapted this rather strange short story entitled *Overture to Eschata*. Ralph wanted a part, but he asked me to just make it a non-speaking walk-on role. I thought long and hard about it, since the story was a death-fantasy thing. In the film,

A shot outside The Criterion Theatre featuring *Run for Your Wife!*

when the modern surgeon raises his eyes from the operating table, we see Baron Frankenstein, with a glinting knife. It's as if the patient has not died but gone back in time to this Victorian chap with long hair and menacing looks—and of course that was Ralph. So I managed to fit him nicely into the script, although when Ralph looked at the script, he said, 'Where are my lines?' 'Ralph,' I gasped, 'you said you didn't want any lines!' He said, 'Oh, don't take me literally, I want some lines!' 'Well,' I told him, 'you can't have any lines now because I don't have a sound crew, we only have a silent camera.' Anyway, it was funny because I thought, that's a star speaking. When my film was shown at Polytechnic, Ralph came to see it, which was lovely, and I got my degree. He was just so supportive in helping people who were starting out, which I thought was very much indicative of the man." [155]

Bates' son Will also remembers the student film. "One of my earliest memories was Dad taking me and Daisy onto the set of a film that our dear friend Tim Goode was making. My dad was playing a surgeon, and the scene involved him cutting someone up. Of course it was the day of the water strikes in London, so the smell was pretty bad and there was blood everywhere. (Tim has since explained to me that it was pig's blood he got from the local butcher.) Sounds ridiculous, but it was so much fun with Dad just fooling around in that crazy surgeon's costume." [156]

Towards the end of 1983 Bates landed his most popular and long-running stage role, that of John Smith in the farce, *Run for your Wife!*, by Ray Cooney. The otherwise ordinary John Smith, taxi driver, has two wives, and leads two lives. Using his job to travel between one woman in Streatham and another in Wimbledon, Smith revels in his situation, until one day a policeman makes inquiries. Bates first played Smith during the play's run at the Criterion Theatre in London and shared the stage with Lionel Jeffries and Brian Murphy. Bates relished the chance to do comedy, and when the opportunity arose for him to resume playing John Smith in 1986, he quickly accepted. Also performed at the Criterion Theatre, this time Bates' castmates included Windsor Davies, Brian Godfrey, Roger Kitter, Peter Blake, Sherrie Hewson, Roy Hudd and Helen Cotterill.

"Before Ralph came to do *Run for Your Wife!*, most of his work had been in dramatic theater and he was basically a very good, solid actor," says Cooney. "He had not done this kind of comedy before, farce, as you might call it. But he turned out to be terrific and he was such a lovely guy to have in the company. The main thing about Ralph is that he was a team player and that is what you need for a daily production like *Run For Your Wife!* Ralph actually became one of the best John Smiths that we had in the history of our production. He was a delight to work and rehearse with. He was also wonderful to direct; Ralph took all the notes, took it on board, and made any changes needed. Of course not having done a play like this before, which is full of joyous laughter, was a new experience for Ralph; he just adored going to the theater every night and hearing that laughter.

"Ralph was chosen to play John Smith for three different runs of *Run for Your Wife!* What happened was after the play's initial success, so that we could continue to get well-known good actors, we decided to do three-month contracts with the stars of the show. So in between their television and movie roles they could do a season in the theater, which was usually a delight for an actor. *Run For Your Wife!* ran nearly nine years in all, eight years of those were these three-month runs that made up 32 sessions. Ralph did two runs at the Criterion Theatre and then appeared in one at the Duchess Theatre when the Criterion was closed for redecoration.

"In person Ralph was quite introverted and quiet. But when he got within the company during rehearsals and afterwards, he was always a joyous member of the team. I think that probably stems from the fact of the work he did prior to *Run For Your Wife!* and that this was a new experience for him. He did some very good serious productions like *Poldark*. I think we did him a good turn actually.

"I was still in touch with Ralph after his runs in the play, as we had a couple of parties at our house and we hosted one special event every year, which was a gathering of all the actors and actresses that we worked with over the years and managed to stay in touch with. Ralph and Virginia were definitely part of that and came to a few of the parties. Ralph was just a lovely man to have around." [157]

One of Bates' frequent collaborators on Cooney's *Run For Your Wife!* was actor and director Leslie Lawton. "Actors went in and out of the play during its nine year run. Changing the cast every three months kept the play fresh and alive. Ralph did a season with comedian Roy Hudd, then a few months later he came back to do another season opposite character actor Brian Murphy. Toward the end of the run I was rehearsing the next cast, but the actor taking over from Ralph was still in another show, which had a lot of matinees. Knowing how difficult it was for me as the director to rehearse with one lead missing, Ralph volunteered to come in during the days the other actor was unable to rehearse and stand in for him. He would then play at night as usual. I can't think of another star who would have done that. It was incredibly extraordinary." [158]

Will Bates remembers the production as a happy time. "I went with my dad to a lot of his plays, particularly *Run For Your Wife!,* which I think I ended up seeing about 50-60 times. On Saturdays my mum would be working at her shop so Dad would have to look after me for the day. I'd go with him to the matinee performance at the Criterion in the West End. I'd sit alone in the Royal box and watch the play (I guess no one in the Royal family had any interest in seeing a Ray Cooney farce on a Saturday afternoon). Sometimes I'd end up staying for the evening performance as well, and my mum would meet us, but we had dinner at Cafe Fish in between. I would hang out with Dad, Lionel Jeffries, Windsor Davis and Roy Hudd backstage. I met some amazing people when I was a kid! Good times. That was pretty much my childhood right there." [159]

Daisy Bates also cited the production as one of her favorites. "I saw him in *Run for Your Wife!* probably 50 times, maybe more. I just loved that show. I would sit with Dad on a Saturday between shows while he rested and ate cake. Windsor Davies would read Welsh poetry to me and Lionel Jeffries would tell me outrageous stories from filming *Chitty Chitty Bang Bang*, while Dad and Roy Hudd ran their lines. It was fun going in and out of their dressing rooms and hearing the stories of their week. All those actors always had their dressing room doors wide open like it was one giant green room. It was a real family, and as terrified as Dad was doing a farce, I remember all the actors being one big supporting group and Angie, the amazing assistant stage manager, keeping them all in check." [160]

British viewers in the early 1980s may have spotted Bates in a TV commercial for biscuits. "Funny enough," Virginia recalls, "Ralph won an award for that." In the commercial Bates explains that the Peek Freans Nice biscuits are so delicate and rich that his wife says they should save them for special occasions. Then he wishes a happy anniversary to a pair of parakeets, and dunks and eats the biscuit. 'What are you saving your Peek Freans for?'

"I collected the award at a smart hotel in Mayfair, as he was unable to go to the ceremony. It was left at the reception in a crumpled paper bag, which I dutifully delivered to our kitchen table. It's the only acting award Ralph ever won in his entire career, a Perspex block from Christie Brown and Co. We still have it." [161]

The Odd Job Man was the BBC's three-part 1984 action series that examined the underside of the secret service. Starring as ex-SAS officer George Griffin was actor Jon Finch, who like Bates got his big film break in a Hammer production, *The Vampire Lovers* (1970). Finch would even work with Bates in his next Hammer, *The Horror of Frankenstein*. The premise of *The Odd Job Man* was that Griffin, now out of official action and in need of a steady cash flow, decides to use his skills taking side jobs for the CIA, while working as an encyclopedia salesman. Needing assistance on his odd jobs, Giffrin teams up with his former commander, Major Drew (Bates). Polly Hemmingway played Griffin's girlfriend Nancy, who gets entangled in his latest mission of trying to find an East German hit man named Tauber (Wolf Kahler). Appearing in the series gave Bates a chance to play a hero for a change, which was unique in his career. *The Odd Job Man* was adapted into three 50-minute episodes by N.J. Crisp from his own novel, and was shot on location in Scotland, which was set up to resemble the Yugoslavian/Romanian border. Apparently Scotland encouraged film companies to use their country in substitute for Communist locations; it also served for the filming of *Tinker, Tailor, Soldier, Spy*. [162]

Toward the end of 1984 Bates was interviewed on radio by director/author Bruce Hallenbeck. The two hit it off immediately and Hallenbeck wrote a script for a film that was to have starred Bates, *Grave's End*. Unfortunately, the project never came to fruition, but Hallenbeck recalled its history and his friendship with Bates. "After my interview with Ralph, we started talking about doing a film together. I had a script called *Grave's End*, so I sent it to Ralph and he loved it. Jokingly, Ralph told me that as far as payment for the film was concerned, 'Give me a bottle of Latour and I'm happy!' He also suggested that Jimmy Sangster direct it, so I put a production package together, but the financing didn't come through in the end.

"Ralph was going to play the villain of the piece, one Reverend (ahem!) Hammer, who controlled a cult of vampires in a little town called Grave's End. Caroline Munro was to have been the heroine. The whole thing was a blatant Hammer homage, with in-jokey names and the whole works. I had letters of intent from Ralph, Caroline, Michael Gothard, Sangster and two special effects aces, John Caglione and Ed French. Everybody loved the script, and the *Grave's End* was actually announced in the 1985 Cannes *Variety* issue, with filming planned for the following year, but this was before everything fell apart in the financing stage. It was one of the most heartbreaking things in my life, alas.

"... For Ralph, he was always affable, enjoyed a good joke and was up for anything. I loved Ralph as an actor. My friend John McCarty said he reminded him of Henry Daniell, and I would tend to agree, but with a wicked sense of humor to boot. Ralph was the perfect Hammer actor, in my estimation: classically trained, dripping with class and elegance, but with that wry schoolboy humor just waiting to come to the fore. His performance in *The Horror of Frankenstein* delights me every time I see it, and his Dr. Jekyll is terrific, especially toward the end when he becomes confused, shall we say, about his/her sexuality. It was a much-underrated performance.

"When I asked him what he thought of replacing Christopher Lee or Peter Cushing as Hammer's [dominant] star, he pooh-poohed the whole idea and said they were irreplaceable. He also told me that while he enjoyed playing George Warleggan on *Poldark*, when you work for the BBC, 'It's like you're paying them.' He told me he received $10,000 dollars (not pounds) for appearing on the series for one year.

"Ralph was just always funny. I remember him sending me pictures of Kate O'Mara, Joan Collins and Stephanie Beacham, along with a note, 'Why aren't I on *Dynasty*?' He was just an all-around great guy in the manner of Peter Cushing. You won't find anyone saying anything bad about him." [163]

A Biography 131

Another role for which Bates was considered but simply did not pan out was in the science-fiction television series, *Doctor Who*. In the episode *Attack of the Cybermen*, with Colin Baker as the Time Lord, Bates was in the mix for the part of the police officer named Russell, which would ultimately go to actor Terry Molloy (who was the third actor to play the Dalek leader Davros in the series). Appearing in the series would have been a family connection, as Bates' wife Virginia had appeared in the first Dalek story serial of the series.[164]

Minder was an action-comedy developed by Euston Films for star Dennis Waterman, who had gained popularity in the police drama *The Sweeney*. The new series aired on ITV starting in 1979, which after a slow start due to a technician's strike went on to become so successful that it ran on and off for 10 years and spawned two television films, including *Minder on the Orient Express* (shown on Christmas Day, 1985) of which Bates was among the star-studded cast. The title refers to a slang term for a body guard, Terry, played by Dennis Waterman. The storyline followed Terry, a former boxer and ex-con, working as a minder for Arthur Daley (George Cole), a used-car dealer and con-man who often needed protection due to the dodgy scams he got involved in. While the character of Terry provided the action, Arthur more often than not provided the comedy, based upon the situations he would get himself into. Cole's character became so popular and the chemistry between him and Waterman worked so well that his role was expanded to more of an equal footing with Waterman's title character. Among the secondary characters, two great standouts were Dave the bartender at the Winchester Club (Glyn Edwards), who had to deal with Arthur's never-ending bar tab and shady deals, and Detective Sergeant Chisholm (Patrick Malahide), who made it his mission to try to put away Arthur, but with not much success. Waterman actually sung the theme song *I Could Be So Good for You* for *Minder*, something he also did for other series he would star in including *On the Up*, *Stay Lucky* and *New Tricks*. The song proved quite popular, and by the series' third season, most people in Britain associated both the series and the song.

In *Minder on the Orient Express*, mob boss Jack South dies of a heart attack, but not before leaving a partial clue to the whereabouts of the proceeds of a multi-million dollar bullion robbery inside the locket of his daughter Nikki (Amanda Pays). Ten years later, Nikki is old enough to have her father's safe deposit box opened, though she is careful as her stepmother is keen on inheriting the fortune her husband had hidden away. With only a team football photo inside the box and with a partial Swiss bank account number in her possession, Nikki intends to solve the mystery. When several thugs try to rob Nikki of the account number on her way to a birthday party at a club, Terry (Dennis Waterman), who is serving as a temporary doorman there, rescues her. Nikki rewards Terry with two free tickets for the Orient Express, where he plans taking his girlfriend, Annie. Meanwhile, Arthur (George Cole) has walked in on an extortion grab by local gangster Brian "Brain Damage" Gammidge, and the police are keen to serve Arthur a subpoena to testify against him in court. Fearing for his life if he is forced to testify, Arthur makes up a story about Terry to anger Annie, so she won't go on the trip and he can take her place to avoid the police. While Arthur makes up another story to placate an annoyed Terry, Nikki has apparently had an ulterior motive for giving him the free tickets, as she too is also on the train on her way to Switzerland, but so are several people also interested in the fortune, including a number of former associates of her father, a scheming widow and a disgruntled bank manager. The grouping of so many crime figures on the train has attracted the attention of Interpol, which sends Sergeant Francois LeBlanc (Bates), assisted by Arthur's regular nemesis Detective Sergeant Chisholm (Patrick Malahide), to observe and report. The combination of so many people with the same motive makes for an all-out melee for the Swiss account number, with Arthur and Terry stuck in the middle.

The feature length *Minder on the Orient Express* special was the highlight of ITV's 1985 Christmas schedule of programming, and it was heavily promoted; Arthur and Terry even made the cover of the *TV Times* 1985 Christmas issue. While the usual banter between Arthur and Terry was evident, the episode also featured a long list of guest stars besides Bates, including Honor Blackman as the scheming widow of one of Jack South's associates, Ronald Lacey as a former money launderer who worked for South and Terry's girlfriend (Linda Hayden), to name a few. Lacey stole most of his scenes as a somewhat creepy frosted blond-haired train enthusiast, with eyes on the South fortune. By 1985, *Minder* was at the end of its first run after five seasons, and the *TV Times* announced *Minder on the Orient Express* would be its last episode. Series creator Leon Griffiths waxed philosophically in a *TV Times* interview on the series' popularity, explaining that he did not set out to make a social statement with *Minder*, but that the series emerged as a metaphor of the cynicism of Margaret Thatcher's run as Prime Minister during the 1980s. [165]

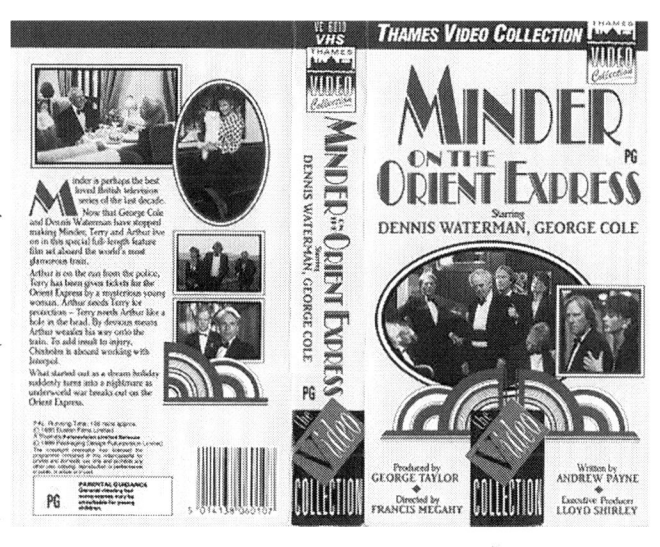

Almost all of Bates' scenes as Sergeant Francois LeBlanc were opposite Malahide's Detective Sergeant Chisholm, so it was a great benefit that they played so well off each other. While Chisholm is by the book and eager for action, LeBlanc is much more laid back and takes every opportunity to enjoy a good meal and a drink. First seen at a station in France sporting a drooping mustache and smoking a cigarette while reading the paper and enjoying a drink, Bates sets the tone for his character. Upon their introduction, it quickly becomes apparent that LeBlanc looks down upon Chisholm and he takes almost every opportunity to embarrass his British counterpart, which proves not that difficult to do. Chisholm's boss has provided him with practically no budget, which prevents him from getting even a simple meal, while LeBlanc relishes his gourmet meals paid for by Interpol. It gets so bad for Chisholm that he has to resort to asking the man he most detests, Arthur, for a monetary loan. In addition, Bates gets to speak French for his role, which also provides him with a way to poke fun at Chisholm with no recourse. The best scene with LeBlanc and Chisholm, however, is after Chisholm points out the mob connection to Nikki South. LeBlanc replies to Chisholm, "I will make sure your superiors get a report of your most useful contribution—it will compensate for your failure to blend in correctly. I refer of course to your suit!" At which point Bates pokes Malahide's suit in disgust. From there the relationship continues to deteriorate until a melee breaks out among the passengers and, as LeBlanc announces himself as Interpol and pulls out a gun, Chisholm calls him a French cretin and punches him in the face, before getting knocked down with a serving tray. In the process, Arthur, Terry and Nikki slip off the train in the confusion, when

A Biography

133

it comes to a sudden stop. One could almost imagine a spin-off police comedy series with Bates and Malahide failing to solve international crimes in each episode. An interesting point is that *Minder on the Orient Express* would be the last time that Bates and his wife Virginia would work on a project together, although they shared no scenes; Virginia had a small role as Debbie Moore in the episode.

Patrick Malahide shared his memories of his on-screen partner from *Minder on the Orient Express*. "I only had the pleasure of working once with Ralph. He appeared as a rather smooth French police officer in *Minder on the Orient Express*, while I was playing the hapless Chisholm. We hit it off immediately and had great fun together on location in Boulogne. Of course, he was fluent in French and we amused each other by concocting a French version of Cockney rhyming slang. *Alors, Ralph, je vais monter les pommes et les poires. Bien sur, Patrique. Tu as besoin peut-etre de l'enigme de Jacques.* That puzzled more than a few French waiters." [166]

Peter Duffell's directing career started in the early 1960s with shorts and television productions. In 1971, he directed two actors who had worked with Bates, Peter Cushing and Christopher Lee, in the Amicus horror anthology, *The House that Dripped Blood*. But it would not be until 1986 that Duffell would get to direct Bates in the television movie *Les Louves*, also known as *Letters to an Unknown Lover*. The film was actually a remake of the 1957 French film noir *Les Louves*, also known as *Demoniac*. Crime writers Pierre Boileau and Thomas Narcejac wrote the story. The two men turned out a number of well-received novels that were made into feature films, including 1955's *Les Diaboliques* (which *Fear in the Night* was based on) and *Vertigo* (1958), which Alfred Hitchcock directed. In *Les Louves*, two Allied soldiers, Bernard (Bates) and Gervais (Yves Beneyton), manage to escape from a prisoner of war camp in German occupied France. Bernard convinces Gervais to travel with him to Lyon where he will meet Helene (Cherie Lunghi), a woman he has been corresponding with via letters for a year and whom he believes is his true love. But Bernard is killed in an accident at the train yard upon reaching Lyon, and the Germans shoot Gervais, but he manages to make it to the home of Helene. When Gervais comes to, he is mistaken by Helene to be Bernard and he assumes his identity. Gervais meets Helene's half sister, Agnès (Mathilda May), whom he finds himself attracted to, though Helene expects him to marry her. Things become more complicated for Gervais as he becomes trapped in Helene's house and Bernard's sister Julia arrives and greets him as her brother. It is then that Gervais realizes that he has swapped one prison for another.

The production, as explained by Duffell, was an Anglo-French co-production filmed with both English and French dialogue for both markets. Bates was part of a bilingual cast, which included Mathilda May in her first major speaking role; she had previously appeared as the space girl in the 1985 Tobe Hooper cult film *Lifeforce*, in which Bates was considered for several of the characters. *Letters to an Unknown Lover*, with its plot twists and turns, benefited from a fine piano score by Raymond Alessandrin, which heightened suspenseful scenes throughout the story. The plot draws the viewers in slowly and once Gervais is ensnared in a deadly scheme, it is as if he is on a rollercoaster with no way off. The device of assuming another person's identity was quite common in film noir, and *Letters to an Unknown Lover* is a prime example. One of the great lines in the film comes from Helene, when she tells Gervais that they have to keep their good name, as that is all they have left after the war. Bates, using a French accent for Bernard, is only in the film in the beginning, but his character sets in motion the whole story involving Gervais and Helene. Bernard has completely fallen for his long distance love and believes that Helene trusts and loves him fully. In a wistful scene in a darkened train car, Bernard is exhausted and his eyes stare up looking about as he thinks about his hope of true love and his future. He also carries a lucky medallion that proves his undoing when he goes to fetch it after dropping it in the train yard. Bates final scene comes very convincingly with the death of his character Bernard. Director Peter Duffell noted in his autobiography that he and Bates struck up a close friendship while filming *Letters to an Unknown Lover*. They both shared a love of cricket and went to Lord's test matches to watch the games. Their friendship would continue and it was Duffell who directed Bates in his very last film, *King of the Wind*. [167]

In October that year Bates was one of the main guests at the Sitges Film Festival in Spain, which specializes in fantasy and horror films and is considered one of the top international festivals for genre films. The festival that year was paying tribute to Hammer Film Productions and guests from the company included Peter Sasdy, Ingrid Pitt, Roy Ashton and Roy Ward Baker. While at Sitges, Bates sat down for an interview with writer Carlos Aguilar and discussed his connection with Hammer: "I never felt at the time that I would become a genre star by appearing in various films for Hammer. I'm only now starting to realize that I do have some presence in British fantasy films. I mention fantasy films deliberately because I don't like the term 'horror films.' You see, when I made those films, in no way was I conscious of what they meant or what they could come to mean. I was working in one, then another, and in between I would do some work on television or in the theater. To me, it was just working as an actor.

"The resurgence of interest in Hammer seemed to begin in the early 1980s, which is when I began receiving invitations to various film festivals devoted to Hammer. I then realized from attending these festivals that many people outside of England knew my work from Hammer and this is wonderful. Nevertheless, I confess to you that during that period of my career, I was only trying to be the best I could in every role and did not particularly think that people would recall these films years later. Acting is very nice work, but it is a job just like any other one. Now when I look back at the films Hammer made I realize how good they were. By re-watching them on television and at film festivals I see how Hammer films have a special and personal style all their own. At Hammer the performers, directors, the make-up crew … everybody was part of a special family and I'm very proud to have been part of that family. It was a privilege and that's also the reason I happily accept invitations to participate in every tribute paid to those films. Likewise, from a personal point of view, Hammer was also very important to me because in one of their films, *Dr. Jekyll and Sister Hyde*, I met for the first time my wife Virginia Wetherell, who had a supporting role in the production. I'm also thankful to Hammer as it is where I met one of my best friends, scriptwriter and director Jimmy Sangster, who is also the godfather of my son Will." [168]

A Biography

Chapter 5
"Well, don't you think that's funny?"

Bates started off 1987 with a choice guest role in the second series of the ITV Yorkshire Television comedy *Farrington* (originally titled *Farrington of the F.O.*). A haphazard British Consulate located in Latin America is taken over by the no-nonsense Harriet Farrington (Angela Thorne). Harriet sets out to run the Consulate in an efficient manner, and she is met with resistance from the staff and Major Percival Willoughby-Gore. In the episode *We're Having a Heat Wave*, Harriet sends off the Major to another position in the embassy after she sees that he is smitten with her recently divorced friend, Sarah. She soon learns from her good friend, Annie, that they are to be visited by J.K. Mapley (Bates), the managing director of British Busts Limited. Thinking Mapley will be the usual "bald, fat, in their middle fifties and about as entertaining as a wet weekend in Whitstable" type, Harriet is surprised to see her new guest is the exact opposite. Mapley makes his interest in Harriet known, but she instead turns down his invitations for dinner. It is only after being confronted about this reality by Sarah that Harriet realizes that she and the Major may finally have something in common—a lost love.

As J.K. Mapley, Bates creates a wonderful "Mr. Right" whom Sarah and Annie swoon over, while Harriet tries to deny her feelings for him. Bates gets to speak some Spanish, impressing the Consulate staff, as well as show his charm and sense of humor. There is one great funny scene in which Mapley convinces an elderly woman, one who thinks the government is after her, that the American Express card that he gives her is actually an anti-laser computer card, which will protect her. Series creator and writer Dick Sharples shared his memories of Bates from working on *Farrington*: "I have fond memories of Ralph. Not only was he a good actor, he was also good company during the one occasion we worked together. I heard he was a direct descendent of Napoleon—he certainly had that look about him—but unlike Old Nappy, he was a quietly laid-back and excellent comedy actor, as in the late John Sullivan's sitcom *Dear John*, when he played a recent divorcee, and also in Ray Cooney's farce, *Run for Your Wife!*, at the Criterion Theatre. Ralph was taken before his time. He was such a nice guy."[169]

In an interview with Ian Woodward for *Woman's Weekly*, Bates himself confirmed he was the great-great-nephew of Napoleon stating, "Ah yes! [This was] A slightly delicate matter. Apparently, one of Napoleon's mistresses, pregnant by him, was forced to marry one of my distant uncles."[170]

Farrington also marked the end of Bates' association with agent John Miller, with whom he had been since 1968. His new agent, Richard Hatton, was a former actor before forming his own agency. Richard Hatton Ltd. was started in 1954 and Hatton was known for discovering a then unknown Sean Connery. His other clients at one time included Robert Shaw, Leo McKern and Michael Crawford. Bates' first production under Hatton's wing would prove to be one of his best-loved roles.

An unsuspecting man returning home from work happens across a handwritten letter on the living room table from his wife. As his eyes scan the content of the letter, his face drops as he realizes that his life as he knows it has just completely changed … he has received a "Dear John" letter. Thus begins John Sullivan's beloved series *Dear John*, which cast Bates as the star of the story, John Lacey. While previous television roles allowed Bates to dip his toes into the water as far as infusing comedy into his performances, it was *Dear John* that completely immersed the actor as a comedy star and shed his past horror image. Yet, the brilliance of Sullivan's writing on the show did not just focus on comedy, but also on the real pathos involved in divorce and its long lasting effects, in which Bates was able to take full advantage. Bates relayed this in an interview with *Radio Times*: "When the script first landed on my doormat, I thought someone had sent it as a joke, because it was so me. It fitted like a glove." [171]

John Sullivan was a television scriptwriter who created a number of memorable and popular British comedies. His career started in 1977 with the writing of the BBC-produced series, *Citizen Smith*, concerning a young Marxist trying to start his own revolution in South London. The success of *Citizen Smith* led the BBC to give Sullivan the green light on his next project. Sullivan's new series was also a comedy, involving a Peckham market trader named Derek "Del Boy" Trotter and his younger brother Rodney, who are constantly coming up with new ways to strike it rich. While the goals of the characters' schemes in *Only Fools and Horses* varied in success, it was Sullivan who truly struck it rich, as the series gained widespread popularity and lasted from 1981-2003. In fact, the series has been voted the most popular U.K. sitcom of all time, according to several polls. Sullivan also won three BAFTA awards with *Only Fools and Horses* for Best Comedy series in 1986, 1989 and 1997. The success of the program allowed Sullivan to continue writing various comedies, and in 1983 he branched out into romantic comedies with *Just Good Friends*. In 1986, and along the similar lines of a romantic comedy, Sullivan wrote *Dear John*, about a recently divorced schoolteacher trying to find himself again with the aid of a group for divorced and separated people known as the 1-2-1 Club. Bates expressed his admiration for Sullivan with interviewer Ian Woodward: "The success of *Dear John* has been absolutely smashing. John Sullivan, the writer of the series, is without

Bates (left) as John Lacey, Belinda Lang as Kate and Peter Blake as Kirk in *Dear John*

A newspaper ad used for *Dear John*

A Biography

Bates lets his hair up on the set of *Dear John*.

a doubt the best comedy writer in television. He's a super guy, too. I'm a bit in awe of him, but I like him a lot. Besides I owe John Sullivan a great deal for giving me a completely new image, as far as TV is concerned." [172]

Dear John, which ran for two seasons before the series was transferred to the United States with a new cast, revolved around its central character of John Lacey, but it also featured the lives of other divorced and separated individuals, who were all members of the 1-2-1 Club. Among the Club was Louise (Rachel Bell), the leader who tends to prod for juicy gossip concerning the sexual issues of the members; Kirk St. Morris (Peter Blake), a loud and obnoxious chauvinist who models himself on John Travolta from *Saturday Night Fever*; Ralph (Peter Denyer), a boorish and naïve man whose Polish wife left him after getting her citizenship; Kate (Belinda Lang), whose frigidness results in three failed marriages and Sylvia (Lucinda Curtis), who makes everyone shudder with her nervous laugh. The ensemble cast played off each other's strengths and weaknesses in various storylines to great comedic effect. Of course, as the main character, the episodes focus on John Lacey and among the best episodes are the following …

Episode one from the first season is *A Singular Man*, a first look at the sad language teacher John Lacey, as played by Bates. Lacey is an emotional wreck after his wife divorces him. To make matters worse his wife has left him for his former best friend, Mike Taylor, who now lives in his former home. John is forced to move out and rents a small flat next to a snooping Polish woman, Mrs. Lemenski (Irene Prador). All of John's friends, such as Roger, seem to think that he is living every man's dream—to be free and date younger women. But in actuality, John is extremely lonely and suffering. Bates displays this to good effect, trying to laugh about his situation with Roger while concealing his hurt feelings. Bates' look for the role of John also conveys his uncomfortable situation—his black hair all disheveled and sporting an oversized coat, in which he seems to get lost. After first proclaiming the 1-2-1 Club pathetic when he sees the advertisement in the newspaper, John nervously goes looking for the group at the town recreational center. This sets up one of the funniest scenes of the whole series when he accidentally sits in an Alcoholic's Anonymous group meeting, much to his embarrassment. During the introduction of the group members, John reveals more of his situation, including that he was married for 10 years with an eight-year-old son, before his wife divorced him and apparently everyone else knew about his wife's affair. Bates certainly seemed to relish the chance to play such a real character and invested much emotion into the character of John Lacey.

Episode five is *Toby*, the name of John's son. Sunday is the only day of the week that John gets to see his son Toby (played by Bates' own son Will, in a clever spot of casting). As he is on limited funds, John has bought a membership to London Zoo that becomes his regular place to bring Toby. During their visit, John explains to Toby how he still loves his mom. After they return to John's former home, John's wife Wendy talks down to him about *only* going to the zoo, before she gets into a row over Mike's staying out late. Wendy convinces John to stay for dinner and, although at first suspicious, John accepts the invitation and tries to be civil. The former spouses reminisce over their good memories, and just when the situation looks like it might turn romantic, Mike returns home. Mike tells John that he was the one who took him under his wing when he moved to London, which seems more like a stab in the back. It is this episode that shows how John would love to believe the fantasy that he could be reunited with his wife and everything could go back to the way it used to be.

In *A New Member*, episode one from the second season, John prides himself on always being honest and responsible, which becomes a problem when Wendy wants him to lie about their marital status so that Toby can get into a prestigious Catholic school. In order for Toby to be accepted, John and Wendy must go together to a special interview with the school headmaster. After wrestling with the issue of lying for the greater good of his son's future, John gives in and agrees to Wendy's plan. The interview starts out well with John discussing his former rugby days and how Toby also plays the sport in school, although soon John digs himself deeper and deeper into a hole of lies, including teaching divinity classes and taking care of rabbits. Just when it seems John and Wendy are in the clear, a condom falls out of John's wallet at the end of the interview, much to his embarrassment. While the episode addresses the issue of what is best for the child of divorced parents, this episode also has some very humorous set-ups and Bates displays his great sense of comedic timing. He was also a master of playing the straight man when something ridiculous happens, while still allowing the viewers to see the wheels turning in his character's head.

Bates has a laugh with fellow *Dear John* actor Peter Denyer.

In *Problems with Toby*, episode two, the son has become very moody and is suffering from a form of depression. Wendy tells John she wants him to stay away from their son for a while, but John is adamant about seeing Toby for his approaching ninth birthday. John gives Toby a rugby ball when they meet, but he is let down to hear that Mike had already played with him. After having a heart-to-heart with his son about sharing feelings, they encounter Kirk (Peter Blake),

A Biography

who quickly has Toby captivated with his outlandish stories of being a government spy. Kirk gets himself invited to Toby's birthday party but the party ends in disaster as Kirk picks a fight with Chuckles the clown. Toby afterwards tells his dad he does not want to see him anymore, which causes John to become stressed and have a blowup with the other members of the 1-2-1 Club. When they finally meet again, Toby reveals to his dad that he actually hates rugby and thought he would disappoint him if he knew the truth. Once John explains he would never be disappointed with Toby's decisions, Toby tells him he actually likes soccer and invites his dad to come to watch him play on the Red Rockets team that he just joined. Out of the entire two seasons, it is this one episode that best shows how divorce can confuse children and how their parents must try and put the pieces back together for them. Bates conveys how heartbreaking it can be for a parent to lose touch with their child and then be rejected by them.

Bates and son William on the set of the *Dear John Christmas Special*

Episode seven, *Kate Returns*, is the last of the second season and is set at Christmas, with a reunion for the 1-2-1 Club, as Kate (Belinda Lang) returns from Greece. John is facing being alone at Christmas, as his son Toby will be spending it with his grandparents. Kirk finally shows that he cares when he saves the members of the 1-2-1 Club from a group of rowdy Hell's Angels at the local pub. Wendy later informs John that Mike broke his leg playing rugby and invites him over for a romantic Christmas dinner. John is excited, but after giving Mrs. Lemenski a record album from her past and sharing a dance with her, she also invites him to Christmas dinner, so she will not be alone. John realizes that under Mrs. Lemenski's gruff demeanor she is actually a kind and lonely soul, and agrees to spend Christmas with her. This final episode ties up some loose ends by giving redemption to a couple of the characters, as Kirk displayed his heart, Mike got his just reward for breaking up John's marriage and John realizes that there are other people suffering from loneliness as well. Bates' performance as John Lacey in *Dear John* was arguably one of the best of his career—thoughtful, funny and full of emotion.

Following the end of the second season of *Dear John*, John Sullivan traveled to the United States where he met with Paramount executives, who bought the rights for an American adaptation of the series. Sullivan had initially planned on writing a third season for the BBC, but he was kept busy working on helping to set up the American series, which would air on NBC and star Judd Hirsch in Bates' original role of John Lacey. The American series ran for four seasons and was re-titled *Dear John USA* when it was shown in England. Bates shared with his wife Virginia that he would have liked to continue doing *Dear John*, but the Paramount producers no doubt wanted an American actor who was more familiar to their audience to star in the new series.

Although the series was demanding in that there were three days of rehearsal for each day of actual studio filming, Bates felt a connection with his character, which made the results worth the effort. One of the reasons Bates must have taken such a strong interest in the role of John Lacey was that he too experienced a divorce not unlike that of his character. In an interview with Sheila Hutchison for *My Weekly* magazine, Bates discussed this quality: "I'm as qualified to play John as the one person in three in this country who divorce. John, to me, is a victim of the situation. Some people think he's a wimp. I don't agree. The situation is real. John has lost everything, his child, his home, and so for a time he goes around pushing doors marked *pull*." [173] In another interview with *Radio Times*, Bates further elaborated how playing John was actually beneficial to him: "I'm a natural pessimist. For most of my life I've been motivated by guilt and fear. It's a legacy from my parents, who were both psychiatrists, especially from my father, who was extremely cautious and could always see both sides of every question. That makes you cynical. But I think *Dear John* may have been cathartic, because I'm slightly less guilty and worried these days." [174] Bates also pondered for Ian Woodward why fans embraced the series: "What's so lovely about *Dear John* is that it's classless and so appeals to people from all walks of life. TV comedy seems to have a much more immediate impact on people's lives than straight drama. People *own* you a bit more, so you get mobbed more often in the playground taking the kids to school." [175]

One of the biggest thrills of working on *Dear John* for Bates must have been having the chance to act with his own real life son. Will explained how his role as Toby came about and the experience of acting with his father: "I had gone along with Dad to the BBC Television Centre in Shepherd's Bush one afternoon. I would tag along with him quite a lot when he had meetings, and there was always something a little magical about walking along those corridors. We'd poke our heads into the *Blue Peter* Garden or have a quick spy on the *Top Of The Pops* stage. Anyway, he was discussing something in the script with the director Ray Butt. They were reading it through, and got to a part where John's son had some dialogue. I think I was just sitting on the other side of the room, probably playing with a Transformer construction toy or something, and Ray just handed me the script and asked me to read it. I read it, and then he

A Biography

asked me if I wanted to do it in front of a camera. I said okay. Maybe the grownups had already discussed it, but it seemed [to be] very spur of the moment to me.

"Working with my dad just felt like I was going to the office with him, which was the best thing ever. It was pretty rare that I'd get to spend that much time with him, to be honest, so those shoot days were very special. As all of the scenes we did were on location, so we had a lot of fun messing around between takes. The first shoot we did was at a house in the suburbs. I remember us all playing cricket in the street at one point, crew versus actors. Another shoot was at London Zoo. Because I was the star's son I think everyone felt it was his or her job to entertain me more or less constantly. We had a lot of fun. Dad just told me to say the lines like they were real; don't ever wait for a laugh. That was pretty much it. I think he was a little worried of me going into the family business. He would sometimes joke around and say, 'Be a plumber, get a proper job.' But I

Bates, clutches a newspaper in front of a flier for the 1-2-1 Club, in *Dear John*.

think in hindsight maybe he just didn't want that experience to influence my choices about what I wanted to be when I grew up. He wanted me to make up my own mind and find the thing that I wanted to do, without the experience of acting in a hit TV show with my dad having too much influence.

"That being said, after the whole *Dear John* thing, I pursued a couple other acting jobs … two to be exact. The first audition was for a movie in French. I was 11 and had recently had my first French lesson at school. The casting director asked how old I was, and I tried to respond in French (I had just learnt to say, 'J'ai onze ans'). The casting director translated my French into better French for the director to understand. I didn't get that job.

"The second audition was for a bubble gum commercial. In the audition I was in a room with five or six other kids. We had to all dance singing our name while standing on our left foot, and then singing our address when we danced on our right foot. The other kids were probably all from drama school and thought this all terribly normal. I was horrified and decided that I didn't want to do this anymore. My dad was in the waiting room, and I told him I didn't think acting was for me. We left and he bought me a saxophone." [176]

One young actress from *Dear John* whom Bates made an impression on was Cathy Munroe, who played one of his apartment neighbors in the initial episode: "Ralph was one not only brilliant actor but a comic genius who was greatly underestimated. I worked on the first episode of *Dear John* for the BBC in 1986, and was in the very first scene with Ralph. I remember him fondly, he was so handsome and extremely charming, especially to an impressionable young girl not long out of drama school. We had a coffee together in the green room; he was quiet and unassuming and was a very generous actor—kind but serious. Until the series developed, I had not realized what a natural comic he was. I think he surprised a lot of people. I feel so privileged to have worked with him, but only once unfortunately." [177]

Among Bates' other castmates from *Dear John* were Rachel Bell, who recalled: "Ralph was great at doing comedy and lovely to be with in rehearsals. But what I remember most about him was his terror about performing. Ralph was always so nervous before taping the series. If you know the BBC Television Centre, it is a big circle. On recording nights, which we did live in front of an audience, Ralph would walk around the Centre in big circles again and again before going on. Poor man. And also poor Virginia, who would be sitting in the audience, knowing how terrified he was. But then Ralph would come out and do this lovely performance. In fact, we gave Ralph the nickname "Worried of Chiswick" (the district in London where his house was), due to his nervous habits, although it was all in good fun and he was really a lovely man.

"One of the things that made *Dear John* so wonderful was the great quality of John Sullivan's writing. He could make you cry one minute and roar with laughter the next. He was a really brilliant writer. That is what made the series and what makes anything really good. It is sad that he is gone as well, as you don't know what else he could have written. You couldn't wait to rip open the next week's script to see what he came up with for the next episode.

"One specific memory that I have of Ralph is an example of the typical generous things he would do. He was the star of the show. Now generally actors don't tell each other what they earn. But Ralph made a point of telling us all what he was earning, so that we could figure out if relatively speaking we were getting a fair deal. This was really much appreciated by the entire cast and was most unusual for a star to go out of his way to help, because salary can be a contentious issue. I think that Ralph had done enough television by then to know that issue could be a problem, which he wanted to avoid for us.

A publicity shot of Ralph Bates for *Dear John*

"We used to have some lovely parties at Ralph's home. I remember Ralph's book-lined study in the middle of Virginia's ornately decorated house. Ralph's study was full of books and 'blokey' stuff. Ralph was a rare breed, a kind and gentle man. He was an unlikely actor, as many are egotistical and bombastic, and he was none of those things. He was quiet and gentle and nervous. He always used to say he only went into acting to get the girls. But that wasn't true, as he never acted like that and he was so devoted to his family." [178]

Wendy Allnutt played John's ex-wife Wendy and recalled: "I absolutely adored working on *Dear John*. To work on a show with a writer of John Sullivan's caliber was just amazing. It was very odd because Ralph had played the Latin lover when we previously worked together, and he did similar romantic type roles in his career, so to meet up with him again when he was almost playing the clown, a sad, downtrodden and henpecked ex-husband, was kind of a surprise to me. You often get cast according to one type and I remember reading the script before committing to the series and saw that Ralph was playing this other type of character, which I found fascinating. Of course Ralph was fantastic in the part, as he was such a good actor. The role was wonderful for Ralph, and not long after the series ended I heard he was ill, and the next thing I knew he had passed away so quickly. I didn't get to know Ralph socially, although once I did go to their fabulous house for a party that they held.

"Ralph always seemed quite relaxed on the set of *Dear John*. When you are carrying a television series like he was, you can kind of expect neurosis and temperament from a leading actor, simply because of the pressure and filming in the studio in front of a live audience. It is very difficult because the warm up happens, and if anything gets held up and the warm up goes on too long, the audience will start to get tired. If something goes wrong, the scene has to be retaken and you are doing all those gags again. But Ralph always seemed to be really cool about the whole thing, and was even better if we did something a second time. This is an art in itself because the whole process can wind people up and they don't know what to do, but Ralph always managed to do it.

"Something in particular I remember was that Ralph's face was sad and bemused playing John, but without letting on he was in on the joke. Sometimes in comedies actors are rather knowing about the joke that is coming up, but we managed to avoid that and let the gag arrive, which to me is the art of being a wonderful actor, especially a comedic one. Ralph was always so good about this, and so when we rehearsed, it was done very seriously that really benefited the series. There was a lot of mileage in the story; all that stuff of dropping off the child with your ex and all these other serious issues were dealt with by a type of lighthearted humor. The episode that remains my favorite was the first in which John ends up in an Alcoholics Anonymous meeting by accident, instead of attending his therapy group. On a related side note, my son wound up knowing Ralph's son Will, as they were both jazz musicians together." [179]

Family friend Tim Goode reflected back on *Dear John* and Bates' love of comedy: "I happened to stay with the family while Ralph was taping the first series. He gave me a pile of scripts and said, 'Read this, it's fantastic.' The writing was very astute and witty and there are some marvelous scenes with Ralph.

"I knew Ralph struggled with farce and initially found it difficult to master. But he persisted and he got it, and adored doing it! He loved doing comedy more than anything else. He actually loved comedians and he was a great fan of them. Tommy Cooper lived on the same road as Ralph and he used to have him over evenings. Cooper supported Ralph in learning the craft and looked after him a bit. Ralph loved Cooper and worshipped comedians like Spike Milligan and John Cleese, whom he very much admired. I think for years Ralph wanted to break out of the kind of dark and sinister type roles and do comedy. He loved comedy of all kinds and he laughed a lot. It was lovely to see that he finally got what he wanted … with *Dear John*. He was extremely pleased with that." [180]

On May 30, 1985 the curtain rose on Alan Ayckbourn's new play *Woman in Mind*. The black comedy was Ayckbourn's first play written using the first person narrative and focuses on a vicar's housewife going through a nervous breakdown. Susan's real life family has either ignored or patronized her and so she develops a perfect imaginary family to take her pain away. She slips between the real and imaginary world but eventually, when the two begin to mix, it results in a downward spiral for Susan. After its initial run at the Stephen Joseph Theatre in the Round, the production was transferred the following year to the Vaudeville Theatre in London's West End. The entire London production was recast in 1987, which is when Bates joined the cast. In the production he played Bill (taking over from actor Peter Blythe), Susan's doctor who cares for her well-being.

Another change was Alan Strachan taking over directing duties from Alan Ayckbourn: "The one production on which I collaborated

In 1985 Bates appeared in *Woman in Mind* at the Vaudeville Theatre.

with Ralph was *Woman in Mind*, Alan Ayckbourn's decidedly dark comedy that premiered at Ayckbourn's Scarborough base before its West End production, under the auspices of Michael Codron, Ayckbourn's regular commercial producer since 1970. It starred Julia McKenzie as the fantasizing vicar's wife Susan, with Martin Jarvis as her unloving husband and Peter Blythe as a local doctor who attends to Susan, recovering from an accident with a garden rake at the opening of the play and who becomes increasingly concerned for her (and, implicitly, attracted to her) as the play develops. Susan becomes increasingly confused between her real and fantasy worlds (the latter an idyll out of House and Garden) and finally spirals into insanity.

"It was critically well received and was still playing to very strong box-office business when the contracts for the leading actors were due to expire after six months. Ayckbourn was not available to re-rehearse with a new company and so Codron asked me to direct it (I had worked regularly for him in the West End, including two earlier Ayckbourn plays, and I also had a good relationship with Ayckbourn, including a successful revival of *How The Other Half Loves* at Greenwich Theatre, which I was then running, and subsequently in the West End). The replacement cast fell into place quite quickly as I recall. Pauline Collins, who was in a previous Ayckbourn play (*Confusions*) which I directed, was everyone's top choice for Susan, and both Michael Jayston as Gerald and Ralph Bates as Bill were my suggestions, quickly agreed by

A Biography

both Codron and the author (who of course has final cast approval). I knew Ralph's work from his TV sitcom *Dear John*, of course, but I knew how adept he was on stage and how deft a comedic touch he had, from seeing him on stage in Ray Cooney's production of *Run For Your Wife!*

"With the exception of two of Susan's fantasy family, the entire second cast was new. This could have been tricky but in fact wasn't. With the holdovers there was no sense of having to boringly go through it all again (Benedick Blythe as Susan's fantasy husband was especially adaptable to a new performance, in some cases very different to those he was acting opposite eight times a week during replacement rehearsals). Of course we had to accept the original design of the set (although costumes were changed) but that didn't present a straitjacket, and it meant that apart from matinee days (when we used a room upstairs at the Vaudeville Theatre, which was the production's home throughout the run. At that point Codron owned the lease on the theater too), we had the luxury of rehearsing on stage.

Bates poses for a shot with Hammer historian Wayne Kinsey at the Hammer International Convention in 1986.

"I remember it as a very enjoyable period, hard work because we only had three weeks and the schedule meant opening on the Monday of our fourth week (no luxury of previews), and it is a complex play. However the cast all cohered remarkably well. Pauline had not known Ralph previously but took to him greatly. Their scenes are very important in the arc of Susan's journey in the play, and they were very strong together.

"Ralph had a wonderfully baffled quality, ineffably polite even when extremely fazed by Susan's strange behavior, and he also somehow created an inner life for the character, suggesting that Bill's own life (married, with two girls) was possibly not without its own strains and stresses. Ayckbourn's dialogue is deceptive, seemingly naturalistic and fluent on the page but in fact full of subterranean and barely voiced thoughts underneath, and, crucially, with a very important rhythm. When actors ignore this rhythm, things can go seriously adrift; it is absolutely not simple pedantry to insist on textual accuracy in handling his plays. Ralph certainly understood this, although three weeks' rehearsal isn't long. Right from the start it was clear that he'd studied the script carefully (he hadn't, in common with the others, actually learned it in advance, rarely a good idea) and he was alert to all the hesitancies, ellipses and other characteristics of Bill's dialogue. I thought his performance was extremely fine (Codron and Alan Ayckbourn did too). Bill could easily, in the wrong hands, be just a stereotypical nervy bumbler but Ralph's creation was touching and very, very human, as well as funny.

"The run was very happy and I popped in quite often to the Vaudeville and gave notes occasionally during the run (although the standard of performance was maintained very well; the company, who all liked each other, all got on, but the production remained disciplined) and it was always a pleasure to stop off in Ralph's dressing room. I think he was happy in the play; he said he was (I got the impression that his stage confidence may have taken a knock at some stage previously) and he also was clearly so happy in his personal life (family photographs prominent in his dressing-room).

"I wish I could have worked with Ralph again. He was that cliché—"a dream to work with"—i.e., he came punctually and was prepared and ready to work as hard and as long as necessary to get it right. If he wasn't sure about a direction, he would query it without aggression; he wasn't the kind to go in for long and introspective analysis, but obviously preferred clear and unambiguous direction, and he certainly needed little in the way of technical direction; he knew all there was to know about the craft of comedy, how to time a line, how best to place oneself for a laugh line to have maximum impact, how to project in a theater like the Vaudeville (acoustically a little tricky because of the low overhang of the circle over the rear stalls), etc. But he was by no means just a technical actor; everything he did was always truthful to the character, and, as importantly, to the play. I think whomever you talk to about Ralph in the theater would echo all of this. It was so sad that just when he seemed to be hungry for stage work again that illness struck. He would have been so good in so many plays, other Ayckbourns, certainly, but also Simon Gray, Rattigan, David Hare, etc. So many parts in which he would have shone." [181]

Michael Shilling played Susan's son in *Woman in Mind* and recalled: "I met Ralph in 1987 when I made my West End debut in Alan Ayckbourn's *Woman in Mind* at the Vaudeville Theatre. It became clear from the first day of rehearsal that I was working with a gentle and kind man who was able to offer supportive words of advice, from time to time, to us, the younger cast members, always with the trademark twinkle in his eyes. I look back with very fond memories on this production and know it was a real privilege to watch and learn from the fine acting of Ralph." [182]

"I was in *Woman in Mind* for the last 11 weeks of its run with Ralph," Jacqueline Clarke remembered. "So apart from the rehearsal period and the playing weeks, my friendship and work experience with him was quite brief. He was a lovely, amiable actor to work with, and I admired his talent very much. I wish we could have continued for longer in such a lovely production." [183]

Woman in Mind was also chosen by Daisy Bates as one of her favorite performances by her dad. "I actually think Dad was particularly good in *Woman in Mind*. To be fair I was very young at the time but the production has left a big impression on me. I remember the play being extremely good. Dad played a doctor and had a sweet scene with a girl and a hand puppet, as Pauline Collins broke down. I remember it all being very moving and beautifully lit.

"Dad was so in awe of Pauline and kept talking about how real she was on stage, and it's just so funny that I ended up working with her two years later in the series *Forever Green* for three seasons. During our time working together on *Forever Green*, she told me lots of crazy stories from the 1960s and also that Dad had loaned her loads of books that showed he was pretty generous. Thinking back, I guess Dad was stylish too; one example being when he told Pauline how to fashionably cut up a tee shirt to make it look more hip. However, this was nothing compared to the effort he took to bleach his jeans on family holidays!" [184]

1988 saw a reunion of sorts of many of the cast members of *Dear John*. Ralph Bates, Peter Blake, Peter Denyer, Rachel Bell and Lucinda Curtis were all brought together for another Alan Ayckbourn play, the comedy *Absent Friends*. The production went on a very successful U.K. national tour to a number of theaters, including the Kings Theatre in Southsea, Portsmouth and the Palace Theatre in Manchester. The play, first performed in 1974, tells the story of Colin (Bates), a recent widower who is invited to a get-together of old friends to take his mind off his loss. Diana (Rachel Bell) is the wife of Colin's friend Paul (Peter Blake) and puts together the tea party to welcome Colin back into their circle of friends. Also invited is Colin's friend Johnny (Peter Denyer), Johnny's wife Evelyn (Amanda Kirby) and Marge (Lucinda Curtis), the wife of the unseen and ill Gordon. But the welcoming party to cheer up Colin has more than its share of issues, involving inter-marital affairs, desires for a baby, general unhappiness and work relationships. They all try to put on their best happy face when Colin finally arrives, but the surprise is on them as their guest is not sad at all and has not only accepted his situation but is quite happy with the time he spent with his fiancée. This unexpected reversal only further adds to the tension of the rest of the group with their own relationships.

"*Absent Friends* was such a fun play to do and we packed the theater all over the place," recalls Rachel Bell. "When we were on tour, whenever he could, Ralph would go home, as he always would rather be home than stay over in a hotel. Ralph just always preferred to be back with his family. He was just a very happy family man." [185]

Following the tour of *Absent Friends*, Bates continued in another theater production, this time for director Leslie Lawton, with whom he had previously worked in Ray Cooney's *Run For Your Wife!* In the comedy *Touch and Go* by actor and playwright Derek Benfield (who had acted with Bates as a Police Inspector in *I Don't Want to be Born*), two married couples, all friends, get themselves into awkward situations, as each member is having an extra-marital affair. Director Lawton explained that the 1989 multi-country tour started in the Middle East in Dubai before eventually making its way to the British Airways Dinner Theater at the Parkroyal Hotel in Kuala Lumpur, the capital of Malaysia. Besides Ralph Bates, who starred as Brian, other actors involved were real life spouses William Gaunt and Carolyn Lyster, as well as former British movie star Barbara Murray. In an interview with Suraya Al-Attas for the Malaysian *New Strait Times*, Bates was asked which acting medium he felt was the most challenging: "Well, I should say theater. I suppose if you can hack it in the theater, you can probably hack it anywhere. I believe anyone who is serious about acting should start in the theater. It's harder for kids now. They want to start straight off into television, doing soaps and stuff like that, and they fail publicly. That's very dangerous. They should be able to learn their craft first and it's better if they fail in the process of learning." [186]

Chapter 6
"It will all pass too quickly"

The celebrated series *Play for Today* ended its run in 1984 and was broken up into two separate series: *Screen One* played on BBC1 and *Screen Two* on its counterpart. Unlike *Play for Today*, both new series were shot on film for possible wider release in theaters. In the 1989 episode *Flying in the Branches*, younger sister Dana (Edita Brychta) visits elder sister Sue (Susan Fleetwood), a Prague refugee living in London since the Russian occupation of 1968. Sue has married an Englishman named Ed (Bates) and forgotten most of her heritage, while Dana, also on a mission to find an English husband to gain political asylum, shares the family's history and customs.

Of Bates' last television role, co-star Edita Brychta shared more about the production, revealing that even though Ralph Bates was well-established, he wanted to learn and hone his craft: "I still cannot fathom that Ralph is gone. He was magic to work with. I hold him in the highest regard and was naturally so devastated to hear of his passing. I'm so deeply saddened. I certainly have the fondest of memories, especially how wonderfully Ralph embraced the fact that his character was immersed into the lives of two Czech sisters, and he truly made huge efforts to learn words and customs from their country. He was a gentle giant. Gentle because he was mild mannered, genuinely kind, and a giant because he had a huge loving heart.

"My favorite scene in *Flying in the Branches* was in the conservatory, when the family's pet parrot escapes from its cage and we have to catch it. (Ralph's bad-tempered parrot Derek played the bird.) Ralph's character Ed was an unhappy person and equates his wife with my character when they first met. So during this one scene there is this incredible sadness and a connection when we are trying to catch the parrot, and he suddenly realizes, 'Oh my God, that's what Sue used to be like.' And Dana sees what a good man Ed was and how lucky her sister was to find him. It is a moment that could be misinterpreted that our characters may be falling for each other, with him looking at me sweetly, but it was an innocent revelation. It was so memorable because that particular scene was one of the most naturally evolving parts of the story, because there was this incredible empathy presented. We did two takes for that scene. The first take went out the window due to a technical glitch, and the director was really impressed at how well the second scene turned out due to the poignancy of what the characters had come to understand.

"Ralph really threw himself into the role. Susan Fleetwood learned a Czech song and Ralph really took it upon himself to learn more about the Czech culture. While waiting for shots to be set up, he would ask me how to say certain words in Czech about the culture, which he would then use in the dialogue. In the parrot scene I touch his hair and Ralph says 'ruka,' which is Czech for hand. Animal sounds are translated

Bates' 1989 agency photo

A photo of St. Mark's Square in Venice, Italy, where Bates' surprise 50th birthday celebration was held.

differently to English, so a rooster crows in English 'cock-a-doodle-doo,' but in Czech it is 'kykyryký.' Ralph was interested in so much that he really was one of the most invested people in the production. He was quiet on the set with an intellectual quality and he never came in with airs or bad moods. I wish that I could have worked with him again." [187]

That February 12, 1990 Bates reached a milestone in life as he turned 50 years old. Virginia recounted her surprise present, along with some help from their friend, producer John Sullivan. "For Ralph's 50th birthday, John Sullivan and I booked a surprise dinner for him in Venice, Italy. While he was taking Wills to school in the morning, I had 20 minutes to pack a bag, get a taxi and, when he returned, we headed straight for the airport. I managed to bluff where we were going until boarding (no security restrictions in those days). Once on the plane, we joined John and his wife Sharon. Ralph was thrilled! We stayed at The Gritti Palace and had the most brilliant time. Doing all the tourist stuff … gondolas, Harry's Bar, galleries. When we visited St. Mark's Cathedral, Ralph lit a candle but set fire to his sleeve. Thankfully John managed to dunk his arm in a font, before the rest of his coat went up in flames! I don't think there was a minute that went by during the three days we were away when I wasn't crying with laughter." [188]

In November of 1990, BBC Radio 4 began broadcasting *The Adventures of Sherlock Holmes*. Clive Merrison and Michael Williams played the classic sleuths Sherlock Holmes and Dr. Watson. Bates joined the cast under the direction of Enyd Williams for the BBC adaptation of Doyle's third story in *The Adventures of Sherlock Holmes* entitled *A Case of Identity*. In the story, Bates played James Windibank, the stepfather to Miss Mary Sutherland, whose fiancé has recently disappeared on their wedding day. Sherlock Holmes is called in along with Watson to find the fiancé, Mr. Hosmer Angel. Although Holmes is able to solve the mystery, the solution is not an easy one for Miss Mary Sutherland to accept, and so Holmes is left with not much besides good advice to offer his client.

Marguerite Henry's 1949 Newbery award-winning novel, *King of the Wind: The Story of the Goldolphin Arabian*, was a last production for a number of people involved in the 1990 film adaptation. It was director Peter Duffell's last film, also the last for Anthony Quayle, Glenda Jackson and Ralph Bates. The Miramax Films production did change some of the details of Henry's book, which was a fictional biography of the Godolphin Arabian, the founder of a line of famous thoroughbred horses including Man o' War, one of the greatest race horses of all time. Henry was a lifelong fan of animals and also a prolific author of children's books, with many of them concerning true stories of horses. The natural love of horses and horse racing has inspired countless films, most notably the various film adaptations of Anna Sewell's 1877 novel *Black Beauty*, *National Velvet* (1944) and 1979 film adaptation of Walter Farely's novel *The Black Stallion*. *King of the Wind* followed in the same vein of an underdog horse overcoming the odds to become a winner.

The assembled cast of *King of the Wind* (1990); Ralph Bates (top left).

In *King of the Wind*, Agba, a mute orphan boy of a Muslim sultanate in North Africa during 1727, finds a strong connection with a newly-born colt in the stable. While the horse master (Nigel Hawthorne) wants to kill the colt due to a wheat ear mark, indicating a bad omen, Agba points out the colt also has a white spot on the hind heel, which is a sign of good luck, thus sparing its life. Agba names the colt Sham, as its golden reddish coat is reminiscent of the sun. Sham's marks of good and bad omens also reflect in Agba's trials and tribulations, as he cares for the horse that he loves so much. Their journey takes them from Africa to France, when the Bey of Tunis gives Sham to French King Louis XV as a gift of good will, working as a cart horse for the royal chef, as a work horse for a cruel merchant, as a grooming race horse for an English dealer and finally as the sire of a young colt named Lath, who just may save the fortunes of the English Earl of Goldolphin (Neil Dickson).

In Bates' very last cinematic role, he returns to his roots and plays a deliciously smug upper crust Frenchman named LeDuc, who acts as a kind of foil to Agba and Sham. First seen when Agba and Sham arrive in France to meet King Louis XV, LeDuc arrives at the town marketplace sporting a big white wig and decadent clothes. A great touch has LeDuc covering his nose with a lace handkerchief to combat the foul odor of the common people and the marketplace. After having Sham escorted to Versailles, LeDuc makes the introduction for King Louis XV. But while the young king expresses an admiration for the Arabian colt, LeDuc is quick to dismiss Sham and apologizes stating the horse is only fit for the knackers' yard. LeDuc tries to make the argument that the Arabian horse is too small and not fit for a man of royal stature like the king. Sham responds to the insults hurled by LeDuc with a hard stomp on his foot. The King is not convinced, however, and LeDuc looks genuinely disappointed when it is decided Sham will be kept in France.

LeDuc returns for the finale when the Earl of Goldolphin brings Lath, the colt bred from Sham, to the Newmarket races for the English King's plate. With Agba now a starter's assistant, the story comes full circle when LeDuc, now the new French ambassador, arrives with his horse named L' Etoile Noir, which is expected to win. The boastful LeDuc is quick to make a high wager of 500 guineas with the Earl and the two horses go neck and neck in a series of heats. Of course with any good horse film, the ending is a come from behind win for Lath, with a little help from Agba and Sham.

Bates' performance as the Frenchman LeDuc is a role that he perfected during his career and his character is certainly one of the highlights of the film. While in the hands of any other actor, LeDuc may have just been a cartoonish caricature, but Bates invested in him a deep feeling of French pride that drives LeDuc and also acts as his own hubris. Audiences also got to see Bates speaking French, as when LeDuc protests and complains in earnest to the English King about his loss in the race. In his book, *Playing Piano in a Brothel*, director Peter Duffell shared an amusing prank that he and Bates played on fellow actor Peter Vaughan, who was cast as a sailor in the film. While admiring his costume, Bates and Duffell commented on what color parrot they should get for Vaughan to perch on his shoulder, which made him quite apprehensive due to a previous negative experience with a parrot when he played the character Long John Silver in *Treasure Island* (1968). [189]

Bates photographed sitting in his favorite chair at home.

Another actor from *King of the Wind* with fond memories of Bates was Neil Dickson: "It was a hugely enjoyable experience working with Ralph. His wit kept everyone amused and on their toes. He even made Glenda Jackson smile. His intelligence was always at the forefront of the work, as was his humor. He had a light delicate touch that I envied. Above all, when I think of Ralph, I smile. He made me laugh. He was fun to be around and he made the work fun. After all these years I can't think of one particular thing that he said that I could repeat … plenty that I couldn't though. Of course I was a fan of his work. I saw *Lust for a Vampire* when I was at Drama school and followed his career from then on. I wanted to be him for a while. I was thrilled when I met him socially in the mid-1980s about three years before we worked together, and he was very kind about a film I'd done that he had seen. He took time to talk about it, which made me feel like a million dollars. We didn't keep in touch and within two years of working on *King of the Wind*, I was whisked off to America to do a television series. The next I heard he had passed away. I was very sad, but when I thought about him, all I could see was that wicked grin ... and I smiled. Bless him." [190]

Ralph Bates was a professional actor for 26 years after his debut in the 1964 stage production of Shaw's *You Never Can Tell*. His splendid career began with a sudden rise into television productions, continued as one of the young, up-and-coming stars of Hammer Film Productions, and then back to television, where he showed up brighter than ever. Throughout his career he returned to the stage, and he used to tell people, "I make a point of treading the boards once a year, if I can, because it's good for an actor." Bates had grown beyond the dark and malevolent romantic and brooding types that he had made his M.O. during the 1970s, and he adapted successfully to dramatic, lighter and comedic parts. At the end of his life, at the age of 50, he had returned to a role he was comfortable playing, that of John Smith in *Run for Your Wife!* This time the production was staged at the Duchess Theatre. However, what should have been a happy return was instead the cause of much worry for Bates and his family, after a perplexing change in his health.

One of Bates' castmates who noticed his change in health was Carol Hawkins: "Although I am a private person and usually do not socialize much when performing, I did get to know Ralph during his turn in *Run for Your Wife!* I found Ralph to be a very gentle and gorgeous person. He was a very generous actor and person to work with, and very lovely. There was no other side to him; what you saw is what you got. I had a role in *Run for Your Wife!* that I performed for many years, and I worked with Ralph in the 1990 run. I called myself a donkey worker because I did all the set ups of the props and gags for all the other actors. I used to have a dressing room next door to Ralph. Unlike American actors, British actors did not have large accommodations; we had little tiny dressing rooms next to each other. And Ralph used to go in and I noticed that he started to get very ill. I used to go to work, set up and have my coffee in my dressing room and sometimes Ralph, who was next door, would be on the floor and his stomach was swollen. My husband is a great supporter of me and used to come up to the theater when he wasn't working to drive me home. Ralph would sit on the floor and tell me he was in so much pain and he didn't know what to do. And no one knew what was wrong with him. My husband and I are also healers, and we used to give him healing to help him get up off the floor, and then he would go on stage for his performance." [191]

"It was during the 1990 run that Ralph got ill," Virginia explained, "Ralph had started rehearsing *Run for Your Wife!* with the cast in September on the West End, at the Duchess Theatre, and they were opening a month later. Almost after the day he first started rehearsals, he begun feeling not well. We just put it down to nerves, him being neurotic, etc. It was after Christmas that Ralph finally asked Ray if he could have a week off to rest. The role of John Smith is an incredibly physically demanding role. And you didn't notice or realize how ill Ralph was when he was doing it. He went on stage night after night, with two shows on a Thursday and two shows on a Saturday. It was incredible. Ray and the whole crew were like a family and they went through it with my family. They never realized of course that Ralph was never going to go back." [192]

Leslie Lawton, who directed Bates and eventually stood in for him when he left *Run For Your Wife!*, also recounted his lead actor's worsening condition. "As I was around Ralph a lot and saw him every day during *Run For Your Wife!*, I had noticed he was not looking well and felt instinctively that there was something seriously wrong with him. I persuaded him to take some time off and seek proper medical attention. It wasn't usual practice to put an understudy on for a lengthy period, so I offered to take over his role for the week, the time his doctor felt it would take for all the tests he needed. Of course Ralph never came back and I ended up playing John Smith for six months. I reported back to him practically on a nightly basis when I got back from the show, and our long conversations, me at home with my post show whiskey, he in his hospital bed, would stretch into the night. I would often pretend to be angry with him: "*One* week you said! *One* week!" I invented a pretend bone of contention. It was traditional in the show that the two stars were billed on advertising from left to right with the actor playing John Smith always on the left (effectively first billing) and the actor playing Stanley Gardner on the right (second billing). Ralph didn't want the "responsibility" of top billing, so whenever he played the role, the billing was reversed. So I often used to rant in the night that it was bad enough that he'd buggered off to languish in his hospital bed and left me to carry the show, but he'd lumbered me with the humiliation of second billing as well. By this time he was often weak from the cancer treatment and he would beg me to stop making him laugh because it hurt so much. He was courageous and extraordinary to the end. And he never lost his sense of humor. In fact I believe he had the last laugh.

"In nine years nothing had ever really gone wrong on the set of *Run For Your Wife!*, pretty remarkable in a play where doors were flying open and slamming closed at breakneck speed throughout the action. But on the matinee of the day Ralph died, everything that could possibly go wrong did. Door handles came off in actors' hands, light bulbs exploded and pictures fell off the walls. It was as if Ralph was rampaging around the stage finally free to break out of the strict discipline and often exhausting routine of live theater night after night. I could feel his presence onstage with me and I loved it.

"He was my favorite kind of actor because he was incapable of telling a lie onstage. His greatest asset as an actor was his honesty. It is a particularly useful gift in comedy where he could make the most ridiculous and outrageous situations look believable. He knew that the secret to getting laughs in comedy is to play the drama. The more seriously you act, the more the audience will laugh. It served him especially well in *Dear John*, where a basically sad situation evoked laughter because the audience cared for John but felt safe to laugh at him, purely thanks to the actor's seemingly effortless technique. Audiences intuit an actor's true nature and they always warmed to Ralph and felt for him, as did his colleagues, none of who ever had a bad word to say about him. He was one of the most universally loved actors I've ever known." [193]

Declining health also prevented Bates from joining director Bruce Hallenbeck's film *Raven's Inn*, a remake of *The City of the Dead* (*Horror Hotel* in the U.S.). Hallenbeck describes the production and circumstances: "I wrote the script to *Raven's Inn* during late 1990. I was working with a producer named Carl Dietz, who produced *Fangs* for me that year, with Veronica Carlson. He asked me if I had any other scripts, and I was a fan of *Horror Hotel*, which I discovered was in the public domain, at least in the U.S. Ralph and I had wanted to make *Grave's End* a few years before, so this gave me a chance to rethink things. I asked Ralph if he wanted to play Alan Driscoll, the Christopher Lee role, and he said, "Of course!" So I sent him the script. I didn't hear from Ralph for a while, and in the meantime attempted to gather other actors together. Debbie Rochon, a young actress in indie horror films at the time, agreed to play Nan Barlow (the Venetia Stevenson role) and I dearly wanted Christopher Lee to be involved, so I wrote asking him if he would be interested in playing the Valentine Dyall role. He wrote back and said that, all things being equal, he would be. And shortly after that, I heard the devastating news that Ralph was terminally ill. I recall Virginia telling me that his reading of the script put him in better spirits. I can only hope it gave him some happiness. After that, I was too sad to carry on with the project, although a few years later I tried to get it going again with Jeffrey Combs, but like *Grave's End*, it was not to be." [194]

As Bates' condition worsened without any immediate answers on the cause, both he and Virginia became focused on finding out the nature of the mysterious ailment and hoping for a possible cure. Virginia explained their struggle and heartbreak: "After about a month of feeling unwell, Ralph eventually went to the local doctor and was told it was just nothing and he was given some medicine, which didn't help, and so then we went to go see a specialist. At that point Ralph had already opened in the play. He was unwell and had terrible discomfort and pain in his stomach and it is a very physical play—it requires a lot of running back and forth on stage—it is farce. He would have to fall over backwards over sofas and getting up. It is a very physically demanding play and he was the lead in it. He kept going back and forth seeing doctors and specialists and nothing was really working. I genuinely thought to begin with that Ralph was being a bit dreary, but his stomach was definitely swelling and he was in pain. Plus it became quite obvious that he was losing weight and started to look thin and drawn. But he had been to top Harley Street specialists in London, and he had been to the hospital and had tests, but at Christmas they had to do two shows on Boxing Day and two shows on Christmas Eve, and we decided to spend Christmas in a hotel literally around the corner from the theater so he could get up, go to the theater, come back and then rest all day. There was also a swimming pool in this hotel and Ralph was comfortable in water, so all day he would be floating in water. As far as we knew and the doctors knew, there was nothing wrong with him and everyone was mystified.

"After Christmas, Ralph had done a show in January for the New Year. At that point I was taking him to the theater and also picking him up, as he couldn't cope with the traveling. When I brought him home he said, 'Look, I'm going to call Ray in the morning and ask him to give me a week off, because I have to get on top of this, I can't do it anymore. I just need to rest and find out what is wrong with me.' Ray told him that's fine, take a week off and Leslie Lawton, who had been directing the play, took his place. The following day Ralph went to the doctor, who sent him to the hospital for tests. He rang me from Charing Cross Hospital while I was at the shop and said, "They want to keep me for tests. I don't have any pajamas so could you please bring me some." So I closed the shop and came straight down to the hospital. Then he was transferred to the Royal Masonic Hospital in Ravenscourt Park, London, which was closer to us, and they did more extensive tests. Even then they didn't find out what was wrong with Ralph for about five days, until they finally did an exploratory test. Just before Ralph went into the operating room, the doctor came in and held his hand and said, 'I'm very sorry Ralph, but I have to tell you that we found traces of cancer.' Ralph and I looked at each other and it was sort of like thank God, at least it is something [physical], as we were almost beginning to think he was going crazy. The doctor left and I spoke with Ralph telling him it would not be such a big deal, as he was young and fit and that we'll beat this. So we went off together into the operating room and I was holding his hand and we were sort of joking as he went in, and then a nurse came up to me and said, "I'm sorry Mrs. Bates but the surgeon would like to have a word with you." I tried to insist that I wanted to stay with Ralph until the last minute, but she was adamant that I needed to talk to the surgeon, so I said goodbye to Ralph, sort of joking break a leg and all that, wishing him luck thinking it was no big deal—a cancer and we would figure it out and get through it. The surgeon came up to me and said, 'I'm very sorry to have to tell you but your husband has got one of the worst cancers that you can have. He has pancreatic cancer.' I have never heard of this type of cancer up until this point. The surgeon then went in and I went back to Ralph's room and was at a loss on what to do. I went to the shop and turned all the lights off and put a note on the door saying closed until further notice, and returned to the hospital.

"After Ralph came out of surgery he was in the hospital for another three months before he died. While Ralph was under I had another visit from a different doctor who talked me through it all. He explained to me all about pancreatic cancer so that I could understand all about the nature of the disease. Now, of course, the disease is much more in the limelight as a number of famous people have died from it, with many people writing about it and organizations set up for help. We are much more aware of it and you can even look it up on the Internet. In those days it was not like now; it was almost unheard of. As a result, after Ralph died, I thought straight away that I was going to start a fund for pancreatic cancer research and that is what we are still doing today. One of the trustees is Dr. John Glees, who was in fact the oncologist who looked after Ralph. Literally the day after Ralph died I made an appointment to see him because I wanted it explained to me and I wanted to know why they had not diagnosed it earlier, and could they have done something if it was diagnosed earlier. He explained to me that the nature of pancreatic cancer is that it is very difficult to detect and, when it finally is detected, it is usually too late as the tumor is too big and inoperable. My whole goal with the research was to find a way to diagnosis the disease earlier and initiate more effective treatments. I later wrote to Glees asking him if he would be interested in being a trustee of the fund that I was creating, and he happily accepted saying it was a terrific idea" [195]

Another person who became one of the trustees of the Ralph Bates Pancreatic Cancer Research Fund was a close friend of the Bates family, artist Sir Peter Blake. After having met in the late 1970s, the two families remained friends and both Blake and Bates shared a common love of the sport of boxing, which Blake elaborated on.

"The first time I met Ralph I was in a local restaurant in London with my family. This little boy came over to our table and he had done a drawing of me in the restaurant and gave it to me. Then his mom and dad waved from across the room, and that was Virginia and Ralph with Daisy, and the little boy was Will. They were all having dinner in the same restaurant and we joined them then for a drink and that is how we first met.

"We remained in touch and it turned out that Ralph was a great boxing fan, and so was I, and he had some connections to get tickets. Now, a fellow actor named Peter Blake also used to come along to the matches with us, so it was Ralph and two Peter Blakes, which was a bit strange. We went to see matches in the late 1970s through 1980s at various places like the Royal Albert Hall, Wembley Arena and York Hall, which is a smaller venue in the East End. At the time, we watched many up and coming middleweights, such as Chris Eubank, Michael Watson and Nigel Benn. We also went to see heavyweight boxing matches featuring Frank Bruno.

"Our friendship continued over the years, and when Ralph was diagnosed with cancer I went to visit him at the hospital. I had recently done a complete set of silkscreen prints for the alphabet, and B was for boxing, which featured Joe Louis, so I brought him a print of that as a present since we had gone to so many matches together. As Virginia and I walked back to the car after my visit, she told me Ralph's cancer was terminal and he only had a few days to live, and indeed he died a few days after that. Ralph was a good actor and such a dear friend." [196]

Bates had always made friends easily and many of his coworkers were very fond of him even years after they worked together on various productions. Among those who shared their memories of Bates' passing were the following—Peter Sasdy: "When I first heard the news of Ralph's death two very different seasonal images came to my mind. The first was a

New Year's Eve in the early 1970s when he joined us in my home in Weybridge during a bitterly cold night for a celebration party. Just before midnight he was chosen as the most handsome dark young man to go outside and return with a piece of coal on the arrival of the New Year. His job was to knock on the door and bring good luck to us all. Out he went into our snow-covered garden as we listened to the 12 chimes, wished everybody Happy New Year ... and completely forgot about Ralph and in the celebratory noise we didn't hear him knocking. It took a few minutes before his face appeared outside one of the windows ... with a big smile half frozen. He came in with a big laugh and we all hugged him to warm him up. The second seasonal thought took me to the morning of the last time we were together. It was a warm sunny morning on the terrace of the hotel in Sitges, Spain, where we were guests of an International Film Festival. We had breakfast together with our wives Virginia and Mia, and talked about Ralph's misadventure the day before when his spectacles had broken. Of course you must know he was rather short-sighted and without his glasses he felt completely lost. All's well that ends well. Our kind Spanish hosts arranged an eyeglass replacement in record time. Ralph was so happy ... and a few years later he was gone." [197]

Bates' grave at Chiswick New Cemetery, London

Shane Briant: "I was in America working when I heard the terrible news that Ralphie was dying in the hospital. I couldn't believe it had all happened so fast. I even wondered if I would ever see him again, but I couldn't let down the cast of the production I was working on and simply fly back to see Ralph. What was the point? So instead I sent him a funny postcard every single day with some ridiculously silly message on it, just so that every day I could hopefully make him smile. Virginia told me years later that he actually looked forward to these cards each day and they *did* make him laugh, despite his pain and grief. I think he was one of the loveliest, kindest men I have ever met and was one of the few men I looked forward to hugging like a brother." [198]

Martin Thurley: "I remember when Ralph was dying and I rang him in the Masonic Hospital. We had a great chat and were laughing so much about freemasonry and so forth, and I said I don't think I'm going to get to see you Ralphie. He joked and said no, it's all right. People I haven't seen in 30 years are surrounding me and I wish they would all go away, as I've only got about a week to go. He had a wonderful sense of humor, even until the end. Ralph was such a great man." [199]

Carol Hawkins: "Peter Blake told me later on about Ralph's diagnosis which happened very quickly. Ralph went to a private hospice in London. I didn't want to go in person to visit Ralph because I was just a working colleague and there were so many closer people to him who needed to see him. So I didn't want to invade his privacy in that hospital in London. So instead I phoned Ralph and had a 20-minute call with him shortly before he passed away. Ralph knew that I was a healer and a medium and we had the most wonderful conversation about death. Ralph knew that having pancreatic cancer was a no-goer. Ralph told me he was very comfortable and told me that he was not frightened of dying. We spoke about life after death and he was very lucid in his conversation with me. It was such a privilege to speak with him and I think Ralph was so brave after speaking with him for that last time." [200]

Joanna Monro: "I went to Ralph's funeral and it was very strange because I literally only knew Ralph from that one job we did together, but there were so many people there who worked with him, as we all wanted to show our respect. We did a benefit concert for Ralph that Virginia organized at the Palladium, which was just called *Dear Ralph*. It was held on Valentine's Day a year after he died. It was extraordinary because so many people came. I helped by handing out programs and selling raffle tickets. Virginia worked so hard on that special event and she was just amazing. Ralph's death was a huge loss and I feel very privileged to have worked with him and that I got to know him and become a friend. We have lost a true gentleman, great actor and a wonderful friend. The world is a much sadder place without him. Ralph was a true gentleman and a joy to work with." [201]

C. Courtney Joyner: "I had wanted Ralph to play the role of the lead villain in our film *Puppet Master III: Toulin's Revenge*. As the film was set during World War II, I wanted it to be in the same spirit as *Night of the Generals* or *Where Eagles Dare*, with an entire European cast. Director David DeCoteau was totally on board for that. We knew already that Guy Rolfe would be playing the puppeteer Andre Toulon, and then Ian Abercrombie and Sarah Douglas came on board. For the role of Major Kraus, I immediately had Ralph Bates in mind. Here in the United States we did not have any exposure to Bates' performances in *The Caesars* or *Poldark*, unless we saw it on public television, so my initial exposure to him was from the Hammer horror films. I had written the script for a film that Martine Beswick was in called *From a Whisper to a Scream*, also starring Vincent Price, so I knew she was a big fan of *Dr. Jekyll and Sister Hyde*. I spoke to David about casting Ralph and he was also a big fan of his, so we talked it over with our casting directors Bob MacDonald and Perry Bullington, who knew Ralph's agent. They reached out to him through his agency and sent him our script for the role, but what we did not know was that he was ill in the hospital from his cancer. We held the role for him and were utterly surprised and saddened when we heard back from his agent who was notified by Virginia that Ralph had succumbed to the cancer. What happened next was a testament to how well Ralph was loved. Actor Christopher Neame came into our office shortly afterwards to audition for the role of Kraus. He knew it was our original intention to have Ralph in the film and he spoke about his long friendship with Ralph, whom he first met while making the Hammer film *Lust for a Vampire*. He then said if we did hire him he was going to donate his entire salary to Virginia for Ralph's benefit, as he wanted to help out in some way. We were all for this but producer Charles Band felt, and I couldn't really argue with it, that the problem was we had so many European actors, and that if we had one more, people would not believe it was made in the United States and that would hurt his sale figures with the foreign distributors, who did not pay as much for home grown products. It was a sad event for us to learn of Ralph's passing that way, but our talk with Neame was touching and sweet that he would step up like that for his friend." [202]

One of Bates' close friends toward the end of his life was Peter Cocks, whom he had a long connection with as they both attended Trinity. Here, Cocks shared his memories of his friend and what made Bates so special: "I first met Ralph as an undergraduate at Trinity. Along with Michael Bogdin and Terence Brady, we were all contemporaries at the college. I met Ralph my first year there around 1960. The actors were not really in my circle of friends, but my connection with them was through Ralph, as we got on very well together.

"After graduating from Trinity, I left to come to the States in 1964. I used to see Ralph when I went home to England, and I kept in contact with him. I always found Ralph extremely funny. He had a great sense of humor. The other thing was that he loved a lot of the old kind of musical vaudeville tradition. Ralph was a big fan of Morecambe and Wise and other comedians like them. Ralph would often do these great impressions of the various comedians that he admired. I watched Ralph perform in some of his plays at Trinity and also afterwards in the West End.

"I had a sabbatical the year that Ralph got ill and passed away. It must have been the first semester of 1991. Around the same time, which was kind of poignant, I started a correspondence with him. I had not written to him that frequently before and I probably did not use to call him that much, as it was expensive to make transatlantic calls then. Ralph and I wrote to each other and we faxed these letters … I remember sending them to Virginia's shop in London. When I found out that Ralph was diagnosed with pancreatic cancer and he would not be around for long, I just flew to London and spent a week with him. He was at the Masonic Hospital, south of the river near Hammersmith. I spent quite a lot of time talking with Ralph about everything and anything.

"I'll always remember that with Ralph it was a laugh a minute. He would always show me things that he was doing or thinking up. I remember one time when Ralph had come to the States to attend Yale drama school. I was in the States as well and spent Christmas with him during 1964. He was married to Joanna at the time, who I also knew from when she was an undergraduate at Trinity. They were living in New Haven, Connecticut and I came over for Christmas dinner. In a typical example of what Ralph would do, he said, 'Cocksy (my nickname), you just stay here in this room and wait a little bit,' and he went off into another room in the apartment. After about five minutes he said, 'All right, you can come in now.' He has one single spotlight on him and he was standing in the middle of the room with a trench coat on and wearing a hat. He made himself appear very straightforward and serious. He stood there motionless and I looked and kept looking at him. Finally I noticed that Ralph had three legs! Then he began to do this great vaudeville act dancing about. He was holding the extra leg through the pocket of his trench coat and then he did this very funny dancing routine. He told me it was from a routine he did for a revue called *Soho Fayre* back at Trinity. This was the kind of thing that Ralph was always doing. I'll always miss him." [203]

Another good friend of Bates, Tim Goode, also recalled their last contact together as well as the funeral mass. "I'd seen Ralph on a television program he had just done. And I thought he didn't look his typical brilliant self, so I rang Virginia and she told me he was doing very poorly. They invited me up for that Christmas of 1990. Ralph suddenly collapsed right after Christmas and was taken to the hospital for tests. I would ring once a week at home and then at the Royal Masonic, where Ralph was later taken. He came home for his birthday on February 12 and I rang him up that day. He said, 'I'd love to see you but I'm not feeling too amicable

> **Valentine's Day Gala**
> at
> THE LONDON PALLADIUM
> Argyll Street, London W1
>
> Sunday February 14th 1993
> at 7.30pm
>
> *Dear Ralph*
>
> in aid of
> The Ralph Bates Pancreatic Cancer Research Fund

at the moment.' Then I got a postcard from him that same week. I had sent him some audio tapes of Beethoven, which I knew he liked. The card was a thank you and to let me know he was doing therapy every week. He signed it, 'What will be, will be, love Ralph.' Ralph's rapidly deteriorating health was very difficult for his children of course. Daisy was involved in her first television series called *Forever Green*. The stars of the show, Pauline Collins and John Alderton, were incredibly supportive of her at that time.

"I was in my garden tending to my flowers when I heard the news on BBC radio that Ralph passed on. I phoned Virginia the next day and attended the Requiem Mass for Ralph. A lot of Ralph's friends from show business came. Virginia had painted Ralph's coffin matte black and she also painted enormous purple lilies all over it. Ralph's coffin was on a stand raised high above the congregation. Virginia and Ralph were so very devoted to each other. Virginia, being who she is, made the event very stylistic. She hired a couple of coaches to get everyone from the church in Chiswick down to the cemetery. I remember Henry Magee went around getting everyone to sign the book of remembrance for the family. Virginia had the burial at the cemetery in Chiswick, which was very moving, and the press were there. Afterwards we all went back to Ralph's place and brought all these wonderful arrangements of hundreds of flowers from the Mass that filled the garden. A number of priests were also at the house. It was a very touching time of remembering Ralph. The grief was not overwhelming, as it was done by then. Windsor Davies held court in the garden like the old trouper that he is. Then at the end of the evening Virginia said, 'What shall we do with all these flowers?' and she decided that we should take them all to the nursing home down the road. And so Will and I helped Virginia take the memorial signs off the lovely flowers and took them down to this large nursing home and gave them all to the residents. We thought Ralph would have liked to have done that, so that's what we did. It was rather special." [204]

Virginia and the trustees of the Ralph Bates Pancreatic Cancer Research Fund sponsored a special variety benefit show to honor her husband and help raise funds. Entitled "Dear Ralph" to go along with Bates' role in the popular series *Dear John*, the benefit show was held on Sunday, February 14, 1993. It was promoted as a Valentine gala to coincide with the holiday and staged at the London Palladium. A massive number of family, friends, coworkers, stars and musicians turned out to host, perform music and skits for the show. Among the acts were musical performances by Steve Hackett and Will Bates, and performances of Roy Hudd's Music Hall and a *Dear John* reunion of Bates' castmates. Leslie Lawton, who had also directed Bates for his last stage appearance in *Run For Your Wife!*, directed the entire event. Sir Peter Blake designed the program cover, Daisy Bates was one of the hosts and Virginia dedicated the show to the loving memory of her husband. Rachel Bell, who took part in the *Dear John* reunion, recalled about the event: "It was an extraordinary experience, as I don't expect to appear at the London Palladium ever again. John Sullivan wrote this long speech that I delivered and then everyone else came on. After we did our bit we all felt rather sad, but it was all for a wonderful cause and we did another benefit the following year. I've never been a part of one of those types of occasions before and it was an amazing experience."[205]

A close-up of the fancy ironworks (the cross imported from France) that adorns Ralph Bates' gravesite

Leslie Lawton, who directed *Dear Ralph,* recalled the effort to put together such a large event: "The London Palladium had *Joseph and the Amazing Technicolor Dreamcoat* playing eight shows a week at the time, and we couldn't get on to the stage until the day of the show. On the morning we had to start by covering up the vast, immovable set of *Joseph* before we could get the orchestra onstage. My stepson Simon Lee (who was Lloyd Webber's musical director) was also musical director for us and brought the musicians over from Germany, as it was easier than trying to assemble a West End orchestra on a Sunday. We managed to get sponsorship for their flights and accommodations and they arrived a few days earlier and rehearsed in the bar of the Shaftesbury Theatre. Sunday was a day off for many of the performers, but we managed to assemble an extraordinary line up of artistes. I only had to mention Ralph's name and they all said 'yes' even before they had heard about the worthy cause it would support. The day was fairly chaotic with people coming in to rehearse when they were free, and I organized the running order around their availability on that day. Maureen Lipman came in and rehearsed, then she rushed home to prepare Sunday dinner. She got back in time to appear at the end of the first half, but she couldn't stay for the finale, as she had to return to feed her family. The cast of *Mr. Cinders* rehearsed in the early afternoon, then they rushed over to the King's Head

Another shot of Bates' grave at Chiswick New Cemetery, London

Theatre to do their 5 p.m. matinee, after which they dashed back to the Palladium to open our show. It was a day of organized mayhem. But the atmosphere throughout was electric and the warmth and feeling for Ralph, both backstage and front of house, was palpable. My abiding memory of the Palladium that night was an auditorium overflowing with love." [206]

Tim Goode, who assisted Virginia with the production of the *Dear Ralph* charity event, also shared his memories: "The Ralph Bates Pancreatic Cancer Research Fund decided having a benefit show was a good way to raise funds. A lot of Ralph's friends wanted to do a show biz tribute to him rather than a memorial, so Virginia hired out the London Palladium and let Ralph's friends do various acts. I spent two months at Virginia's shop in London prior to the event basically writing to and organizing everyone who wanted to do a tribute to Ralph. We had a fantastic cast; we had so many people. Virginia got Leslie Lawton, whom Ralph had been directed by in *Run For Your Wife!*, to direct the event, as he had experience doing big theater events. Virginia and I leafleted fliers for *Dear Ralph* the night or two before the event, announcing the show on Valentine's Day.

"We went around putting fliers under the windscreen wipers of cars by the Soho Theatre. We also stuck up fliers in the middle of the night on walls and got caught and nearly got arrested because we didn't know the rules about posting fliers. Virginia and I were doing this all on our own and had no idea it was illegal. We had a load of the posters printed off, a bucket of paste in the front of my car and a brush and we went and slapped them up on walls, bollards and road crossings. On one occasion we were in Kensington doing this and a policeman walked around the corner on his beat, and upon seeing us said, 'What on earth are you doing?' We didn't realize we were doing anything wrong and he explained that this type of flier posting was done by organized crime groups, who come out to slap something up and run off, and there was a £2,000 fine for it. We of course apologized and said it was for a charity event we were putting on and that we did not know. He took pity on us and said, well, just don't put any more up.

"*Dear Ralph* all came together into a wonderful show and Leslie Lawton did an amazing job directing everyone. Virginia sat in the royal box to view the show, but I was too nervous and stayed backstage most of the time with people like Gerald Harper and Peter Egan. I think the show ran over about an hour, as so many people were involved to do tributes. The Palladium didn't mind and we all had a great time. In fact, we actually sold out, which we were told, by the staffers of the Palladium, was unheard of for a charity event that was privately organized. So it turned out to be an enormous success, and was a wonderful professional tribute to Ralph. The show was so successful that the following year a second *Dear Ralph* Valentine Gala was held, this time a day before the holiday and staged at the Shaftesbury Theatre. Will and his band again played and the Hollies also performed. Daisy repeated as one of the hosts, and Christopher Biggins was the Master of Ceremonies. But after the first show ended that Valentine's Day evening, Virginia, Will, Daisy, myself and a few friends in dresses and tuxedos

Don Fearney's "open day" at Bray Studios, 1999: Veronica Carlson (left) displays her portrait of Ralph Bates, which was auctioned for Bates' cancer fund. Virginia Wetherell Bates stands holding the painting at the right.

went to the cemetery around midnight and opened a bottle of champagne over Ralph's grave. And we toasted him and we lit some candles on his grave. That was a most memorable moment of remembrance." [207]

Among all the many friends and colleagues who have shared their memories of Ralph Bates, the most qualified people able to properly remember him are his family. Both of Bates' children shared the best advice their dad gave them and how they think he would like to be remembered. Daisy Bates related: "Dad was a really available father who had a lot of time off, so we talked a lot. On the way to school and back or over the long childhood holidays, he advised me on everything really. Nothing was off limits with him. Dad discussed how much he loved university and how it formed him. I know he very much desired for me to have that same experience as well. Dad had hilarious stories from university involving all his close friends, Peter Cocks, David O'Clee and my godfather Roger Ordish. He told so many great stories.

"At the time I was studying classical ballet and that conversation (and many more subsequently) helped me to let go of all that and think about a way to get to university, after all that ballet training. He was concerned that my ballet training might be too narrow focused and make it difficult to branch into another career if I changed my mind, so he took me to Charterhouse where he'd been lecturing students for his old university friend Dr Ian Blake. Dad was so impressed by these boys and their ideas so he took me down there to see for myself. I wound up leaving ballet school and pursued a more academic education that started at Charterhouse, and a whole new world opened up for me.

"Dad was so humble I don't think he would have cared much how anyone saw him. I genuinely believe he was a very proud dad. Family meant everything to him and he really

Ralph Bates' son Will Bates, composer

indulged in his home life before heading off on the road again to the next job. He wasn't an actor that really enjoyed the work while it was going on, and I now realize that's quite unusual for a working actor.

"I think he just couldn't wait to get home to his family. He had this big heart that meant no one was excluded from our kitchen table. Driving across the country from a regional theater was nothing to him if he thought he could have a night at home with us. So quite honestly, I think he would like to be remembered as a great family man that really lived a full life. He really was … the best. He was gone too soon all the same." [208]

Will Bates explained: "My dad taught me lots of things. Don't drop your T's, always hold the door open for a lady and stand up when they enter or leave the table, don't do as I do, do as I say. He taught me about the crippling effects of fear. He greatly admired boxers, and used to say how boxers and standup comics to him were the ultimate in fearless performers.

"I think the thing that influenced me most was something he said about six months before he died. He asked me what I wanted to do with my life. He had never asked me that before. I was 13, and I told him I wanted to play the sax. He told me I didn't have the discipline; it seemed like he didn't think I could do it. So after he died I spent a lot of time trying to prove him wrong. Years later when I told my mum what he'd said, she said how much he would have loved to hear me play and compose, and that his saying that was just another, 'son be a plumber,' thing. But I think the drive that he had unwittingly given me, along with the support and encouragement that my mum gave me, pretty much set me on my path.

"As it turned out, I didn't end up being a sax player for a living, but it did teach me to be the composer I am now. So in a way I guess he was right. But I also know that he'd probably love the shit that I write, and the weird life I now have as a result.

"My dad was such a contradiction that I honestly find it a hard question to think how he would like to be remembered. He had such admiration for people in other professions. I think because of his medical family he would sometimes show a kind of reluctance that he became an actor; that he should be a doctor, or do something significant like Uncle Louis!

"I think he longed to really *make* something. He would often tell me how much he admired writers; how without the writing there really is nothing. He loved Sullivan for that, and Jimmy [Sangster], along with a lot of his other friends, were writers.

"But really, I think he was just impressed by people who were at the top of their field; people who had perfected their craft. I think he would have been proud to have the respect of those people, and to know that he was a good dad. And he sure was." [209]

Even though he was on the planet for just 51 years, Ralph Bates truly lived his life to the fullest, as a dedicated and constantly working actor, as a loving father and husband and as a good friend to many. His eager sense of humor and caring loyalty to his friends is well documented by the contributors to this biography. One can only imagine where the actor's life would have led, had he not passed away so young. His career was climbing high again by 1991, with fans enjoying repeats of *Dear John* and a triumphant third season return to *Run For Your Wife!* Further television series and stage productions were certainly in store for him, and perhaps even a return to feature films. He may have even been up to taking on a sinister part in Hammer's 2007 revival. All such thoughts make Bates' passing from pancreatic cancer the more poignant. Out of tragedy came something positive—a research fund in his name which continues to promote awareness of pancreatic cancer, as well as earlier detection and, hopefully, effective treatment.

The Ralph Bates Pancreatic Cancer Research Fund (RBPCR Fund) contributes to continuing research at St. George's University of London in Tooting, south London, where Professor Gus Dalgleish is the director of the pancreatic cancer research team.

Ralph Bates' daughter Daisy Bates, actress

For fans of British film and television, Ralph Bates will never be forgotten. He made the most of the time he had, and he has left a legacy of kindness mixed with a good sense of humor to those who knew him well. If there is one thing his fans can do to thank him for all his wonderful performances, it is to visit the RBPCR Fund at http://www.ralphbatespcr.org.uk/ and learn more about the disease, to protect you and your loved ones. Donations are most welcome to further fund research that will one day prevent pancreatic cancer from taking anyone else too early from life.

Death of An Actor
In memory of Ralph Bates, 1941-1991

© Ian Blake 1991

February
Operation Desert Storm.

"Half an hour ago we passed the deadline."
Politicians ramble on, discuss
in solemn tones 'advisability
of war' of 'siege mentality';
declare themselves opposed
to 'long campaigns,'
to 'conflicts long drawn-out.'
A five star general settles the debate,
"My boys simply wanna kick some ass."
"A blitzkrieg gets it over."
"Weeks not months."

Out in the smoking sand
sharp granules chap the lips,
find their way to every mug of tea,
smart carelessly ungoggled eyes with tears.
Muffled missile-launchers,
guns on netted tanks,
lift their muzzles east
like scenting wolves,

Intelligence advises 'end it now.'
Politicians wisely nod grey heads.
"End it quick, before the summer comes."
Meaning end *them* quick—
the half-run lives
of soldiers in the sand-hills
half their age,
writing letters home
to friends, Mum, wives?

With politicians, on the news today—
sailing south to fight for their ideals,
not old enough to buy pints in a pub—
a cheerful sailor,
still too young to vote.

*

Now I hear that,
half an hour ago,
they operated.
Deadline.
Weeks not months.

March
Curtain call.

After all the rehearsals
for dying on stage—
***Hamlet*, *Macbeth*,**
Hammer Horror chillers,
all those Who-dunnit thrillers.
Empty echoing suburban halls
smelling of Boy Scout meetings;
old, left-over hoards
of clothes for Jumble Sales;
Young Mothers' coffee;
draughty, creaking, boards.
Knocking out the half-remembered lines.
Darkened spotlights.
Smoking in empty wings.
Thumbing dog-eared copies
for mis-remembered cues,
but knowing, deep-down,
it will always be
all right
on the night—
now, unexpectedly,
the down-turned page.

*

Your part ran out.
Before "Beginners Please!"
No way of knowing
'What they are like to-night'
before 'going
on.'

Nothing can prepare
for that last loneliness—
that final audience there,
whom you love most of all
who most love you—
separated for the last time by
your final curtain call.

A Biography

April
Memorial

In this bright afternoon,
sun far too hot
for solemn suits.

*

Weathered into dull discolouring.
memorials to the past:
Dearly beloved.
Died in 1965
aged 77
Now with God in Heaven.
Now with her husband who,
Aged 58.
Departed this life 1937.
Thirty years,
a World War
and the world he knew
away,
before she lay
with him again
at last.

*

Not quite knowing
what we should do,
after the priest has finished,
we wait around the hole
thinking of you.

Family drop in flowers.
Birds sing. The sun
burns down.
Slowly, one by one,
we drift towards your grave.
Trickles of earth fall
softly to the bottom of the shaft
on that black lid and peace
for you.
For us too, too, release.
So ends the day
the traditional way
silently saying it all.

Ralph Bates

Afterwards

Outside this garden wall
traffic muffles past,
unseen mothers walk
their unseen children home from school.
Among the early flowers in here
we talk—
we who are,
and now *were,* all
your friends.

Years which till now,
seemed only yesterday.
have fled away.

How suddenly it ends.

Afterword
Pancreatic Cancer

The pancreas is a large gland that lies within the abdominal cavity, behind the stomach, and is composed of a head part, a body part and a tail part. The pancreas produces digestive juices and can be the origin of one of the worst cancers known to man (termed Pancreatic Adenocarcinoma). The majority of these cancers are diagnosed after the age of 65, but they can occur earlier, as was the case with Ralph. This cancer type is lethal because most patients discover its presence too late (after spreading to other internal abdominal organs) and in the majority of cases the cancer has usually spread to the liver (liver metastases). The reason for this is that initial symptoms are vague, such as some unexplained weight loss, a bowel action that may appear fatty, floating and light-colored within the lavatory pan, and is usually difficult to flush away. Patients commonly describe unexplained upper abdominal or back pain, but this already may be a late feature of more widely spread disease.

Only about one in 10 patients present with early disease, with the tumor still confined to the pancreatic gland itself, are therefore still operable. A CT scan of the abdomen will usually show the primary pancreatic cancer and whether a spread to other organs, such as liver or lymph nodes or into adjacent blood vessels, has occurred. The first line of silent spread is usually the liver, but the cancer can spread directly into neighboring blood vessels and this is sadly also common. Other areas of spread are within the abdominal cavity (also called peritoneal cavity) and this type of initial spread was the cause of Ralph's death. He had complained of tummy pains which were dreadful and these pains were ascribed incorrectly to "stage fright and anxiety" at having to appear on stage every night in the West End. When cancer of the pancreas is inoperable, as sadly was the case with Ralph, then we only had in those days chemotherapy treatments, which were usually only partially effective, never curative. Even today advanced metastatic pancreatic cancer is incurable with most patients not surviving more than one year, and the chemotherapy treatments are unpleasant due to drug-induced side effects. At the present time, only in those patients where the cancer is confined only to the pancreas, can the potentially curative Whipple operation be attempted by the pancreatic cancer surgeon. There are very recent reports of combining chemotherapy drugs with vaccine therapy, and this combination reportedly nearly doubles survival times from around six months to over a year. Other newer therapies include using monoclonal antibody-type chemotherapy. Targeted radiotherapy (radiation) can also be helpful to relieve the back pain caused by the cancer. Sadly most patients are diagnosed late, often with jaundice, very significant weight loss, fatty stools and unexplained diabetes and severe pain.

Soon after Ralph's death, Virginia and myself and others founded the Ralph Bates Pancreatic Cancer Research Fund, and we are actively involved in supporting research. I remember when Ralph died my own elderly mother cried, as she loved his TV series *Dear John*. Many, many others throughout Great Britain and the world also cried on hearing this terrible news.

Dr. John Glees

Notes/Bibliography

1. Debre, Patrice. "Louis Pasteur," *Flammarion*, 1994.
2. Geison, Gerald. *The Private Science of Louis Pasteur*. Princeton University Press, 1995.
3. *The History of Stoke Park*, Glenside Museum website, edited by Adrian Kerton.
4. *British Journal of Psychiatry* archive.
5. www.visitcolchester.com
6. Personal interview with Jonathan Johnson, 2016.
7. *Dr. Jekyll and Sister Hyde* pressbook, 1971.
8. *The Beaumont Review*, December 1955.
9. *The Beaumont Review*, November 1956.
10. *The Beaumont Review*, December 1957.
11. Personal interview with Elisabeth Eidinow, 2013.
12. Personal interview with Henry Stevens, 2016.
13. Personal interview with Robin Mulcahy, 2016.
14. Personal interview with Michael Parker, 2016.
15. Personal interview with John Wolff, 2016.
16. Personal interview with Barrington Tristram, 2016.
17. Personal interview with Elisabeth Eidinow, 2013.
18. "Ralph Bates, The Man with the Ruthless Charm" by Ian Woodward, *Dear Ralph: A Valentine Gala*, February 13, 1994.
19. Personal interview with Bruce Arnold, 2016.
20. "Sound and Fury," *Trinity News*, December 3, 1959.
21. "A Strong Passion for Acting" by Suraya Al-Attas, *New Strait Times*, February 17,1989.
22 Personal interview with Joanna Van Gyseghem, 2013.
23. Personal interview with Terence Brady, 2012.
24. Personal interview with Michael Bogdin, 2014.
25. "Players Triumph in Belfast," *Trinity News*, May 3, 1962.
26. "The Revue," *Trinity News*, May 31, 1962.
27. Personal interview with Ian Blake, 2016.
28. "Ralph William Pasteur Bates," *Trinity News*, March 5, 1964.
29. "Cuchulain by W.B. Yeats," *Trinity News*, February 27, 1964.
30. "Players Sweep the Board at U.D.A.," *Trinity News*, April 23, 1964.
31. "Ralph Bates: The Young Look Frankenstein," interview with Pip Evans, *Photoplay Film Monthly*, January 1971.
32. Personal interview with Michael Bogdin, 2014.
33. Personal interview with Joanna Van Gyseghem, 2013.
34. Personal interview with Michael Bogdin, 2014.
35. Personal interview with Joanna Van Gyseghem, 2013.
36. Yale University Library.
37. Personal interview with Jon Jory, 2015.
38. Ralph Bates interview with Sam Irvin, *Bizarre #3*, 1974.
39. "Going for Laughs" by Ian Woodward, *Woman's Weekly*, August 23, 1986.

40. "Ralph Bates: The Young Look Frankenstein," interview with Pip Evans, *Photoplay Film Monthly*, January 1971.
41. Personal interview with Joanna Van Gyseghem, 2013.
42. "Dublin Festival," by Harold Matthews, *Theatre World*, November 1964.
43. Personal interview with Joanna Van Gyseghem, 2013.
44. Personal interview with Terence Brady, 2012.
45. Personal interview with Michael Bogdin, 2014.
46. Stephanie Rolt, Records Assistant, *The Theatres Trust*.
47. University of Glasgow special collections.
48. Personal interview with Richard Wilson OBE, 2014.
49. Personal interview with Felicity Kendal, 2014.
50. Personal interview with Wendy Allnutt, 2014.
51. Personal interview with Judith Noble, 2016.
52. Watson-Wood, Peter. (2012). *Serendipity … A Life*. Authorhouse. pp. 104
53. Personal interview with Wanda Ventham, 2014.
54. Personal interview with Joanna Van Gyseghem, 2013.
55. Ralph Bates interview with Carlos Aguilar, 1986.
56. Personal interview with John Miller, 2015.
57. Personal interview with Joanna Van Gyseghem, 2013.
58. Personal interview with Angela Pleasence, 2014.
59. "West End Women: Women and the London Stage, 1918-1962," Maggie Barbara Gale, Psychology Press, 1996.
60. Personal interview with Ellen Sheean, 2016.
61. Personal interview with Felicity Kendal, 2014.
62. Ralph Bates interview with Sam Irvin, *Bizarre* #3, 1974.
63. Ralph Bates interview with Carlos Aguilar, 1986.
64. Personal interview with Peter Sasdy, 2014.
65. Meikle, Denis; Koetting, Christopher T. (2009). *A History of Horrors: The Rise and Fall of the House of Hammer*. Plymouth: Scarecrow Press.
66. Personal interview with Linda Hayden, 2013.
67. "Frankensteins—and Son," Jimmy Sangster interview, *ABC Film Review*, August 1970.
68. "Ralph Bates: The Young Look Frankenstein," interview with Pip Evans, *Photoplay Film Monthly*, January 1971.
69. "Frankenstein Rides Again" by Margaret Pride, *Reveille*, July 18, 1970.
70. Personal interview with Jeremy Burnham, 2014.
71. Video: *A Look at The Filming of a Hammer Horror*. April 28, 1970.
72. Personal interview with Dave Prowse, 2013.
73. Personal interview with Veronica Carlson, 2013.
74. Ralph Bates interview with Sam Irvin, *Bizarre* #3, 1974.
75. Ralph Bates interview with Serena Cairns & Bruce Hallenbeck, *Little Shoppe of Horrors* #8.
76. Personal interview with Joanna Van Gyseghem, 2013.
77. Personal interview with Phil Campbell, 2014.
78. Personal interview with Judy Matheson, 2014.
79. Ralph Bates interview with Sam Irvin, Bizarre #3, 1974.

80. *Dr. Jekyll and Sister Hyde, ABC Film Review*, June 1971.
81. *Dr. Jekyll and Sister Hyde* pressbook, 1971.
82. Ton Paans interview with Ralph Bates, *Little Shoppe of Horrors* #16, August 2004.
83. *Dr. Jekyll and Sister Hyde* publicity, 1971.
84. Ralph Bates interview with Sam Irvin, *Bizarre* #3, 1974.
85. Ralph Bates interview with Carlos Aguilar, 1986.
86. Personal interview with Martine Beswick, 2014.
87. Personal interview with Brian Reynolds, 2014.
88. Personal interview with Brian Clemens, 2014.
89. "Going for Laughs" by Ian Woodward, *Woman's Weekly*, August 23, 1986.
90. "Selling Junk Means Independence" by Romany Bain. *TV Times*, November 20, 1980.
91. "Going for Laughs" by Ian Woodward, *Woman's Weekly*, August 23, 1986.
92. Ralph Bates and Virginia Bates interview with Sam Irvin, *Bizarre* #3, 1974.
93. Julian Glover interview with Andy Roffey, 2013.
94. Personal interview with Virginia Bates, 2014.
95. Personal interview with Viviane Ventura, 2013.
96. "Hitchcock and the Making of Marnie" by Tony Lee Moral, Scarecrow Press, 2013.
97. Personal interview with Braham Murray, 2015.
98. Personal interview with Mia Farrow, 2015.
99. Ton Paans interview with Ralph Bates, *Little Shoppe of Horrors* #16, August 2004.
100. Ralph Bates interview with Sam Irvin, *Bizarre* #3, 1974.
101. *Fear in the Night* pressbook, 1971.
102. Ralph Bates interview with Sam Irvin, *Bizarre* #3, 1974.
103. Personal interview with Shane Briant, 2013.
104. Personal interview with Garrick Hagon, 2013.
105. Personal interview with Virginia Bates, 2015.
106. Personal interview with Gerald Harper, 2014.
107. "Hollywood Has an Appealing New Star—Old Gooseberry," July 25, 1976. NYT
108. "Possessed Infant Turns into Killer in British 'Devil,'" June 24, 1976. NYT
109. Ton Paans interview with Ralph Bates, *Little Shoppe of Horrors* #16, August 2004.
110. Personal interview with Peter Sasdy, 2014.
111. Personal interview with Renée Glynne, 2013.
112. Personal interview with Anne Rutter, 2016.
113. *The History of British Literature on Film 1895-2015*, Greg M. Colon Semenza and Bob Hasenfratz, Bloomsbury Publishing Inc, 2015.
114. Ton Paans interview with Ralph Bates, *Little Shoppe of Horrors* #16, August 2004.
115. Ralph Bates interview with Sam Irvin, *Bizarre* #3, 1974.

116. Ralph Bates interview with Carlos Aguilar, 1986.
117. Personal interview with Daisy Bates, 2015.
118. Personal interview with Gareth Jones, 2015.
119. Personal interview with Shelagh Bourke, 2015.
120. Personal interview with Tim Goode, 2015.
121. "Poldark," *The Sunday Times*, 1975.
122. Personal interview with Robin Ellis, 2014.
123. Personal interview with Jill Townsend, 2014.
124. Personal interview with Hugh Dickson, 2014.
125. Personal interview with Jean and Stephen Gates, 2014.
126. Personal interview with David Delve, 2014.
127. Personal interview with Donald Douglas, 2014.
128. Personal interview with Will Bates, 2015.
129. "Ralph Bates, The Man with the Ruthless Charm" by Ian Woodward, *Dear Ralph: A Valentine Gala*, February 13, 1994.
130. Biographical Entry: Bates, Ralph Marshall (1902-1978), British Medical Journal, 1978.
131. Personal interview with Paul Spurrier, 2014.
132. *Jet Set* playbill, 1979.
133. Personal interview with Martin Thurley, 2014.
134. Personal interview with Peter Blake, 2014.
135. Personal interview with Michael Briant, 2013.
136. Personal interview with Virginia Bates, 2015.
137. Personal interview with Terrence Hardiman, 2015.
138. *TV Review*, January 18, 1984, *Sunday Age*, Melbourne Australia.
139. "Selling Junk Means Independence" by Romany Bain. *TV Times*, November 20, 1980.
140. Personal interview with Steve Hackett, 2013.
141. Personal interview with Tim Goode, 2015.
142. Personal interview with Brian Cox, 2014.
143. Personal interview with Ian Cullen, 2013.
144. "TV: *Mrs. Reinhardt*, Edna O'Brien Adapation," by John J. O'Connor, *New York Times*, December 7, 1981.
145. "Intriguing Expose" by Peter Hepple, *The Stage*, October 1, 1981.
146. Personal interview with Joanna Monro, 2014.
147. "Fortnight of Fear" by David Wheeler, *Radio Times*, December 11-17, 1982.
148. "TV: *Two Weeks in Winter, A Docudrama about Poland*," by Walter Goodman, *New York Times*, December 13, 1982.
149. Personal interview with Christopher Olgiati, 2014.
150. Theatre Review: Hedda Gabler, *The Post*, May 18, 1982.
151. Personal interview with Tim Goode, 2015.
152. Personal interview with Virginia Bates, 2015.
153. Personal interview with Virginia Bates, 2015.
154. Personal interview with Peter Bowles, 2014.
155. Personal interview with Tim Goode, 2015.
156. Personal interview with Will Bates, 2015.

157. Personal interview with Ray Cooney, 2014.
158. Person interview with Leslie Lawton, 2015.
159. Personal interview with Will Bates, 2015.
160. Personal interview with Daisy Bates, 2015.
161. Personal interview with Virginia Bates, 2015.
162. "Odd Jobs for Dunkeld and Doune," Andrew Young, June 2, 1983 *Glasgow Herald*.
163. Personal interview with Bruce Hallenbeck, 2014.
164. Personal interview with Tony Crawley, www.crawleyscastingcalls.com, 2016.
165. "Minder How You Go" by Jo Vale, *TV Times*, December 1985.
166. Personal interview with Patrick Malahide, 2014.
167. *Playing Piano in a Brothel* by Peter Duffell, Bear Manor Media.
168. Ralph Bates interview with Carlos Aguilar, 1986.
169. Personal interview with Dick Sharples, 2013.
170. "Going for Laughs" by Ian Woodward, *Woman's Weekly*, August 23, 1986.
171. "Dear John," *Radio Times*, September 5, 1987.
172. "Going for Laughs" by Ian Woodward, *Woman's Weekly*, August 23, 1986.
173. "Dear Ralph … We Think You're Wonderful, Too" by Sheila Hutchison, *My Weekly*, July 12, 1986.
174. "Dear John," *Radio Times*, September 5, 1987.
175. "Going for Laughs" by Ian Woodward, *Woman's Weekly*, August 23, 1986.
176. Personal interview with Will Bates, 2015.
177. Personal interview with Cathy Munroe, 2016.
178. Personal interview with Rachel Bell, 2014.
179. Personal interview with Wendy Allnutt, 2014.
180. Personal interview with Tim Goode, 2015.
181. Personal interview with Alan Strachan, 2014.
182. Personal interview with Michael Shilling, 2014.
183. Personal interview with Jacqueline Clarke, 2014.
184. Personal interview with Daisy Bates, 2015.
185. Personal interview with Rachel Bell, 2014.
186. "A Strong Passion for Acting" by Suraya Al-Attas, *New Strait Times*, February 17, 1989.
187. Personal interview with Edita Brychta, 2014.
188. Personal interview with Virginia Bates, 2016.
189. *Playing Piano in a Brothel* by Peter Duffell, Bear Manor Media.
190. Personal interview with Neil Dickson, 2014.
191. Personal interview with Carol Hawkins, 2014.
192. Personal interview with Virginia Bates, 2014.
193. Personal interview with Leslie Lawton, 2015.
194. Personal interview with Bruce Hallenbeck, 2015.
195. Personal interview with Virginia Bates, 2015.
196. Personal interview with Sir Peter Blake, 2015.
197. Personal interview with Peter Sasdy, 2014.
198. Personal interview with Shane Briant, 2014.
199. Personal interview with Martin Thurley, 2014.

200. Personal interview with Carol Hawkins, 2014.
201. Personal interview with Joanna Monro, 2014.
202. Personal interview with C. Courtney Joyner, 2016.
203. Personal interview with Peter Cocks, 2014.
204. Personal interview with Tim Goode, 2015.
205. Personal interview with Rachel Bell, 2014.
206. Personal interview with Leslie Lawton, 2015.
207. Personal interview with Tim Goode, 2015.
208. Personal interview with Daisy Bates, 2015.
209. Personal interview with Will Bates, 2015.

Photo and Art Acknowledgments

Photographs not credited here were either studio publicity shots or acquired from the Midnight Marquee Press Photo Collection. Opening numbers below are page numbers where the photo is located.

2 – *The Horror of Frankenstein* Norwegian brochure. Stig Rolsasen collection
8 – Ralph Bates and Virginia Wetherell Bates in *Dr. Jekyll and Sister Hyde*. Author collection
9 – Virginia Wetherell Bates
10 – Ralph Bates and Richard Klemensen. Richard Klemensen collection
12 – Will Bates, Virginia Wetherell Bates and Christopher Gullo – Author collection
15 – Louis Pasteur. Virginia Bates collection
16. Bates' paternal grandparents. Virginia Bates collection
17. Ralph Bates Sr. Virginia Bates collection
17. Bates as a young boy. Virginia Bates collection
18. Bates as a young boy riding in his model toy car. Virginia Bates collection
19. Orwell Park Prep School photo. Jonathan Johnson collection
20. Orwell Park magazine. Jonathan Johnson collection
21. Trevor Bailey cricket coaching. Virginia Bates collection
22. Beaumont College production of *The Housemaster*. John Tristram collection
23. Bates with his school mates. Virginia Bates collection
24. Bates makes a diving play. Virginia Bates collection
25. Bates reading at school. Virginia Bates collection
26. Lord's Ground score card. John Tristram collection
27. Bates in a rowboat. Jonathan Johnson collection
28. Bates at Braiswick Lodge. Jonathan Johnson collection
29. Bates and school chums. Virginia Bates collection
30. Bates and Babette in a rowboat. Jonathan Johnson collection
31. Bates and Babette outside. Jonathan Johnson collection
33. Scottish poet and author Ian Blake
34. Joanna Van Gyseghem. Getty Images
36. Bates' theater contract for *You Never Can Tell*. Virginia Bates collection
37. Bates in *You Never Can Tell*. Virginia Bates collection
38. Bates in *Night Must Fall*. Virginia Bates collection
39. Bates in *Twelfth Night*. Virginia Bates collection
40. Bates in *The Creeper*. Virginia Bates collection
40. Bates in *A Christmas Carol*. Virginia Bates collection
41. Bates in *A Christmas Carol*. Virginia Bates collection
41. Bates in *Maria Marten*. Virginia Bates collection
42. Bates in *Naked Island*. Virginia Bates collection
43. Bates in a publicity photo for *The Caesars*. Author collection
44. Bates as Caligula with the guards in *The Caesars*. Virginia Bates collection
45. Bates as Caligula showing his anger in *The Caesars*. Virginia Bates collection
46. Bates in close-up publicity shot for *The Caesars*. Virginia Bates collection
47. Bates in a Colchester Reperatory production. Virginia Bates collection
48. Judy Geeson and Bates in *Happy Ever After*. Author collection

49. Bates in *Trilby*. Virginia Bates collection
50. Bates in a publicity headshot. Virginia Bates collection
51. Bates and Jean Anderson in *Alice Rhodes*. Virginia Bates collection
53. Bates as Lord Courtley in *Taste the Blood of Dracula*.
54. *Taste the Blood of Dracula* film poster. Ian Ashley Price collection
55. Dagger used by Bates in *Taste the Blood of Dracula*. Tim Goode collection
55. Bates' Lord Courtley presiding over a black mass in *Taste the Blood of Dracula*.
56. Bates' Lord Courtley coming to a bloody end in *Taste the Blood of Dracula*.
57. *The Horror of Frankenstein* film poster. Daniel Bouteiller collection
58. Bates as Victor Frankenstein with his laboratory equipment in *The Horror of Frankenstein*. Author collection
58. Bates with Jon Finch in *The Horror of Frankenstein*. Virginia Bates collection
59. Bates with Kate O'Mara in *The Horror of Frankenstein*. Author collection
59. Bates with the monster played by Dave Prowse in *The Horror of Frankenstein*. Author collection
60. Bates as Victor Frankenstein in *The Horror of Frankenstein*. Virginia Bates collection
61. Bates with Veronica Carlson in *The Horror of Frankenstein*. Virginia Bates collection
61. Bates in another scene with Veronica Carlson from *The Horror of Frankenstein*. Virginia Bates collection
62. Bates with director and friend Jimmy Sangster on the set of *The Horror of Frankenstein*. Virginia Bates collection
62. Peter Cushing telegram to Bates. Virginia Bates collection
63. Peter Cushing and Bates face-to-face in a publicity shot for *The Horror of Frankenstein*. Tim Goode collection
64. Bates and Graham James in *The Horror of Frankenstein*. Author collection
65. *Lust for a Vampire* film poster. Daniel Bouteiller collection
66. Bates as Giles Barton in *Lust for a Vampire*. Virginia Bates collection
66. Jimmy Sangster directing the cast of *Lust for a Vampire*. Virginia Bates collection
67. Bates and Yutte Stensgaard being directed by Jimmy Sangster in *Lust for a Vampire*. Virginia Bates collection
67. Bates checking his script alongside Judy Matheson on set of *Lust for a Vampire*. Judy Matheson collection
68. *Dr. Jekyll and Sister Hyde* film poster. Daniel Bouteiller collection
69. Bates and Martine Beswick publicity shot for *Dr. Jekyll and Sister Hyde*. Author collection
69. Bates in a promotional advertisement for *Dr. Jekyll and Sister Hyde*. Virginia Bates collection
70. Bates in another promotional shot for *Dr. Jekyll and Sister Hyde*. Author collection
71. Bates and Susan Spencer in *Dr. Jekyll and Sister Hyde*. Author collection
71. Bates as Dr. Jekyll facing himself in *Dr. Jekyll and Sister Hyde*. Virginia Bates collection
72. Bates passing his own wanted poster in *Dr. Jekyll and Sister Hyde*. Author collection
73. Bates and Martine Beswick in a publicity shot for *Dr. Jekyll and Sister Hyde*. Virginia Bates collection
74. *Dr. Jekyll and Sister Hyde* film poster
75. Peter Wyngarde in the television series *Jason King*
76. *Play for Today*
77. Tony Curtis and Roger Moore in *The Persuaders!*
78. Bates and Mia Farrow in the theater production of *Mary Rose*. Virginia Bates collection

79. Peter Cushing letter to Bates. Virginia Bates collection
81. *Fear in the Night* film poster. Daniel Bouteiller collection
82. Bates and Judy Geeson on the set of *Fear in the Night*. Virginia Bates collection
82. Cast and Crew of *Fear in the Night*. Virginia Bates collection
83. Judy Geeson and Bates being directed by Jimmy Sangster on *Fear in the Night*. Virginia Bates collection
83. Bates clowning around with Judy Geeson on the set of *Fear in the Night*. Virginia Bates collection
84. Bates, Shane Briant and their wives Virginia and Wendy. Shane Briant collection
84. Bates, Virginia and Babette in Johnson family garden. Jonathan Johnson collection
85. Bates as Michel Lebrun in *Moonbase 3*. Author collection
86. Bates with cast members of *Moonbase 3*
87. Bates in an intense scene from *Moonbase 3*
88. *The Protectors*
89. *I Don't Want to be Born* film poster with alternate title *The Devil Within Her*. Author collection
90. Bates as Gino Carlesi with Joan Collins as his wife in *I Don't Want to be Born*. Author collection
91. Susan Richards, Bates and Joan Collins in *I Don't Want to be Born*. Author collection
92. *Thriller*
93. *Persecution* film poster with the alternate title *Sheba*. Daniel Bouteiller collection
94. Bates as David Masters lurching over in *Persecution*. Virginia Bates collection
94. Bates trying to maintain his sanity in *Persecution*. Virginia Bates collection
95. Bates with the title feline in *Sheba* aka *Persecution*. Author collection
95. Bates' *Persecution* script with original shooting title. Tim Goode collection
96. *Crown Court*
99. Bates as George Warleggan in *Poldark*. Author collection
100. *Poldark*
101. *Poldark* DVD collection with Bates on the cover
102. Bates with the cast of *Poldark*
104. *Hammer House of Mystery and Suspense*
106. Playbill for the theater production of *Double Edge*. Author collection
107. *Penmarric*
110. *Secret Army*
111. *Secret Army*
113. Bates in his dressing room for the theater production of *Sleuth*. Virginia Bates collection
114. *Turtle's Progress*
115. Bates and Susannah York in *Second Chance*. Author collection
116. Bates, Virginia, their children and Dave Prowse at the first Hammer Convention. Richard Klemensen collection
117. Bates with the goblet from *Taste the Blood of Dracula* at the first Hammer Convention. Richard Klemensen collection
118. Bates with props from *Taste the Blood of Dracula* at the first Hammer Convention. Richard Klemensen collection
119. *Mrs. Reinhardt*
120. Bates and cast of the theater production *Instant Enlightenment Plus V.A.T.* Author collection

122. Bates and Toyah Wilcox on the set of *Tales of the Unexpected*. Virginia Bates collection

123. *The Agatha Christie Hour*

126. Bates' boat *The Sea Daisy*. Virginia Bates collection

127. Playbill from the theater production of *Gigi*. Author collection

128. *Run for Your Wife!* production at the Criterion Theatre. Virginia Bates collection

133. *Minder on the Orient Express*

137. Bates as John Lacey, along with fellow castmates Belinda Lang and Peter Blake from *Dear John*. Author collection

137. Newspaper ad used for *Dear John*. Virginia Bates collection

138. Bates letting his hair up on the set of *Dear John*. Virginia Bates collection

139. Bates with fellow *Dear John* castmate Peter Denyer. Author collection

140. Bates and son William on the set of *Dear John*. Author collection

141. *Dear John* DVD

142. Bates as John Lacey at the 1-2-1 Club in *Dear John*. Virginia Bates collection

143. Bates publicity shot for *Dear John*. Virginia Bates collection

145. *Woman in Mind* production at the Vaudeville Theatre. Author collection

146. Bates with Hammer historian Wayne Kinsey. Wayne Kinsey collection

148. *Absent Friends* theater poster. Author collection

149. Bates' 1989 agency photo. Author collection

150. St. Mark's Square, Venice where Bates had his 50th birthday celebration. Virginia Bates collection

151. Bates with the cast of *King of the Wind*. Author collection

152. Bates in his favorite chair at home. Author collection

157. Bates' grave at Chiswick New Cemetery. Virginia Bates collection

160. *Dear Ralph* pamphlet. Virginia Bates collection

161. The ironworks at Bates' gravesite. Virginia Bates collection

162. Bates gravesite at Chiswick New Cemetery. Virginia Bates collection

163. Virginia Bates and Veronica Carlson holding Carlson's portrait of Bates before going to auction at Bray Studios. Wayne Kinsey collection

164. Will Bates

165. Daisy Bates

Index

Absent Friends 147-**148**
Adventures of Sherlock Holmes, The 85, 150
Agatha Christie Hour: The Magnolia Blossom **123**-124
Allnutt, Wendy 42, 144
Bailey, Trevor 20-**21**
Bartlett, John 43-44
Bates, Daisy 10, 32, 84, 96-97, 103, 105, 107, **116**, 125, 129-130, 147, 160-**165**
Bates, Elisabeth (Babette) 16, 18, 23, 26, **30-31**, **84**
Bates, Lilian Adrienne 15-16, 18
Bates, Ralph Agent 40, 46-47, 136; America 32-35, 116; Award 130; Childhood 16, **17-18**; Colchester 16-18, 21-23, 107; Cricket 20, **21**, 22-24, 26, 82, 87-88, 135, 142; Fiftieth birthday 150; French background 16, 27, 29, 82-83, 125; Grave **157**, 160, **161-162**; Marriage 33-34, 87; Napoleon 136; Nickname 76; Pancreatic Cancer 24, 155-156, 165; Professional acting debut 36; Ralph Bates Pancreatic Cancer Research Fund 160, 162, 165; School acting debut 25; Typecasting 70, 83, 95
Bates, Ralph Marshall 15-16, **17**-20, 20, 107
Bates, Virginia (Wetherell) **8-9**, 10, 12, 71, 73-76, 84, 87-88, 95, 96-97, 103-104, 110, 113, 116-117, 119, 122, 125-128, 130, 132, 134-135, 141, 143-144, 150, 153-**163**
Bates, William 10, **12**, 22, 83-84, 103, 105-107, **116**, 125, 129-130, 135, 138, **140**, 141-142, 144, 150, 160-161, **164**
BBC2 Playhouse: Mrs. Reinhardt 119-120
Beaumont College 21-25
Bell, Rachel 138, 143-144, 147-**148**
Beswick, Martine 68-**69**, 70-**73**
Blake, Ian 32-**33**
Blake, Peter 110, 138-139, 147-**148**, 156
Blake, Sir Peter 156, 161
Bogdin, Michael 28-29, 31-33, 37-39
Bourke, Shelagh 98-99
Boy Meets Girl: Love With a Few Hairs 42
Brady, Terence 24, 28-30, 37-39
Braiswick Lodge 18-19, 21
Briant, Michael 112
Briant, Shane 28, **84**, 157
Broad and Narrow 37-39
Brychta, Edita 149-150
Burnham, Jeremy 59
Caesars, The 16, **43-46**, 48-49, 57, 87, 99, 127, 158
Campbell, Phil 63-64
Carlson, Veronica 60-**61**, **163**
Christmas Carol, A **40-41**
Clarke, Jacqueline 147
Clemens, Brian 68, 72-73, 92
Cocks, Peter 159

Colchester Repertory 27, 36, **47**
Conflict: Othello 41-42
Cooney, Ray 129-130, 155
Cox, Brian 118-119
Creeper, The **40**
Crime Buster: The Third Thief 43
Crime of Passion: Lina 78
Crown Court **96**-97
Cullen, Ian 119
Cushing, Peter 47, 53, 57-**63**, 66-67, **79**-81, 83, 118, 131, 134
Dangerous Knowledge 104-105
Dear John 42, 72-73, 110, 115, 122, 136, **137-143**, 144-145, 147
Dear Ralph **160**-162
Delve, David 104
Dickson, Hugh 103
Dickson, Neil 152-153
Double Edge **106**-107
Douglas, Donald 105
Dr. Jekyll and Sister Hyde 8, **68-74**, 75-76, 80, 92, 119, 127, 135, 158
Duffell, Peter 134, 150, 152
Ellis, Robin 99, 103
Farrington: We're Having a Heat Wave 136
Farrow, Mia **78**-80
Fear in the Night 49, 68, 80, **81-83**, 84, 91, 101, 134
Fifty-First State, The 48-49
Forget Me Not: Rich 105
Gas Company, The 33
Gates, Stefan 103-104
Geeson, Judy **48,** 80, **81-83**, 101
Gentle Touch, The: Who's Afraid of Josie Tate 125-126
Glees, Dr. John 156, 170
Glover, Julian 76
Glynne, Renée 91
Gigi 126-**127**
Goode, Tim 99, 117-118, 128-129, 144-145, 159-160, 162
Grady: Somebody Else's War 64-65
Gyseghem, Joanna Van 27-28, 30-**34**, 36-40, 46-48, 50, 62, 73, 76, 88
Hackett, Steve 116-117, 161
Hagon, Garrick 87
Hallenbeck, Bruce 131, 154-155
Hammer Films 2, 30, 40, 53-66, 68-69, 74, 78, 80-84, 89, 91-93, 95-96, 105-106, 112, 115-118, 131, 135, 146, 158, 165
Happy Ever After: The Fifty-First State 48-49
Hardiman, Terrence 113-114
Harper, Gerald 83, 87-88
Hatton, Richard 136

Hawkins, Carol   153
Hayden, Linda   57
Hedda Gabler   125
Here I Stand: Margaret Clitherow   105
Horror of Frankenstein, The   **2**, **57**-**64**, 68, 81, 131
House of Caradus   108
House on the Hill, The: Man of Straw   92, 117-119, 128
I Don't Want to be Born   55, 81, **89-91**, 148
Instant Enlightenment Plus V.A.T.   **120**-121, 124
It's Childsplay   105
ITV Playhouse: Would You Look at Them Smashing all Those Lovely Windows?   50
ITV Play of the Week: One Fat Englishman   42
ITV Play of the Week: Sarah   42
ITV Play of the Week: The Blue Moccasins   42
ITV Playhouse: Rogues' Gallery The Misfortunes of Lucy Hodges   43
Jason King: Variations on a Theme   **75**-76
Jet Set, The   109, 112
Johnson, Jonathan   17-21
Jones, Gareth   97-98
Joyner, C. Courtney   158
Kate: A Good Spec   51
Kendal, Felicity   42, 51-52
King of the Wind   135, 150, **151**-153
Kinsey, Wayne   **146**
Klemensen, Richard   **10**
Lawton, Leslie   130, 148, 153-154, 161-162
Lee, Christopher   53, 56-57, 66, 74, 83, 131, 134
Letters to an Unknown Lover   134-135
Loir, Dr. Adrien Charles   14-15, 125
Love Story: Alice   78, 92
Lust for a Vampire   **65**-**67**, 95, 106, 152, 158
MacDermot, Julia   40
Malahide, Patrick   134
Malleson, Miles   40
Maria Marten   **41**
Mary Rose   47, **78**-80
Matheson, Judy   **67**
Mayday   43-44
Miller, John   46-48, 80, 136
Minder on the Orient Express   132, **133**-134
Monro, Joanna   121-122, 158
Moonbase 3   **85**-**87**
Mrs. Reinhardt   **119**-120
Mrs. Thursday: Charity Begins at a Ball   40-41, 78
Mulcahy, Robin   23
Munroe, Cathy   143

Murray, Braham 79-80
Naked Island 42
Night Must Fall 38
Odd Job Man, The 131
Olgiati, Christopher 124
One Fat Englishman 42
Orwell Park Prep School 17, **19-20**
Othello 42
Panorama: Two Weeks in Winter 124
Parker, Michael 23
Pasteur, Louis 14-**15**
Penmarric *107*, 108-109
Persecution **93-95**
Persuaders!, The: Nuisance Value 76-77
Picture of Katherine Mansfield, A 85
Play for Today: Thank You Very Much 76
Players Dramatic Society 27-29, 31-32
Pleasence, Angela 50
Poldark 43, **99-102**, 103-105, 122, 130-131, 158
Private Lives 97-99
Protectors, The: Petard **88**-89
Prowse, David **59**, 60, **116**
Ralph Bates Pancreatic Cancer Research Fund 156, 165
Reynolds, Brian 71-72
Run for Your Wife! **128**-129, 148, 153-154
Rutter, Anne 92
Sangster, Jimmy 58, **62**, **66-67**, 68, 81, **82-83**, 99, 105-107, 121, 131, 135
Sarah 42
Sasdy, Peter 54-56, 135, 156-157
Screen Two: Flying in the Branches 149
Second Chance **115**-117
Secret Army **110-111**, 112-113
Sharples, Dick 136
Shilling, Michael 147
Six Wives of Henry VIII, The 49
Sleuth **113**-114
Softly Softly Task Force: The Visitor 105
St. Mary's of Colchester 17
Stevens, Henry 22
Storyboard: Lytton's Diary 89, 127-128
Strachan, Alan 145-147
Street and Sand 33
Tales of the Unexpected: Blue Marigold **122**-123
Taste the Blood of Dracula 47, **53-56**, 57-58, 70, 115, **117-118**
Ten Commandments, The: Hilda 68
Thriller: Murder Motel 92

Thurley, Martin 109, 157
Touch and Go 148
Townsend, Jill 103
Trilby **49**
Trinity College 21, 27-31, 33, 38, 127, 159
Tristram, Barrington 24-26
Turtle's Progress: Box Nine **114**
Twelfth Night **39**
Ventham, Wanda 45-46
Ventura, Viviane 77
Wednesday Play, The: Hello, Good Evening and Welcome 43
Wicked Women: Alice Rhodes 50-**51**
Wilson (O.B.E.), Richard 40
Wolff, John 23-24
Woman in Mind **145**, 147
Woodlanders, The 42, 51-52
Woman's Place?, A 107
Yale University 34-35
You Never Can Tell **36-37**, 153
Z Cars: Distance 92

About the Author

Christopher Gullo is a history teacher, volunteer lieutenant fireman and part-time background actor. Bitten by the horror bug since he watched *The Evil of Frankenstein* at the tender age of seven, Gullo became a fan of British horror films. He would go on to become the second president of the Peter Cushing Association, dedicated to his favorite actor, and which has over 9,000 active members. Gullo's love of film, history and research has led him to also become a biographer, writing books on actors Peter Cushing and Donald Pleasence, besides composing numerous magazine articles. He lives in Long Island, New York with his wife Beth and son Anthony.

If you enjoyed this book,
send $2.00 for a catalog of other
Midnight Marquee Press titles
or visit our website at
http://www.midmar.com

Midnight Marquee Press, Inc.
9721 Britinay Lane
Parkville, MD 21234
410-665-1198
mmarquee@aol.com

Printed in Great Britain
by Amazon